Advance Praise for
Madmen, Intellectuals, and Academic Scribblers:
The Economic Engine of Political Change

"Ideas matter. *Madmen*, with its engaging stories, is perfect for anyone interested in public policy, or how our world could be a better place."
—**Tyler Cowen**, George Mason University, blogger at The Marginal Revolution, and author of *Discover Your Inner Economist*

"There's no shortage of writing about bad government policies, but Leighton and López go several steps deeper, by exploring the incentives that foster bad policies, the institutions that foster bad incentives, the ideas that foster bad institutions, and the social processes that foster the spread of bad ideas. Better yet, they offer wise prescriptions for change and colorful stories to illustrate their wisdom. This is a book that manages all at once to be sage, important, and great fun to read. I highly recommend it."
—**Steven E. Landsburg**, Professor of Economics, University of Rochester and author of *The Armchair Economist*

"This book is an inspiring reminder that great thinking matters. It's a delightful, accessible, and thought-provoking book for anyone interested in big ideas at the intersection of economics and politics."
—**Charles Wheelan**, University of Chicago and author of *Naked Economics: Undressing the Dismal Science*

"Leighton and López have written a captivating book that explains the process of social change, from ideas to outcomes. Their theoretical framework—centered on the figure of the 'political entrepreneur'—is illuminating and original. It will spark productive conversations among those who are interested in social change and the wealth of nations."
—**Giancarlo Ibarguen**, Entrepreneur and President of Universidad Francisco Marroquín

D1211342

"Come along with Leighton and López as they speed date significant economic and philosophical influencers and chart the triumph of markets. As an erstwhile political practitioner in radical market reforming mode, I was relieved to find that I could dodge the moniker of 'madman' and classify myself as a 'political entrepreneur.' Racy and relevant, this book is a call to reforming arms."
—**Honourable Ruth Richardson**, former Minister of Finance, New Zealand

"*Madmen* makes clear there are several necessary conditions for a political shift to take place. We tend to think of change as resulting from a single hero or villain, but the story is more complex. The tales in this book show what it takes to effect change, while weaving a yarn that is entertaining and memorable."
—**Michael C. Munger**, Duke University and author of *Analyzing Policy*

"Leighton and Lopéz supply intellectually sound arguments, grounded in public choice and of Austrian economics, to explain why democratic governments often fail to produce policies that are consistent with the public's interest. Most impressive are the authors' evident grasp of— and ability to synthesize—complex arguments about the properties of 'good government.'"
—**William F. Shughart II**, University of Mississippi and co-author of *Policy Challenges and Political Responses*

Madmen, Intellectuals, and Academic Scribblers

Madmen, Intellectuals, and Academic Scribblers

The Economic Engine of Political Change

Wayne A. Leighton and Edward J. López

STANFORD ECONOMICS AND FINANCE
An Imprint of Stanford University Press
Stanford, California

Stanford University Press
Stanford, California

Special discounts for bulk quantities of Stanford Economics and Finance are available to corporations, professional associations, and other organizations. For details and discount information, contact the special sales department of Stanford University Press.
Tel: (650) 736-1782, Fax: (650) 736-1784

Printed in the United States of America on acid-free, archival-quality paper

Library of Congress Cataloging-in-Publication Data
Leighton, Wayne A., 1965– author.
  Madmen, intellectuals, and academic scribblers : the economic engine of political change / Wayne A. Leighton and Edward J. López
    pages cm
  Includes bibliographical references and index.
  ISBN 978-0-8047-8097-1 (cloth : alk. paper)
  ISBN 978-0-8047-9339-1 (pbk. : alk. paper)
  1. Political planning—Economic aspects. 2. Policy sciences—Economic aspects. 3. Political entrepreneurship. 4. Economic policy. I. López, Edward J., author. II. Title.
  JF1525.P6L45 2012
  320.6—dc23
                                                                                    2012016315

Typeset by Thompson Type in 10.5/14 Bembo

For our families, especially our wives, for their love, guidance, and patience.

Political change happens when entrepreneurs exploit loose spots in the structure of ideas, institutions, and incentives.

Contents

Preface

In the fall of 2011, a movement called Occupy Wall Street went viral. Protesters in New York were joined by others in hundreds of cities across the country and the world. They were complaining about the "one percent," the wealthy Wall Street types. They argued that the rules apparently did not apply to these privileged few, who were coddled by a government that was supposed to be regulating them instead. A few years earlier, a CNBC reporter went on a live television rant about the government's bailout of Big Auto, igniting the Tea Party, which soon emerged as a force in U.S. politics. In this case, protesters complained that government was too big: that it regulated too much and spent too much. From Occupy Wall Street to the Tea Party, angry citizens in the United States had had enough. They wanted things to be different.

In late 2010, some 4,000 miles away in Tunisia, a poor merchant set himself on fire to protest thuggish police confiscating his wares. Sympathetic protesters flocked to the streets, and soon that country was engulfed in the flames of revolution, which then spread to Egypt, Libya, and Syria.

The Arab Spring offers perhaps one of the most dramatic and enduring modern examples of people clamoring for change and dying to get it, sometimes literally. For decades, the rules of the game in countries like Egypt, Libya, Syria, and Tunisia were whatever their dictators said they would be. Few people liked the status quo, but fewer did much about it. Then it was time for a different idea.

These days, many people around the world seek political change. A lot of them are tired of the status quo, which they see as unjust, or unfair, or simply unproductive. To them, it also is time for a different idea.

As economists who study politics, we've spent years thinking and writing about how economic insights can provide a better understanding of political change. We are impressed with the scholarly books on political history and the popular economics books that make this serious subject easy and even fun. In fact, we step off from the argument found in nearly all of the pop-econ best sellers: Incentives matter. They matter because they shape human behavior. We then dig a little deeper, and we show that to understand political change, we need to understand what ultimately shapes incentives.

Our understanding of political change is as follows: Incentives are shaped by the rules of the game, which economists call institutions, and these institutions in turn are shaped by the ideas in a society. In other words, ideas matter. In the course of this book, we provide a brief history of the different ideas people have held about what should be the rules of the game so people can live better lives. We then offer a framework to think about how ideas matter, when it is that political change happens, and why at other times the status quo endures.

Whether a society is experiencing an evolution of rules over many years or a revolution that will topple a dictator tomorrow, political change is a process. As we look at the world around us, we think it's a process worth understanding.

Wayne A. Leighton, Guatemala City, Guatemala
Edward J. López, San Jose, California
December, 2011

Acknowledgments

The story of this book began in the fall of 2005 when the two of us began a conversation about how to teach political economy, both to our students and to the public. We agreed that the available books tended to be written for professional, technical readers and that there was an opportunity to convey the economics of politics in an engaging, more readable, yet still serious way. As we shared our conversation with friends and colleagues, the idea for this book began to take hold. And it never would have come to fruition without their gracious help. In particular, for comments that improved individual chapters we would like to thank Roberto Blum, Peter Boettke, Victor Borme, Tyler Cowen, Chris Coyne, Kenneth Godwin, Joshua Hall, Lissa Hanckel, David Henderson, Giancarlo Ibárgüen, Carlos Méndez, and Sarah Skwire. For helpful comments on multiple chapters we would also like to thank William Ferguson and an anonymous referee. Michael Munger and William Shughart provided valuable comments on the entire manuscript. Don Crooks, Ben Dyer, and Jeff Fong provided excellent research assistance, and Laralyn Murphy helped with formatting. There are many more people whose conversations along the way helped sharpen our thinking and how we build our arguments. We are grateful to them all, but they are in no way responsible for errors, omissions, and other missteps that remain entirely our own.

We also would like to thank several organizations that supported us while researching and writing this book, namely Universidad Francisco Marroquín; Liberty Fund, Inc.; the Social Philosophy & Policy Center at Bowling Green State University; and Stanford University Press.

None of this would have been possible without the expert guidance of our editor, Margo Beth Fleming, whose vision and wisdom kept us moving in the right direction and whose commitment and attention to detail got us across the finish line.

Most of all, we thank Elizabeth Andrion and Jamie López for reading every word, improving every chapter, and always keeping us grounded in what is truly important.

1

Ideas and the Rules of Politics

Coaches abused basketball again today.
—*The Washington Post*, March 8, 1982

It was March 7, 1982, and the cold drizzle falling on Greensboro, North Carolina, was no match for college basketball fever. The hottest ticket in the country was the Atlantic Coast Conference (ACC) men's basketball championship, with nationally ranked number-one North Carolina taking on number-three Virginia, in a rematch of their two-game split of the regular season. This game had it all. Both teams had come in with only two losses all year. A total of five future National Basketball Association (NBA) players, three of them future all-stars, would take the court, and the greatest basketball player of all time, Michael Jordan, was in his debut season for Carolina.[1] A rare national television audience was about to tune in. And inside the Greensboro Coliseum, 16,034 screaming fans felt lucky just to be there when the game tipped off. The anticipation was palpable. The excitement could not have been greater.

But, by the end of the game, the fans were booing, the players on both sides were disappointed, and both coaches were taking flack for thinking too much and playing too little. With seven minutes and thirty-three seconds left to play and his team ahead by one point, North Carolina's coach, the legendary Dean Smith, told his team to play keep-away. With Virginia's coach Terry Holland keeping his squad close to the basket in a zone defense, the North Carolina players were free to dribble and pass and stall and do everything but shoot. As the game clock ticked away, and a glorious game turned foul, the chorus of boos rose in crescendo beyond the rafters of the Greensboro Coliseum. One thoughtful sportswriter summed up the despair: "Imagine the final 12 minutes of Hamlet if the cast started reciting the Congressional Record. Or Hemingway writing the last chapters of his classics in pig Latin. Coaches abused basketball again today, ruined what could have been a game for the ages by thinking."[2]

The ACC championship wasn't the only "slowdown" game that year where fans booed; it was just the biggest. Average scoring nationwide had been declining for seven straight years and had reached its lowest point in more than three decades. The various conference leagues were becoming increasingly worried about the quality of play and a possibly shrinking fan base. The National Collegiate Athletic Association (NCAA) began looking into the rules of the game and how "stall-ball" was not only possible but in fact a winning strategy too tempting for coaches to pass up. Desperate for a good idea, they turned a figurative eye to Danny Biasone, an Italian immigrant who had settled in Syracuse, New York, and in 1954 invented the twenty-four-second shot clock.

Danny Biasone owned a bowling alley and had built up enough of a fortune to start a professional basketball team. In 1946, his Syracuse Nationals began to play in what would soon become the National Basketball Association. In 1950 the NBA had its own "stall-ball" fiasco, when the Fort Wayne Pistons beat the Minneapolis Lakers by the dubious score of 19–18. A shrewd businessman, Danny Biasone protected his investment by inventing the shot clock. Like many revolutionary ideas, his was simple. He divided the 2,880 seconds of a forty-eight-minute game by the average number of shots per game, which was 120. He arrived at an average of one shot taken every twenty-four seconds. By the new rule, if the team on offense failed to shoot the ball within twenty-four seconds of taking possession, the whistle would blow, and the other team would get the ball. When the NBA introduced Biasone's rule in 1954, the number of shot attempts and average scoring increased by 15 percent—in one year![3] The idea rescued pro basketball and ushered in its modern era.

Chances are the NCAA brass didn't actually consult Biasone in 1982. It didn't have to. By that time the NBA was a very successful sports enterprise, and the shot clock for college basketball was on everyone's mind. But the idea hadn't gone anywhere yet (except for one minor college league, the Sun Belt Conference, which had recently begun using a forty-five-second shot clock). In fact, basketball coaches around the country hated the idea. Just twenty days after the Carolina–Virginia letdown, the NCAA rules committee held a survey, and coaches voted against a thirty-second shot clock by a whopping 343 to 53. Even so, the NCAA rules committee pressed on, saying the shot clock was necessary "as a result of a decrease in scoring, what many people thought was an excessive use of zone defenses and because some teams were holding the ball a little too long . . ."[4] After a few years, as different leagues experimented with different rules, the NCAA eventually settled on a thirty-five-second shot clock. The days of stall-ball and angry fans were over. College basketball became immensely popular—and profitable. By 1989, CBS television paid $1 billion for the right to broadcast the postseason tournament, and by 1999 the network upped the ante to $6 billion, making college basketball one of the biggest revenue sports in U.S. history.[5]

The Rules of Politics

You may wonder why a book about politics begins with a story about basketball. But a close look reveals that there is more than basketball at play in the shot clock story. Sports are like controlled experiments in human behavior; they have much to tell us about the way people interact and why. The coaches and players are highly motivated, and how they play depends a lot on the rules of the game. When a new idea changes the rules of sports, players and coaches have new and different incentives. In basketball, a shot clock increases the costs of holding the ball for too long, while a three-point line increases the benefits of long-range shooting. When the rules of sports change, we get an unobstructed view into how incentives shape people's strategies and tactics, which largely determine how the game turns out.

The rules of politics work the same way. Voters, politicians, corporations, and all other political actors are driven largely by their incentives in politics, which in turn are determined by the rules of the political game at a given time and place. Politicians vote for government spending in ways that will get them more votes. Interest groups prefer to work with policymakers on specialized issues that don't attract negative publicity. And voter turnout is low on rainy days. As in basketball, the rules of politics determine how the game of social life is played. And, when the rules of politics change, this change gives political players new incentives. So the shot clock story is about more than basketball. It's an allegory for our story of political change, a microcosm of our broader tale, starring *madmen*, *intellectuals*, and *academic scribblers*.

These characters come to us from the pens of two prominent twentieth-century economists, John Maynard Keynes and Friedrich August von Hayek. Both articulated theories by which new ideas, sooner or later, sway public opinion and overwhelm status quo interests. In Keynes's landmark 1936 book, *The General Theory of Employment, Interest, and Money*, he said that "madmen in authority" unwittingly heed the counsel of "academic scribblers." By "madmen in authority," Keynes refered to policymakers—those people whose hands grip the policy levers and can change the rules of the game. In the shot clock story, they are the NCAA rules committee. In politics, they would be politicians, bureaucrats, and other decisionmakers in public policy. As for Keynes's "academic scribblers," they are philosophers, economists, and other thinkers whose main job is to produce ideas. In the book's final sentence, Keynes said it is ideas, not vested interests, that are ultimately "dangerous for good or evil."[6] Keynes said the academic scribblers win. They, not the vested interests who currently benefit from the status quo, ultimately control the madmen in authority.

Keynes's perspective is top down: The ideas of academic scribblers might originate in ivory towers, but they become concrete and influential as they work their way down to shape what broader circles of people believe. Madmen in authority might speak to the masses in everyday language, but, whether they know it or not, the depth of their message was penned by some bygone academic.

What about the *intellectuals* in our tale? For this we turn to Keynes's great adversary, Hayek, whose approach to ideas was similarly top down. But Hayek added a middle layer between the madmen and scribblers. In a 1949 essay, "The Intellectuals and Socialism," he argued that opinion makers who trade in ideas—whom he called "intellectuals"—select the academic ideas they like, edit and repackage them, then disperse these ideas into society. The problem, according to Hayek, is that intellectuals hold biased views. In Europe and the United States following World War II, where Hayek lived and worked, the intellectuals favored socialism, and the public discussion promoted by the press strongly favored this perspective. In other times and places, if intellectuals hold biased views toward some other set of ideas, we should expect the public discussion to tilt in that direction. Hayek argued that the intellectual class acts like a sieve between academic scribblers who generate ideas and the absorption of these ideas into the body of public attitudes, beliefs, and opinions, where madmen in authority make their appeal.

In short, Keynes and Hayek gave us a top-down process for thinking about the rules of the game and how they change. In basketball or public affairs, change usually is a tale of madmen, intellectuals, and academic scribblers, offering different ideas, changing the rules of the game, and giving people new incentives. If the NCAA rules committee plays the part of madmen in the shot clock story, with their hands on the levers of policy ready to change the rules of the game as needed, then the sports writers, with their allusions to Hamlet and Hemingway, are the intellectuals. And Danny Biasone, with his back-of-the-envelope arithmetic, plays the academic scribbler.

Coaches and players aren't chessboard pawns, of course. Neither are voters. Rather, they are individuals with their own goals, aspirations, talents, and limitations. And they have their own ideas about how the world should work—ideas that are shaped by life experiences, culture, age, and other influences that seem rather bottom up compared to the scribbles of some bygone academic. College coaches resisted the top-down shot clock idea in part because it was foreign to their long-held beliefs. College hoops, they believed, had done fine without a shot clock for eighty years. There was no time limit on possessions in Dr. James Naismith's original thirteen rules of the game. This shot clock idea—it just wasn't *right*.

So, apparently, the status quo can be a formidable foe. It consists of established, vested interests that benefit from the status quo rules. And it also has people's long-held beliefs on its side, which presents us with a challenge. We have Keynes and Hayek telling us that ideas eventually trump interests and change the world. Yet we look around and see that a lot of things do not seem to be changing, or seem to resist changing, even when we can imagine a better solution. So which is it? Do ideas really matter? Do they change the world? If so, how? And when?

Changing the Rules of Politics:
How and When Ideas Overcome Vested Interests

What major rule change or reform by the U.S. government has been most beneficial during your lifetime? Maybe you'll think of the Civil Rights Act, or the Endangered Species Act, or the Family Medical Leave Act. If you focus more on foreign policy, you might nominate the Shanghai Communiqué that came out of Nixon's trip to China, or the Strategic Arms Reduction Treaty with Soviet Russia to phase out nuclear missiles. If economic growth is your priority, your top pick might be the deregulation of the airline and trucking industries in the 1970s or the auction of radio frequency spectrum in the 1990s that ushered in the age of mobile communications.

Now flip the question over. What is the most wasteful and unjust policy in memory that was carried out by the federal government? If you or a loved one has ever desperately needed an organ transplant, you might nominate the National Organ Transplant Act of 1984, which created the shortages, waiting, and dying that we now have. Or perhaps your house has been taken by eminent domain, in which case you might point out that urban renewal programs destroyed the neighborhoods of millions of people in the twentieth century, especially African Americans and the poor among us.[7] Or perhaps you're a frequent flyer, in which case you might nominate the Transportation Security Administration's (TSA's) enhanced pat-downs and full-body imaging. If a family member is one of the 4 million people in jail or on parole for drug possession, your thoughts might drift to the war on drugs, which turned forty years old in 2011. And so on.

Quite a mixed bag, this government business. The fate of the human condition depends on how ordinary people respond to the rules of the game. And the rules of the game, in turn, depend largely on how governments respond to ideas circulating in society. The process of political rules adapting to a changing world—what we call political change—creates the new incentives that generate outcomes that we hope will improve the human condition and yet sometimes make it worse. Yet, for all its importance, political change doesn't easily surmount status quo forces.

Understanding political change is both simple and complex. It is simple because we need only focus on incentives to begin explaining the political world, yet complex because changing incentives is not like flipping a light switch. Incentives are embedded in institutions—the many rules of the game that make up politics, law, religion, art, and all other aspects of a society. Like athletes who get better through weight training, which tears muscle tissue so that it may grow back stronger, changing political rules requires tearing a people's institutional fabric. It is only natural to expect resistance to that, even if the result is beneficial.

And, like all human creations, a society's institutional fabric evolves. It is the product of a particular people in a given time and place in history. And it is in this context that new ideas are accepted or rejected. Consider, for example, the experiences of the English before and after the Industrial Revolution, of the Germans in the decades prior to World War II compared to the decades following it, of U.S. citizens before and after the terror attacks of 2001, or of the Chinese under Mao compared to the same people after decades of historic economic growth. In all these cases and more, the circumstances of time and place changed dramatically, creating a climate receptive to different ideas.

With this insight, we get a better view of how ideas matter and what conditions are needed for ideas to trump interests. Both Keynes and Hayek believed that top-down ideas are the driving force in political change, despite the opposition of vested interests or the current beliefs of the masses. An earlier giant in economic thought, John Stuart Mill (1806–1873), saw things differently. Ideas are of no consequence by themselves, Mill argued, unless "outward circumstances conspire with them."[8] According to Mill, ideas matter—in fact, they matter a lot—but they alone do not explain why change happens. It is not inevitable that ideas eventually sway public opinion and overwhelm vested interests. Something must happen to make the ideas relevant at a given time and in a given place.

In politics as in sports, change comes when conditions make it possible for new ideas to trump *both* vested interests and long-held beliefs. And *crisis* is the word that most easily evokes Mill's "outward circumstances." In college basketball, more (and more prominent) coaches gradually succumbed to the temptation to play stall-ball, and as this game-killing practice lost its stigma, a crisis emerged. After thirty years in the waiting, the time had come for Danny Biasone's big idea.

If you listen to politicians and pundits enough, crises both real and imagined will become exceedingly common. That's because madmen in authority are expected to *act* in response to a crisis, and the bigger the crisis the bigger the change expected—or allowed. During the Great Depression, unusually severe economic conditions created a political environment that was much more receptive to starting new government programs, including programs that likely would not have garnered equivalent support in earlier years. More recently, as President Barack Obama took office in the wake of the subprime and financial crises, his chief of staff offered the following advice: "Never let a serious crisis go to waste. What I mean by that is it's an opportunity to do things you couldn't do before."[9] Market advocates are tempted to draw the same connection between crisis and change. Milton Friedman, for example, said that truly major reform always requires some form of crisis.

But certainly Mill's "outward circumstances" can emerge without a crisis. Sometimes reforms evolve slowly in small increments until they snowball into major reform, as did the regulatory changes that helped create the housing boom in the first place. Sometimes simply unpleasant or inefficient conditions can move toward Mill's tipping point. For example, during the deregulation of the commercial airline industry in the 1970s, inflation and economic malaise certainly meant there was interest in reforming inefficient regulations. But these inefficiencies were nothing new; they had been brewing for decades. And even though the established players (Keynes's vested interests) in the industry strongly opposed reform, a major episode of deregulation still ultimately happened.

Nor is crisis *sufficient* for political change, as any advocate of budget reform or nationalized health care in the United States can attest. On both of these issues—health care and fiscal policy—politicians and pundits have been screaming "crisis" for decades. Yet neither issue has experienced a major reform that has stuck (in the sense of not being reversed by courts or future legislation). So although "crisis" most easily evokes Mill's "outward circumstances," we think it's neither necessary nor sufficient to effectuate major political change.

In all cases of political change—those that expand government and those that reduce it, those that spring from crisis and those that slowly emerge from bad conditions—an opportunity to do something big emerges. Certain people see those opportunities and act on them. A scribbler pens just the right idea. An intellectual spins an issue for public consumption. And then it becomes in the interests of the madmen in authority to do something about it—to change the rules of the game. In this book, we call all those people political entrepreneurs. Building on Mill, Keynes, and Hayek, we argue that change happens when it becomes in the interest of the madmen in authority to adopt new ideas and oppose established interests. As Mill explained it in 1845, "When the right circumstances and the right ideas meet, the effect is seldom slow in manifesting itself."[10]

Preview of the Story

Changing the rules of the game isn't easy, in basketball or in politics. But when bad rules give people incentives to do bad things, political change is needed to improve outcomes. In every chapter of this book we focus on three questions that are the key to understanding political change:

1. Why do democracies generate policies that are wasteful and unjust?
2. Why do failed policies persist over long periods, even when they are known to be socially wasteful and even when better alternatives exist?
3. Why do some wasteful policies get repealed (for example, airline rate and route regulation) while others endure (such as sugar subsidies and tariffs)?

The first question has a lot packed into it. To come up with an answer, you need sound ways of thinking about justice, as well as a standard for thinking about waste. As if that weren't enough, answering this question also requires a theory of how democracy works and why it often seems to fail. To get our arms around these big questions, we spend Chapters 2, 3, and 4 introducing you to some of the biggest thinkers in politics and economics that history has to offer.

For starters, Chapter 2 gets some advice from people who would know about justice: philosophers. Why visit with our philosopher friends? Think back again to our question about the most unjust government policy you can remember. In your answer, did you consider the purpose of government? Should its ultimate purpose be to promote freedom, or virtue, or justice, or some other good? Even more, what is a good society? How should we properly separate private and public life? What is the best form of government? Is it one with a strong executive or even a monarch, one with most powers delegated to a democratic assembly, one with a clear and respected division of powers, or some other arrangement? These are the timeless questions that point to where a people's political hearts lie and what they think the ideal political world would (or should) look like. Without these, we can hardly even pose the first question, much less develop a good answer.

To navigate the philosophical maze between us and our three motivating questions, Chapter 2 tells the story of history's greatest political philosophers and how their ideas do battle with one another. We'll hear their arguments and controversies, and we'll spice it with the details of their lives and how their life circumstances influenced their academic scribbles. We'll cover a lot of ground in a few pages, from the ancient Greeks to Renaissance philosophers and the minds of the Scottish Enlightenment, and from the American Founders to the Progressives. The chapter is like a drive-by tour ("please don't feed the philosophers!"), and we won't tarry. Our goal is simply to harvest from these ideas their implications for identifying and implementing good rules in society.

The second element of our leading question involves waste, otherwise known to economists as "inefficiency." In Chapter 3, we tell the story of modern economic theory joining the battle of political ideas by showing how government can (at least in theory) promote more efficient outcomes. As it turns out, modern economic theory is an outgrowth of the philosophers we will meet in Chapter 2. Almost chronologically, Chapter 3 thus picks up where two millennia of political philosophy leave off, to tell the story of neoclassical welfare economics. This is academic stuff, but it's also a big part of the real political world, because much of what government does is justified by economic theory. For example, the idea from welfare economics is that markets are good at most things, but, for a class of very important things, markets don't work well. So governments must intervene to correct market failure.

But economists also compete in the marketplace of ideas. Just as neoclassical welfare economists were finalizing the details of their theory in the 1950s, a new brand of thinking started to sprout, a brand of thinking known as public choice theory. In Chapter 4, we introduce this new theory—an *economic* theory—of politics. The basic idea of public choice is that economists shouldn't have one set of theories for a person making a commercial decision and a separate set of theories for that same person making a political decision. Economists working in the public choice tradition argue that if we're going to look at market failure, then it makes sense to see if there is government failure, too. With this perspective in mind, it becomes clear why democracies so often generate inefficient policies and why they allow them to persist.

In short, Chapters 2 through 4 provide a brief tour of political and economic thought, starting with ways to think about what is just, unjust, and wasteful in a society; moving on to consider measures of wastefulness in the market and how government might address it; then proceeding to review why government policies themselves may be wasteful. We then use this foundation to answer our first two questions: why democracies generate bad policies and why they so often persist.

The problem is that traditional public choice leaves us hanging on the question of why *some* policies get repealed and *others* do not. To that end, Chapter 5 lays out a framework for thinking about political change. Our framework matches the elements of political change (ideas, rules, and incentives) with the characters who make it happen (madmen, intellectuals, and academic scribblers), paying close attention to the circumstances at a particular time and place. In brief, the framework is the sum of four basic points about how and when political change happens:

1. Incentives determine people's behavior.
2. Institutions frame incentives.
3. Ideas influence institutions when "outward circumstances" become favorable.
4. Entrepreneurs make change happen.

In short, political change happens when entrepreneurs notice loose spots in the structure of ideas, institutions, and incentives and then find ways of implementing these new ideas into society's shared institutions. The entrepreneurs in political change may be philosophers, opinion makers, political leaders, or other types of influencers. What they have in common is an interest in better ideas—ones that improve the human condition—and having them become part of society's institutions, which in turn has an impact on incentives and outcomes.

To illustrate our thesis with applications to the real world, Chapter 6 details four case studies about significant episodes of political change, examining how rules were revised and how outcomes changed as a result. The welfare reform of the 1990s, for example, was said to be launched in response to the crisis of welfare policy in the country. This reform was preceded by significant academic research as well as other reform efforts, and we review the history of this experience. In contrast, the deregulation of airlines in the 1970s was not directly tied to an immediate crisis but instead the result of a confluence of factors. We will give the experience careful attention. Similarly, telecommunications reform in the 1990s helped spur the mobile communications revolution by making more spectrum available, but it was not the product of any crisis in the industry or its regulation. Rather, a budget crisis gave the critical push to a political change that had been building for years, a story we recount in detail.

All three of these examples—welfare reform, airline deregulation, and the reform of spectrum policy—produced economic gains. But the results of political change are not always positive. A prominent example is the housing bubble that emerged from 1997 to 2006, which was prompted in part by regulatory policies that had incrementally altered the incentives of people in housing and lending markets. As our fourth and final case study, the housing crisis shows the great negative consequences that can emerge when unproductive political entrepreneurship becomes systemic. We close Chapter 6 with a discussion of the changing policies related to this market and their serious consequences.

Finally, Chapter 7 makes use of the framework developed here to examine the role of political entrepreneurs—those who see and seize opportunities to effectuate political change. While the end result may be tremendous social benefits or massive waste, the act of political entrepreneurship always involves someone seeing an opportunity within the circumstances at hand and then acting. We look briefly at political entrepreneurs who have tried to change the world, and we derive a handful of principles that most successful political entrepreneurs are likely to have in common.

Over the course of these chapters, we dig deep to lay a foundation for thinking about good rules, and then we show how incentives matter in politics and how ideas, interests, and entrepreneurship effectuate political change over time.

2

The Never-Ending Quest for Good Government

We do not say that the production of potatoes is economic activity and the
production of philosophy is not. We say rather that, in so far as either kind of activity
involves the relinquishment of other desired alternatives, it has its economic aspect.
There are no limitations on the subject matter of Economic Science save this.

—Lionel Robbins, *An Essay on the Nature and*
Significance of Economic Science (1932)

Imagine you are taking part in one of the great revolutions in history. Maybe
it's the American Revolution, and you're helping Jefferson, Madison, Hamilton, and the others draft what will become the most enduring constitution
in the world. Perhaps it's 1789 in France, and you have joined the *philos-*
ophes in crafting a new political order that will send tremors across Europe
and beyond. Or perhaps it's 1918, and you are taking part in the Bolshevik
Revolution at Lenin's side. On a cheerier note, imagine you are in Prague
in 1989 during the revolution that peacefully split Czechoslovakia into two
countries, one for the Czechs who call it the Velvet Revolution and one for
the Slovaks who call it the Gentle Revolution.

In other words, imagine you are helping to shape the rules of politics.
What you decide will have deep and lasting consequences. Future generations will be more likely to live in prosperity, or poverty, based on the kind

of government you establish. The likelihood of war abroad or civil unrest at home will be greater, or lesser, based on the decisions made by you and your fellow revolutionaries. How will you decide what to do? As a leader in such a revolution, the *ideas* you hold—your beliefs and attitudes, preferences and prejudices—will matter. What is the best form of government? How should it be structured? Should it even be structured at all, or might the best rules simply emerge through the evolution of voluntary cooperation? In short, what should government do? What should it *not* do?

The way that you, as an individual, answer these questions depends on a lot of factors: your education, your sense of right and wrong, what you talk about with your friends, how you read history and literature, and whatever else you think is important. Your beliefs about the best form of government are a distilled version of the unique blend of influences in your life. Some of these influences are easy to identify: In the eighth grade, Mrs. Parsons inspired you to write a paper on Japan's political system. Other influences are more subtle and intermingled: the combination of people and events that have personally influenced you, the authors you have read, the figures who have influenced them, the influences on their influences, and so on. Whether knowingly or implicitly, we all approach the big political questions in life carrying with us a rich history of influential figures—some say baggage. The point is, you are not the first person to grapple with these issues, and neither are we. These questions have occupied the core attention of political philosophers for over two thousand years. This chapter provides a brief tour through some of their thoughts. The sheer beauty of political philosophy is that these questions endure. Its horror is that, for all our trouble and sometimes violent political conflict, humanity has arrived at precious few political truths after all this time.

Truth is a big word when it comes to politics. For example, is it *true* that democracies generate policies that are unjust, as our first motivating question from Chapter 1 seems to assume? Is it *true* that good rules of the game—that is, good political institutions—can lead to better outcomes from government? To give satisfying answers, we need an ideal against which to compare the actual. And this standard comes from our philosopher friends who, over the millennia, have laid the foundations of the economist's trade. In this light, there is no doing economics without also doing philosophy. Interestingly, if we take this chapter's opening quotation seriously, nor is it possible to do philosophy in an economic vacuum. Economics and philosophy, it seems, are connected at the hip.

Writing a little more than a decade before Lionel Robbins's 1932 book, Justice Oliver Wendell Holmes says the production of truth is like a competitive marketplace of ideas:

> When men have realized that time has upset many fighting faiths, they may come to believe even more than they believe the very foundations of their own conduct that the ultimate good desired is better reached by free trade in ideas—that the best test of truth is the power of the thought to get itself accepted in the competition of the market, and that truth is the only ground upon which their wishes safely can be carried out. (*Abrams v. United States* 250 US 616 [1919] at 630)

And like competition among college basketball teams, or competition among producers of potatoes, the outcome depends on the rules of the game. In philosophy, the most important rule is whether people have freedom of thought and expression. This is a very old argument. For example, in his *Areopagitica* (1644) John Milton pleads with his fellow Englishmen, ensnared in civil war, to practice tolerance. The Truth, he says, depends on it. "Let her and Falsehood grapple; whoever knew Truth to be put to the worse, in a free and open encounter?" You can find the same basic argument anywhere from Socrates, to John Stuart Mill, to Thomas Jefferson. Lionel Robbins says it's foregone alternatives that make a philosopher's trade an economic one. Channeling Danny Biasone's shot clock, we add the important point that the economics of ideas is about the rules of the game, too.

Morality, Rules, and the Good

For many political philosophers, the quest for political truth starts with figuring out what behavior is moral. Think about this for a moment. The study of politics begins with the study of individuals—who are we, what is in our hearts, how do we use our minds, how do we make moral decisions, are we inherently sociable or violent? These are delicate questions, but we have to understand that individual morality is at the heart of the big political questions. What makes political philosophy *political* is that it considers what types of rules a society should adopt to achieve what its people, as moral individuals, think is good. Morality, rules, good: These are the three basic ingredients in play.

If you follow scandals among contemporary American politicians, you might not think moral behavior and government go together. People in government do a lot of very bad things; they always have, and they always will. Some of the worst evils governments have committed arose from attempts to legislate morality. Yet many important, desirable rules about behavior within a society are made and enforced by government. Murder and blackmail are illegal, and that's a good thing. Perhaps government is simply people's collective way to recognize and reinforce what they were already doing peacefully and cooperatively anyway. Murder and blackmail were wrongful acts before they became illegal. Government can codify and perhaps even promote the framework of rules within which people in a society cooperate, prosper, and flourish in any number of ways that they, as individuals, believe are good.

It sounds rather simple in that light, this whole political philosophy endeavor. Choose the good, eschew the bad. But the devil is in the details.

In this chapter, we ask you to follow a brief tour of the history of Western political thought, from the ancients all the way up to the twentieth century. To make it fun along the way, and to grasp the details of our philosopher friends much better, we also tour their historical context. The societies in which they lived and the events of their times influenced the ways in which their ideas were founded, nurtured, and either accepted or rejected, often with horrible violence. Ideas have consequences. Circumstances do, too.

To lay this foundation for the rest of the book, we begin where the philosophers begin.

The Greeks and the Idea of a Democracy

Every art and inquiry, and similarly every action and
intentional choice, is held to aim at some good.
—Aristotle, *Nicomachean Ethics*

Some of the earliest and most influential philosophers thought a lot about the best form of government and how people should live within a society. These thinkers include Socrates, Plato, and Aristotle, otherwise known as the primary contributors to the School of Athens.

As is often the case with ideas that change the world, the historical, cultural, and physical settings matter. The physical setting was the land of Homer's *Odyssey*, among the city-states of ancient Greece. The historical setting was Athens of 470–430 B.C.E., a brief period of peace and prosperity marked by war both before and after and one of the most celebrated societies in history. The war (490–470 B.C.E.) that preceded this era saw Athens and Sparta join forces to avoid becoming the latest addition to the Persian Empire. The peace that followed soon gave way to the Peloponnesian War (430–400 B.C.E.), in which the former allies Athens and Sparta fought each other.

The School of Athens flourished during this brief era of peace, as did the society itself. The city-state of Athens had a prosperous economy for the time, using its port and navy to trade with neighbors. But it was the type of government that was unique. Athens had one of the "purest" democracies in world history. This observation merits some clarification, however, as women, slaves, and foreigners did not participate in the political process. Athens was a pure or direct democracy in the sense that all free adult male citizens could participate in the general assembly, which voted on a variety of matters small and large. There were no representatives, as everyone simply represented himself. Nor was there a president, an executive branch, or any alphabet soup of executive-branch agencies. There was a type of judiciary, a supreme court made up of perhaps a thousand citizens who rotated on an alphabetical basis and which, not incidentally, was rather hard to bribe with so many members. Democracy, indeed. Many political philosophers and even more politicians have commended the virtues of Athenian democracy, before moving on to argue for representative or monarchical government. Yet no society in history has been as famous or as democratic as ancient Greece, even though it was a remarkably brief period.

Looking back on this experiment in "pure" democracy, we may be tempted to thank the most famous Greek philosophers for their ideas. They might well respond with an "I told you so." Socrates, Plato, and Aristotle certainly have unkind words for democratic institutions, and some modern scholars attribute the disappearance of democracy and its sluggish emergence in the West to these criticisms. At the least, the ideas of the School of Athens had a major influence on decisions about the best form of government in the history of Europe. Yet even that is understating their influence. Listen closely in political debates today, and you can hear the whisper of these ancient Greeks.

What is wrong with democracy? We turn first to Plato (427–347 B.C.E.). According to Plato, democracy is seemingly perfect because it reflects the will of the people. But it too easily turns to disaster, like anarchy or the rule of the mob. Exhibit 1 in Plato's attack on democracy is the execution of his mentor, Socrates, by the Athenian "majority" that ruled the day. "I only wish it were so," says Socrates as he nears death, "that the many could do the greatest evil; for then they would also be able to do the greatest good—and what a fine thing this would be! But in reality they can do neither; for they cannot make a man either wise or foolish . . ."[1]

Democracy is not the best form of government, Plato argues, because its end is merely freedom, not virtue, that higher value taught by Socrates. If they are focused on freedom, people are less likely to do what is right, or virtuous. Plato claims that a just society could be achieved if the people were truly virtuous, but they are not. Few achieve virtue. Those few, according to Plato, should lead.

To Plato, then, the ideal government requires that a philosopher become the king, or that the king become a philosopher. Surprisingly to the modern reader, Plato says that it doesn't matter which of these two approaches is taken. This is because the philosopher who is properly educated and subsequently made king would make decisions for the benefit of all citizens and, by the power of the crown, would be sufficiently powerful to execute these decisions. Similarly, a king already has such power and, if subsequently educated, would produce the same benefit.

The philosopher-king might be a single ruler or even a small group of rulers. What matters to Plato is that they be properly trained. That is, those persons who Plato reckons should lead society are *made*, not born. The leaders would be properly educated and thereby deserving of their privileged position. As rulers they would be philosophers, so they would act in the best interests of all the people. Education and merit aside, the exclusivity—some might say elitism—of such a government is almost entirely foreign to us. There would be no private property among the ruling class, and there would be no formal means by which the rest of society could express their approval or disapproval of the rulers. No rulers would be voted off the island like some game show contestant. And no feedback would be solicited.

But we would be hasty to dismiss Plato's model of government simply for being undemocratic. In fact, Plato offers a thoughtful critique of democracy (perhaps best thought of as "democracy gone wild"), and it's a critique that has remained relevant for centuries. It was on the mind of the founders of the U.S. system. In the modern era, Plato also can be claimed as an ally of autocratic leaders and quasi-dictators across the world. In less-developed countries with poorly developed democratic institutions—from Africa to Asia to Latin America—many have exploited Plato's virtue-over-freedom concern to establish rules that maintain a strong executive against a legislature or judiciary trying to limit their control. Nor are less-developed countries with inadequate political institutions the only places where one can see a powerful executive express concern about constraints imposed by democracy. Just look at the United States.

Supporters of President George W. Bush argued that the Twenty-Second Amendment, which limits presidents to two terms in office, made it difficult for the president to protect the United States from terrorist attack. Only a few years earlier, supporters of President Bill Clinton argued that he could, with or without support from Congress, send U.S. troops to Kosovo in an effort to prevent genocide. And President Obama reasserted the president's right to carry out extrajudicial killings, while continuing his predecessor's policy of holding suspected terrorists indefinitely and without trial. Various interests have argued that the "War on Terror" should allow the U.S. president to engage in conduct outside the scope of court review in pursuing and interrogating individuals, including U.S. citizens, who are deemed to be a threat to national security. In this modern incarnation it is security rather than virtue that leaders have used to justify ever-greater degrees of political power.

The branches of Plato's core argument go in many directions, neither starting nor ending in the United States. But the philosophical root is the same. A strong leader, educated and virtuous, should protect the people and should not be constrained by the democratic masses or other institutions. Thus, you might invoke Plato if you are, for example, a president with an interest in taking some action that is politically unpopular or legally questionable, but that you think is important for your citizens to flourish. Or perhaps you want to protect oppressed people in a faraway country, saving innocent lives. You might want to save your country from recession, or save the planet from extinction, or even save your job in the next election. Or you might simply think that decisions about the big questions of governance should be made by the "best and brightest" in society. In short, many of our modern arguments about limits on political institutions in general and democracy in particular have their roots in Plato.

The ideas of Plato's most famous student, Aristotle (384–322 B.C.E.) have had a similarly grand impact on political philosophy. Like Plato, Aristotle also is concerned about the good and the conditions needed to achieve it. Their differences are notable, too. In terms of political philosophy, Plato emphasizes the need for education, especially for the rulers, while Aristotle stresses the need to overcome moral weakness.

Aristotle is famous for many insights, including his advice for how to live a virtuous life. He recommends making decisions in accordance with a "golden mean"—the avoidance of extremes in favor of a middle or moderate position. Aristotle also applies the "golden mean" concept to political philosophy. There is a "golden mean" between rule by the elite and rule by the mob, a type of constitutionally limited government that lies between aristocracy and pure democracy. But living in accordance with the "golden mean" does not, in the philosophy of Aristotle, lead one to advocate democracy. Rather, he prefers aristocracy and is greatly troubled by democracy.

To see why Aristotle prefers aristocracy, let us consider his approach. He places along a continuum those governments that are most likely to bring the good, or virtue, to the most people. These are good governments. Then he lists those that do not bring the good, which are the bad governments. As shown in Table 2.1, the bad governments include tyranny, oligarchy, and demagogy. The good governments include monarchy, aristocracy, and some form of limited democracy. All of the good forms of government are good only if the rulers are virtuous.

It is important to note that the number of rulers does not necessarily imply good or bad government. A monarch who does not act with virtue and abuses the people is a tyrant. An aristocracy that does the same is an oligarchy. A well-governed and limited democracy that wanders away from virtue heads toward demagogy. While some might call this latter condition a state of anarchy, the label is misplaced, as anarchy implies no government, while demagogy implies the presence of a government, only one that essentially is "led" by everyone and is, thus, without order.

Aristotle argues that, in a sense, the best form of good government is monarchy, but when it goes bad and becomes tyranny, it is the worst of the bad. The problem is that the temptations for a king to move in this direction are strong. Similarly, democracy gives way far too easily to anarchy.

One could argue that the modern's penchant for democracy simply represents a millennia-long evolution along Aristotle's continuum, from monarchy to aristocracy to democracy. But this would not be Aristotelian. Rather, Aristotle's golden mean is in the middle, with aristocracy. If we focus on the choice among good governments and, at the same time, recognize the tremendous costs that accrue when these governments go bad, then the golden mean appears reasonable, as it does to Aristotle. The ideal is a small group of

Table 2.1.   Forms of government in classical thought.

	Rule by One	Rule by a few	Rule by many/all
Bad (less likely to promote virtue)	Tyranny	Oligarchy	Demagogy
Good (more likely to promote virtue)	Monarchy	Aristocracy	Democracy

leaders, educated and virtuous. It's a position somewhere between Plato and the modern political world.

Today's developed democracies don't give much attention to monarchs versus aristocrats, tyranny versus virtue. But the tensions between Plato and Aristotle are still evident. Take, for example, the modern approach in the United States to blend expertise with power, as evidenced by the growing list of policy areas to which the White House has assigned top administration appointees (known ironically in the news media as "czars").[2] Between them, Presidents George W. Bush and Barack Obama have appointed a combined 113 people to posts that include the well-known drug czar, intelligence czar, and climate czar. There are also czars for weapons, war, terrorism, manufacturing, green jobs, AIDS, global AIDS, bird flu, mine safety, food safety, copyright, and autos. There are even czars for faith and reading, along with czars appointed for executive compensation, bank bailouts, and stimulus accountability. Not to be outdone, Congress has given experts the power to govern areas of life that include regulation of markets, disaster aid, retirement pensions, agriculture subsidies, tax credits for everything from child care to divorce, and far more.

The contribution to political theory made by the Greeks is dwarfed only by their contributions to philosophy in general. In the practice of politics, Athens provides one of history's clearest examples of direct democracy. But it is the theory, the ideas, that have been most influential. Plato and Aristotle offer harsh criticism of the Athenian model, casting a skeptical eye on democratic institutions and influencing ideas about government for over 2,000 years. Their ideas still influence us today.

The Romans and the Idea of a Republic

Apart from ancient Greece, few other societies contributed more to early political thought than ancient Rome. While Rome was one of the first societies to be influenced by Greek thought, its early political organization in fact preceded the School of Athens and endured in one form or another for much longer, almost a millennium. The reign includes the Roman Republic (509 B.C.E.–49 B.C.E.), followed by a period of conflict and transition (49 B.C.E.–29 B.C.E.) and the Roman Empire (29 B.C.E.–476 C.E.). While the fall of Rome in 410 C.E. is often cited as the beginning of the end of the Roman Empire, it is worth noting that this was the first time in nearly 800 years the great city had been successfully invaded. There was something particularly enduring about this society.

The Roman Republic began with the fall of a monarch in 509 B.C.E. The Senate, which had existed in a weak form under a strong monarch, assumed control. A leader from the Senate would be named consul, later to be called praetor, and would assume executive responsibilities. The Senate itself carefully defined these responsibilities, and a Roman "executive" in this era had little in common with the executive branch of modern governments. But for many centuries, this arrangement allowed the Senate to provide a political counter to continuous rule by a single monarch. Members of the Senate were aristocrats of noble birth and significant land holdings. They were complemented by assemblies that granted representation to talented but nonaristocratic members of Roman society, called plebians, and other assemblies that had less-expansive authority but even broader representation of citizens.

It is this Roman experience—including its ideas about government and how this government worked in practice—that has influenced political thought across centuries. And it is one thinker in particular, Marcus Tullius Cicero (106 B.C.E.–43 B.C.E.), who did the most to communicate its ideals. Cicero lived at the tail end of the Roman Republic, and he died as the Republic was dying. It was in this era that Julius Caesar assumed powers of a dictator, with the ability to appoint additional members to the Senate and even veto its decisions. In the civil war that engulfed Rome following Caesar's assassination, Cicero would be one of its most prominent victims.

Though he was a skilled politician, it is Cicero's philosophy of politics that has endured. He wrote two books that specifically address political philosophy. Neither has survived fully intact, but excerpts from the writings show a mind grasping at the question of the best political order.

Given that this question of the best political order was addressed by the Greeks, it is not surprising that Cicero has a decidedly Greek approach, though one tailored to the Roman experience. He studied under schools that claimed to be descended from Plato. Like those of Plato and Aristotle, Cicero's ideas reflect a strong dose of skepticism, as well as the sense that life should be based on reason, not pleasure. As a good skeptic, Cicero doubts the certainty of any particular philosophy. As a successful politician, he seeks to pick ideas that would work to create a better society.

Cicero starts by examining the proper nature of a commonwealth—an assembly of people who associate with respect to the administration of justice and the common good. Like his Greek forebears, he recognizes that a commonwealth may be a monarchy, aristocracy, or democracy and that when they go bad their respective counterparts are tyranny, oligarchy, and demagogy. He observes that, because of the risks associated with any one form of government, a successful regime includes a mix of all three. That is, the best government would combine a king (monarch), with some authority granted to nobles (aristocracy) and other matters left to the people (democracy). The title of Cicero's first book, *Republic*, indicates where he is going, while the title of his second, *Laws*, reflects the importance of a set of rules that enforce and maintain that type of good government.

While the concept of a republic as presented by Cicero is not identical to what latter political theorists would envision—including James Madison's conception of the American republic—some elements are clear. A republic is neither a monarchy, as most governments known to the Greeks and Romans had been, nor a direct democracy in the style of the Greek city-states. It is a democracy with some degree of representation. This observation surely would have been obvious to the Romans, who had been living with their republic for almost five centuries. But Cicero adds something more. He is clearly aware of a decline in the ideals of the Roman Republic, and it would be but a few years after his death that the Roman Republic became the Roman Empire.

It is in this criticism and concern that Cicero articulates one of the most important concepts in political philosophy, the *balance of power*. He is the first philosopher to very clearly do so. The idea of a balance of power was unique because it went beyond the mutually exclusive types of government—monarchy, aristocracy, or democracy—to a careful mix of these or similarly powerful and competing institutions. The challenge, then as now, was to ensure that no single person or institution of government had too much power. This balance of power within representative democracy would later be recognized as a key element to many successful political systems, to government based on a republic.

It should be noted that a republican form of government does not mean a government run by Republicans, as that label is understood in the present-day United States, any more than a democratic form of government means a government run by Democrats. In the United States, Republicans represent an evolving set of political principles held by politicians who have included Abraham Lincoln, Dwight Eisenhower, Ronald Reagan, George H. W. Bush, and George W. Bush, while Democrats likewise represent an evolving set of political principles held by politicians who have included Thomas Jefferson, Franklin Delano Roosevelt, Jimmy Carter, Bill Clinton, and Barack Obama. In contrast, democratic and republican forms of government are ideal types, against which real governments may be compared. Because they are run by imperfect and fallible human beings, real governments are never ideal governments. The Roman model was no exception.

It would be foolish, therefore, for Republicans in the United States to present themselves as modern-day Romans and just as foolish for Democrats in the United States to style themselves as modern-day Greeks. On the other hand, both Greek and Roman influences pervade Western political systems. For example, the American Founders designed a representative government with a strong emphasis on checks and balances among competing institutions. Within the legislative institution, the more exclusive branch, often called the most exclusive club in the world, is the U.S. Senate, named after its Roman counterpart. A tour of Congress reveals exhibits and materials that show a clear philosophical lineage back to Greece and Rome. One can even see the Greco-Roman influence in the architecture of capitol buildings in Washington, D.C., in the American state capitals, and in many parts of Western Europe as well.

Cicero tried to save the Roman Republic, but he was too late. While many scholars have sought to understand why Rome fell, an equally valuable question is why its republican form of government endured for half a millennium, followed by an empire for another 500 years. Put in modern terms, what did the Roman republic do particularly well? What mistakes were made that modern society would be wise to avoid?

Some of the wealthiest and most stable democracies in the world have answered the first question by applying key elements of the Roman system, with a republican form of government and, importantly, a careful balance of powers. With regard to its failures, plenty has been written, including Edward Gibbon's classic, *The History of the Decline and Fall of the Roman Empire*, published in 1776. While Gibbon takes six volumes to provide a complete answer, suffice it to say that he casts a lot of blame on a loss of virtue among the citizenry—a critique one might expect from the Greek philosophers— along with the outsourcing of military services to mercenaries, a decreased interest in worldly affairs, and greater concern for the afterlife due to the rise of Christianity in the empire. In fact, religion would play a key role in political philosophy in the years to come.

The Middle Ages: Monarchs, Popes and Political Thought

After Rome fell, the rules of politics were set not by a strong central government but by small, unconnected societies scattered across the former empire. The Catholic Church would be perhaps the most powerful political force in the region for the more than 800 years known as the Middle Ages. In addition to substantial political power, the Church held a virtual monopoly on the training of intellectuals—almost all of them monks and priests—and thus largely controlled the development of new ideas, whether in theology, philosophy, or politics. Like most monopolies throughout history, it was not a source of great innovation.

Two of the most important Church philosophers of the Middle Ages also serve as bookends for the period. Writing near the beginning is St. Augustine of Hippo (354–430). Near the end is St. Thomas Aquinas (1225–1274). Both play key roles in shaping theological as well as political thought.

St. Augustine is one of the most prolific writers and deepest thinkers in the history of Christianity. His many contributions cover important issues of the day, such as the concept of original sin, free will, and the relationship between faith and reason. But Augustine's insights on *politics* play a key role in Western thought as well. He views the Church and state as separate authorities, with the Church responsible for the Heavenly City and deriving its authority from God and the state responsible for the Earthly City. His ideas would strengthen the Church as compared to other institutions of the day, especially monarchies.

In one of his more famous works, *The City of God*, Augustine responds to the argument that Rome fell because of the rise of Christianity. In doing so, he shapes an argument about the proper role of the state, drawing on his broader worldview that situates the Church as the central human institution. That view was to hold sway for a thousand years.

Augustine's argument encompasses the Church, the State, the Heavenly City, and the Earthly City. The Heavenly City is that which awaits those who live according to the Christian faith, while the Earthly City is for those who live only for this present life. The Church and State set rules for individuals to live their earthly lives, but only the Church extends its concern to earthly conduct that will get one to heaven as well. Augustine is skeptical of the State, considering it far too susceptible to human sinfulness, much as the Greeks worried about human selfishness as an impediment to a successful democracy. He pays less attention to human imperfections within the Church itself. As we'll see in Chapter 3, the mainstream of economic theory in the twentieth century also would pay little attention to human imperfections within political institutions.

In effect, the European political system during the Middle Ages was comprised of two institutions that would maintain an uneasy balance. One was led by a pope, while the other was led by an emperor or monarch. For most of the period, few thinkers looked on the Church with open criticism, probably because they were affiliated with it. And few thinkers bothered to look critically at the role of government, apart from jealously guarding papal interests as against the emperor or monarch. With a monopoly stranglehold on the marketplace of ideas, change would come slowly.

As the most important philosopher at the end of the Middle Ages, St. Thomas Aquinas (1225–1274) is an early example of the Church scholars known as the Scholastics, who emphasize the integrity of the individual in social thought. His influence is so great that Aquinas remains today a significant force in Catholic theology, and his political thought plays the pivotal role, more than anyone else of his day, of rediscovering the philosophy of Aristotle for the Christian world. The Crusaders returned from Muslim lands with Arabic translations of Aristotle. In addition, monks in Toledo translated the Arabic versions of Greek philosophy that already had become part of the Islamic Golden Age. These works influenced Aquinas and other scholars of the era, who in turn would affect Christian thought for centuries.

If we examine the life and works of Aquinas through the economic lens of Lionel Robbins, it makes sense that his political philosophy is remarkably Aristotelian. As a Catholic at a time when the Church was splitting, Aquinas may see the theme of Aristotelian balance as an advantage to his arguments about the best political rules. He argues that, just as the Church has authority, so should some men rule over others, owing to their superior virtue and knowledge of the good. A monarchy is the best form of government in theory, but it degrades to the worst form when the king eschews virtue. Given human nature, the best form of government, therefore, balances monarchy, aristocracy, and some form of democracy. In short, it produces a type of political Aristotelian mean that is reminiscent of Cicero's justification of the Roman forum.

It is of no small consequence that Aquinas and the rest of the Scholastics are sympathetic to interests of the pope over that of kings. But in framing their arguments, they also tend to advance the interests of people ruled over by both popes and kings. Given the papacy's competition with monarchs for political control, this is good politics, as it helps place the crown in a more subordinate position relative to the papacy. This is a significant step because it implies that the king is not automatically good. Justice, in other words, may depend on countering the power of kings. With this relative weakening of the crown, however, over time democratic institutions that were more representative of the people emerge to challenge both kings and popes.

Aquinas goes so far as to argue that under certain circumstances it may be proper to overthrow a king who had abused his power and was, much as Aristotle might have said, not good. Of course, it was not the case that kings and queens were suddenly at risk of being deposed by unhappy subjects, and Aquinas clarifies that the Church and it alone was to pass judgment on an unjust monarch. Nonetheless, the idea that a monarch could be judged by any mortal, even the pope, is an important step toward checks and balances against the abuse of power.

The Middle Ages saw the rise of ecclesiastical authority over the authority of kings, which helped lay the moral groundwork for future political ideas that would limit and separate political power. These ideas were becoming institutionalized during Aquinas's lifetime. Most significantly, in 1215, the Magna Carta limits the power of kings by granting certain rights to subjects. The Magna Carta is, of course, largely considered the foundation of constitutional law in the English-speaking countries of the world today. The English cherish it as the foundation of their democracy based on common law and fundamental rights. The U.S. Capitol displays a copy of the Magna Carta document for all visitors to see. Such is the reverence in the United Kingdom that, when this country was considering whether to lengthen the time a suspected terrorist could be held without charge, one prominent politician referred to it as "the day the Magna Carta died." The originally specified rights have evolved to serve more as general principles than specific political rules, although certain rights like habeas corpus and limits on eminent domain are direct descendants with practical relevance to the balance of the individual rights against government (whether in the form of a king, prime minister, or president), even eight centuries later.[3]

The Renaissance: Romance and Realism in Politics

Many have imagined republics and principalities that never really existed at all. Yet the way men live is so far removed from the way they ought to live that anyone who abandons what is for what should be pursues his downfall rather than his preservation; for a man who strives after goodness in all his acts is sure to come to ruin, since there are so many who are not good.

—*Niccolò Machiavelli, The Prince*

The European Renaissance of the fourteenth through the sixteenth centuries is largely seen as a rebirth of thought in theology, philosophy, and politics (the word *renaissance* literally means "a new birth" in Italian). It shaped art, architecture, literature, science, and religion in enduring ways. It also influenced politics. Perhaps no political thinker is more identified with Renaissance thinking than is Niccoló Machiavelli (1469–1527). He is history's greatest political realist. Francis Bacon (whom we'll meet presently) certainly thinks so, describing the world as indebted to Machiavelli for writing about what people *do*, not what they *ought* to do, as Machiavelli's most famous work, *The Prince* (written in 1513, published in 1532), bluntly renders matters in the quotation opening this section.

For almost two millennia before Machiavelli, Western political thought was heavy on romance, neglecting to question whether it is in the interests of rulers to pursue the good. By examining the *ruler's* tradeoffs when considering different courses of action, Machiavelli may be the first philosopher of political *economy*—in the parlance of today's social sciences, he uses "positive" theory (what is) rather than "normative" theory (what should be). And being the first philosopher to eschew the idealistic in favor of the practical, Machiavelli's ideas changed the way the world looks at politics. The most authoritative translation of Machiavelli's *The Prince* states that it is "the most famous book on politics when politics is thought to be carried on for its own sake, unlimited by anything above it."[4]

Machiavelli's fame endures more commonly in the expression "Machiavellian," often used to refer to a win-at-all-costs politician, a scheming professor in a university academic department, a backstabbing co-worker, or even that meddling member of your homeowners' association. But these pejoratives are mostly unfair because they fail to appreciate Machiavellian means versus ends. When Machiavelli writes of ends, they are generally of the sort that would be admired by the modern reader. But when he speaks of means, we are shocked, shocked! Perhaps this is because he is the first to do so in such a candid and direct way.

Machiavelli's honesty is seen most clearly in *The Prince*, his most famous and most hastily written work. Here, he writes to the teenage Prince Lorenzo de Medici, newly installed as the Florentine leader and holder of Machiavelli's fate as the latter writes from a prison cell. Gambling mightily, Machiavelli decides to tell his audience the brutal truth: that all of political philosophy is flawed because it offers no practical insight about how to act in the real world. Rather, classical political thought is too focused on theoretical models, on ideals.

A clear example of this excessive focus on ideals is Plato's allegory of the cave. Plato's lesson is that politics should be guided by a "reality" that is not seen except by those few who are able to escape from the cave. This is Plato's model of the enlightened leader who is supposed to understand the world as it really is. But in the real world there are no leaders who are so thoroughly enlightened. Thus, what Plato offers is not realism; it is idealism of the first order.

Machiavelli is a radical departure from Plato. In understanding republics, or any form of government in which real, fallible human beings rule we should not abandon "what is for what should be." The practical lesson is to recognize the limits of good intentions. This is especially true in politics, where good intentions and true friends are fleeting. As two former U.S. presidents, Harry Truman and Bill Clinton, were fond of saying, if you want a friend in Washington, get a dog.

A deeper lesson, perhaps, is that circumstances of time and place limit the ruler's ability to pursue the good. Sometimes a little wastefulness and injustice is the least negative course of action. Conditions aren't always favorable to rule as a philosopher-king would. One is not to make a profession of pure goodness but to make a profession of acting wisely in a world full of both good and bad people who are doing good and bad things. The point is to succeed in navigating such a world. Do the "right thing" by acting and speaking nobly and truthfully, but only when this makes it possible to achieve one's ends. When necessary, you must know when, and how, to employ dark means and make a deal with the devil—or one of the many corrupt popes in those days, or even a foreign prince if he has enough armies.

In *The Prince*, then, Machiavelli provides one of the first and most famous primers on the means to political advantage. Then as now, however, the means we use to gain such advantage and promote our goals can be a force for good or evil, so we would do well to understand the process by which this change occurs. In this sense, Machiavelli provides a blueprint for entrepreneurship in social and political change, a theme we take up in Chapter 5.

But Machiavelli offers more than a means for negotiating one's way in the world. He also offers a more general framework for good government. To see this, however, one has to read his less famous work, *The Discourses*. There, he sets out the basic elements of his ideal form of government. Unsurprisingly, it is heavily influenced by Greek and Roman thought, especially the latter. Democracy is good, but it can be unruly. Monarchs may be wise, but they are often tyrants. A better government does not give too much power to one group but instead balances monarchy (princes), aristocracy (nobility), and democracy (the people as a whole). In so doing, Machiavelli sets forth the idea of checks and balances, an idea that goes at least to Cicero and (as we'll see presently) that Locke and Montesquieu would advocate more formally in coming centuries, all of which would influence the American Founders.

Thus, while most people think the Machiavelli of *The Prince* explains the cutthroat politics in their nation's capital, Machiavelli of *The Discourses* also says much about the best rules for the political game when looked at realistically instead of romantically.

The Spanish Scholastics: Early Interest in Individual Rights

We've already previewed the Scholastics' intellectual tradition, initiated primarily by St. Thomas Aquinas. In the sixteenth century, this intellectual tradition was reinvigorated by the Spanish Scholastics, in what is sometimes called the School of Salamanca. They rose to prominence in the early to mid-1500s, as Spain grappled with questions related to its expanding empire. Francisco de Vitoria and the Jesuit scholars Juan de Mariana, Luis de Molina, and Francisco Suarez are counted among its most famous contributors.

Like Aquinas, the Spanish Scholastics advocate a doctrine of natural rights based on a mix of revelation and reason. What is most significant, however, is that these thinkers extend this concept of rights to individuals outside of their own society, with remarkable results. Specifically, Spain is the first empire in history to seriously question its conquest of other lands and other peoples.

Aiming their pens at the papacy and the Spanish Crown, the Spanish Scholastics argue that the natural rights of individuals are not to be taken from them by anyone, including the Church. They further argue that these rights are inherent to the individual and exist regardless of the individual's sin or lack of grace. Among these fundamental rights is the right to one's own person— such as the right to not be a slave—and the right to one's land and possessions.

Prior to the Spanish Scholastics, it was unheard of to argue for such rights for the subjugated peoples of conquered lands. No less an authority than Aristotle presents two contrasting forms of human existence, master and slave. Ironically, it is that famous Scholastic, Aquinas, who helps reintroduce Aristotle to European thought. Yet Aristotle's position would hold sway for another three centuries in many parts of Europe and the Americas. The Spanish Scholastics of the sixteenth century simply were ahead of their time, planting the seeds of future rules by engaging the philosophical and moral ideas of their day.

The impassioned and forceful arguments of Vitoria on behalf of people who were not his countrymen—but were subject to the rule of his countrymen— have led a number of observers to call this Spanish Scholastic the father of international law. Others in this school of thought argue for the rights of the individual within a country. In particular, Juan de Mariana is remembered today for arguing that a ruler who had become a tyrant could be deposed, including by force.

While less directly related to political economy, the Spanish Scholastics also make contributions to economic theory, especially in the area of money and inflation (and as gold flows in from the Americas, they have much to study). They also offer an early defense of usury. So valuable were these insights that some scholars argue that it is the Scholastics of Spain, rather than the Calvinists of England, who do the most to lay the intellectual foundations for capitalism. At the least, they are laying the groundwork for a deeper appreciation of individual rights in political philosophies to come.

The Enlightenment: Individual Rights Meet Social Contracts

The Age of Enlightenment is known for its seminal contributions to philosophy and subsequent influence on political discourse. A hundred years earlier, Machiavelli had broken new ground in turning political thought toward realism, though it cannot be said that he changed philosophy itself. That would be left to Francis Bacon (1561–1626) and René Descartes (1596–1650).

Bacon is seen by many scholars as the first to argue generally that ideas based on reason should replace ideas based on faith. Perhaps his most important contribution to philosophy is empiricism, which emphasizes rational thought and use of the scientific method (building on Galileo and the Renaissance scientists). Bacon's ideas are not only a big step away from Church authority; they are a necessary step for the scientific and industrial revolutions to come.

Descartes is to France what Bacon is to England, a major philosopher who helps liberate inquiry from the limits of mysticism and idealism. Whereas Bacon introduces empiricism, Descartes opens the door to rationalism, based on Cartesian logic. His focus on the individual as a rational being is a philosophic concern more than a political one, but it affects political philosophers to come. From Descartes, the individual can recognize him- or herself as a rational, thinking being apart from the rest of the world. Ultimately, Descartes establishes the individual as the starting point of all modern philosophy and the end to which all political philosophy must lead. This is a leap of historic proportions, and, as we'll see in the next chapter, starting in the 1870s all of economic theory begins with the analysis of the individual.

For political philosophy as well as science, Bacon's empiricism and Descartes' rationalism provide the foundation on which future thinkers will build. By replacing revelation based on scripture with reason based on observation, they change philosophy and science. They also open the door for

political philosophers to argue that laws should be based on reason, not revelation, and help further the argument that rights should attribute to individuals. Some of the most important political philosophers in history will make
their contributions in the wake of these changes.

The State-of-Nature Approach

One example is Thomas Hobbes (1588–1679). Here is a leading representative of a key branch of political philosophy, one who sees government as a
necessary element to create order in civil society. Hobbes's view of human
nature is important because, unlike Aristotle, he does not see humans as
essentially political beings. Rather, he sees them as fearful, with fear of a
violent death especially relevant. For those in the state of nature, there is no
protection from the aggression of others and thus no incentive to plant that
which may be sown by others or to build anything that may be taken by
others. Property cannot exist in such a state. Conditions would be bleak, a
war of all against all, and hence Hobbes is most famously remembered for his
commentary on the state of nature prior to civil society, in which life would
surely be "solitary, poor, nasty, brutish, and short."

Hobbes argues that to ensure protection and establish peace—goals that
would later influence the American Founders—there must be a mutual but
minimal laying down of rights. That is, each person must give up as much
freedom as every other person, starting with the right to kill the other. This
mutual agreement to ensure self-preservation is the basis of the social contract,
which for state-of-nature theorists like Hobbes makes civil society possible.

In giving up rights, Hobbes explains, a certain amount of power is relin-
quished to a government or sovereign. The sovereign is to protect the rights of
the citizens, and the citizens are to respect the legitimacy of the sovereign. In
fact, the citizen is to submit entirely to the sovereign, limited only by the right
of self-preservation. Hence, a subject cannot be made to kill him- or herself or
testify against him- or herself. Hobbes recognizes the enormity of the power
to be given to this governing entity, which he compares to Leviathan in the
Book of Job. (The notion of Leviathan as a powerful, imposing government
is another way Hobbes's thought has worked its way into modern language.)

Like the Greek and Roman philosophers, Hobbes looks at different government types, including monarchy, aristocracy, and democracy. But unlike
Aristotle or Cicero, he is not terribly worried about a monarch turning into
a tyrant. To Hobbes, the monarch, especially one who can expect to be succeeded by his or her heirs, has private interests that align with the interests
of the people. Leading a country to ruin would also ruin the monarchy, and

hence a monarch will avoid such folly. One wonders if North Korea's Kim Jong Il or Zimbabwe's Robert Mugabe got the wrong message from Hobbes during their princely educations.

Hobbes is less sympathetic to democracy. He argues that a democracy involves multiple leaders and factions, with ever-changing interests and allegiances that seldom serve society as a whole and often degenerate into anarchy. Aristocracy falls somewhere between monarchy and democracy, with some of the strengths and weaknesses of each. In this sense, then, Hobbes has something in common with Aristotle.

In practice, however, Hobbes's loyalties are clearly with the crown. He lived in the days leading up to the Glorious Revolution of 1688, when the English crown ceded significant power to parliament. He knew Charles I and spent time in exile in Paris with Charles II. Hobbes is skeptical of the balance of power across government, such as between a king and a parliament, exactly what the Glorious Revolution helped achieve. To Hobbes, the English Civil War is a classic struggle for power between the king, the lords, and the parliament. The inevitable result of such a struggle is anarchy, which makes shared powers no better than the pure democracy that ultimately begets anarchy. To illustrate the perils of democracy, Hobbes translates Thucydides, the Greek historian of the Peloponnesian War. Hobbes hopes the Athenian democracy's loss to Sparta will encourage the English to favor monarchy over democracy. It didn't.

If Hobbes is the philosopher most closely associated with a powerful government, John Locke (1632–1704) is the philosopher most closely associated with a limited one. He builds his theory of government in response to Hobbes, with whom he vehemently disagrees. But Locke's is not a minor difference of opinion; it is a radically different worldview.

Perhaps surprisingly, Hobbes and Locke start with similar opinions on the origins of government. Like Hobbes, Locke views government as a product of a social contract. This is in contrast to the view of government as established by God, a favorite argument of monarchs and those who favored the divine right of kings. Hobbes and Locke offer the view of humanity emerging from a "state of nature" and establishing a social contract. Both the divine right of kings and the social contract give legitimacy to government as well as a reason to obey it, but for very different reasons.

Like Hobbes, Locke assumes an original "state of nature" that precedes the state itself. Everyone in this state of nature owns or has property in his or her person as well as his or her labor. All other property, such as that which an individual discovers or creates, derives from this fundamental notion of property. Similar to Hobbes, Locke sees that the challenge to the individual in the state of nature is to protect property in him- or herself and that which he or she has created. To some extent in Hobbes and even more in Locke, property rights also are seen as a means to address scarcity, an economic reality in all societies.

Locke sees all humans as being inherently equal, and in this he would greatly influence the American Founders. By equal, Locke means equal in rights, not ability, and he plants the seed for the notion of equality before the law. More importantly, Locke is distinguished from Hobbes on the allocation of power under the social contract. Hobbes sees individuals coming to an agreement in which they vest a king with sovereignty and, in return, the sovereign protects their rights. Locke sees individuals coming to an agreement in which the rights of the individual to live exactly as he or she pleases is subsumed into a larger whole in order to protect those rights, with this larger whole also recognizing the rights of all other members of the community. Hobbes's sovereign is not party to the social contract but instead is the all-powerful recipient of authority to govern. Locke's government, in contrast, is party to the social contract. By implication, a Lockean government may be legitimately overthrown for failing to abide by that social contract.

Hobbesian ideas have taken a backseat to some of Locke's work, especially the ideas put forth in Locke's *Two Treatises of Government*. The *First Treatise* provides a refutation of the argument for divine right of kings. Having sufficiently attacked the argument for monarchy, Locke proceeds in the *Second Treatise* to provide his own approach to government. Today, students of political philosophy often bypass the *First Treatise* and head straight into the *Second Treatise of Government*. It is here that one sees clearly the fundamental difference between Hobbes and Locke. Hobbes's tradeoff between anarchy and order contrasts with Locke's tradeoff between liberty and oppression. It is in this sense that Locke is sometimes referred to as the first political philosopher of liberty.

On the other hand, Hobbes has not exactly gone out of fashion. In fact, it is common for political leaders—usually those in the executive branch—to invoke a concern about a state of anarchy as they claim more power, reminiscent of Hobbes. The modern student of political philosophy again is likely to think of George W. Bush and the suspension of habeas corpus for suspected terrorists. This is a classic example of the emphasis on order at the expense of liberty. But, again, this is not a historical first for the United States. At the start of the Civil War, Abraham Lincoln suspended habeas corpus in Maryland in an attempt to limit insurrection and restrict those who were likely to encourage that state to secede. During World War II, Franklin Delano

Roosevelt oversaw the forced detention without trial of tens of thousands of Japanese Americans. It is an old debate about anarchy versus order.

The Emergence of Political Economy

While seventeenth-century England witnessed a rich debate between Hobbes and Locke, more than just the English made important contributions to political philosophy. In particular, a Frenchman, Montesquieu (1689–1755), writes admiringly of the English political system and was soon admired by those who would establish the model of government adopted by the English colonies in America.

Like Locke and Hobbes, Montesquieu sees human development progressing from primitive relations among individual savages to association in groups, with government emerging to address conflicts within or between groups. He provides a critique of the different forms of government, including a monarchy and a republic, and emerges with a model that is somewhat similar to but more developed than that supplied by Locke. Like Machiavelli, he rejects the Aristotelian approach of evaluating a government based on the virtue of the rulers, as in a king versus a tyrant.

Montesquieu instead provides key details about how a republic may be structured. For a democratic as opposed to an aristocratic republic, the people delegate to their representatives the authority to make certain decisions, such as those related to foreign affairs. These representatives should be chosen from those with a minimum amount of wealth. However, participation in the judicial system, as in serving on juries, should be open to all citizens. The model has important democratic elements, but with limitations, and it is far from being a direct democracy.

Montesquieu also takes the division of power further than Locke and much further than Aristotle. In the Aristotelian model, there are executive, judicial, and deliberative (or legislative) roles, but these need not be distributed among different branches of government or even among individuals. Locke argues strongly for a division of powers, but the executive and judicial roles are to be combined. In contrast, Montesquieu stresses the value of clear separation of executive, judicial, and legislative functions. The U.S. experience flows directly from this insight.

Still another Enlightenment thinker who would influence the political rule-makers of his day is one of the most influential philosophers of all time, David Hume (1711–1776). In his lifetime, Hume was known for his six-volume *History of England*. Today, he is known more for his many contributions to philosophy, ethics, and political thought.

With regard to political economy, Hume is often remembered for his remark that reason must be a slave to passion. It is easy to take this comment out of context, as Hume does not make of it what later thinkers, especially Rousseau, would make of Romantic philosophy. Rather, Hume builds on the arguments of Hobbes and Locke, arguing that what is good or ethical must be consistent with the passions. As we have seen, Hobbes views self-preservation as the greatest passion, with law deriving from the use of reason to preserve life. Hume disagrees, arguing that ethics does not derive from reason applied to the passions, but is itself derived from passions, or what Adam Smith would call moral sentiments.

Hume also differs from Hobbes and Locke in how he views the "state of nature" and the emergence of society. He argues that the benefits of working together to protect rights to property and life, as well as the benefits of the division of labor, are not obvious to those living in a state of nature. Rather, people first form families, a consequence of sexual desire, and only then do the benefits of association begin to be obvious. With time, the benefits of reciprocity become clear, especially in a world of scarcity.

In the course of living in society, we of course are self-interested, but the position of Hobbes and Locke that there is a "selfish" system of morals is not quite correct, not in Hume's view. Rather, we recognize injustice when others fail to reciprocate or honor contracts, and we sympathize with others who are treated this way. Over time, a sense of right and wrong develops among the majority of the people. This ethical system is, nonetheless, beneficial to those who participate in society and thus is in some sense derived from people's rational self-interest. Government exists, Hume says, to enforce this emergent, organic concept of right and wrong; that is, to ensure justice.

The benefit of reciprocity and just conduct accrues to everyone in society and is in our self-interest. However, it also will be in one's self-interest to take advantage of certain situations, often for short-term individual gain at the expense of the harmed party or parties. In other words, people can cheat instead of playing by the rules. This is Hume anticipating the free-rider problem (which, as we will see in Chapter 3, is a building block of market failure theory). In establishing a government, Hume believes that it is best to assume that all humans are self-interested, not public spirited. The law should not depend on benevolence instead of self-interest because the latter is likely to dominate. Unlike Locke, however, Hume does not construct a social-contract theory of government, in which government exists and is justified by the consent of the governed. He agrees that government probably first developed from the state of nature based on consent. But Hume points out that government as we know it today, and as it has been known in recorded history, is not based on such consent. Rather, one type of government replaces another within a society, or one society conquers another and imposes a new form of government. The individual members of the society were not asked, one by one, to consent and thus join the society.

While Hume does not adopt Locke's "natural law" approach to government, he agrees with many of Locke's conclusions, including the right of citizens to overthrow an oppressive government that does not meet its fundamental obligation to protect rights. As for how the government should be structured, Hume is not far removed from Hobbes and Locke. Power should be separated among a head of state (or monarch) and a legislature, which might include a smaller "aristocratic" upper body and a popular assembly. The separation of powers, with checks and balances, should help control the weaknesses of each power. If checks and balances are properly established, Hume thinks that even a society with a monarch at its head could advance the interests of all members. This led Thomas Jefferson to conclude that Hume had done more to advance the ideas of the Tories, with their traditional support of the English crown, than the Whigs, with their traditional support of the legislative branch having greater power relative to the executive branch. Hume nonetheless has more in common with the Whig philosopher John Locke, albeit without the social contract theory.

The Idealized State and the General Will

In contrast to the political philosophy of Hobbes, Locke, and Hume, but no less an influence on modern governments, is Jean-Jacques Rousseau (1712–1778). No other eighteenth-century philosopher stands more solidly against the Enlightenment. Rousseau argues that progress in the arts and sciences does not lead to a betterment of the human condition but instead to moral corruption. Nor was the moral, or the good, to be found in religious faith. In this regard, Rousseau accepts Hume's skepticism. Unlike Hume, however, he does not seek to replace faith with reason, and in fact thinks reason inferior to the heart.

Rousseau starts with the state of nature, but unlike his peers he ends with an idealized state, one to act as a model for guiding efforts to reform the current conditions but not necessarily one intended to be achieved in practice. Whereas Hobbes sees life in the state of nature as brutish, Rousseau sees it as idyllic, sufficient to satisfy basic wants. Rousseau considers efforts to better meet human needs, such as through science and technology, to be futile, corrupting, and ultimately enslaving. His famous treatise, *The Social Contract*, thus begins with an even more famous phrase: "Man is born free, and everywhere he is in chains."

The source of these chains, and thus the source of all evil, is property, which also is the starting point of society. With property, there can be no equality. Here one stumbles on the question of whether Rousseau means equality of result (indeed impossible when property exists) or equality before the law (possible, as described by Locke and others). Rousseau focuses on the latter, but ultimately produces a model that strives also for the former. In *The Social Contract*, he makes clear that the individual's rights should be "alienated" to the whole community. The happy (if theoretical) result is equal conditions for all and thus no incentive for anyone to impose burdensome conditions on anyone else. Rousseau's model contrasts vividly with the "inalienable" rights in the Declaration of Independence. It also differs dramatically from Locke's or Montesquieu's view of a government with a balance of powers emerging from the state of nature or even from Hobbes's more tolerant view of a powerful government protecting against anarchy.

A closer parallel to Rousseau is found in Plato, especially in educating citizens to know and do the good, where the good is a means to freedom. Rousseau is fond of the democratic city-state as developed by the Greeks. He clearly prefers Sparta to Athens. In understanding Rousseau's focus on the city-state, one sees why he considers democracy feasible. He recognizes the problems of monarchy, aristocracy, and democracy, and he views the best approach to achieve freedom partly to be determined by the size of the society. A larger population may need a more powerful government, such as a monarchy, but the risks to freedom would be greater. A city-state, with democratic government, is preferred. This democratic government does not, however, have the balance of powers addressed by Locke and Hume.

In Rousseau's vision, the rights of individual citizens give way to the general will. This is not identical to the perfectly natural state of humanity, because there is more than one person in society and thus more than one will. Rather, the general will is only constrained by what all may want and thus is very natural or free. The state represents all members, which is what makes it legitimate. This perspective, which has profoundly influenced so many governments, does not tell the modern reader exactly what kind of government to support. Either an authoritarian system or a democratic one may be appropriate, as long as it represents the general will. That said, Rousseau argues passionately that democracy as practiced in most forms is illegitimate and too likely to be subject to self-interest. One can see why Rousseau prefers Sparta to Athens.

Rousseau is adamant that society must reflect the general will of the people, however difficult this is to define. While skeptical of monarchy, he nonetheless believes that a "great leader" may be needed to establish this ideal society. The leader will impose the rules necessary to advance the general will and establish a new, ideal regime. This is not an evolutionary process; it is a revolutionary one. Rousseau's influence on the French Revolution is as clear as Locke's influence on the American Revolution.

The tension between the philosophies of Locke and Rousseau continued through the end of the Enlightenment, and they continue today, as can be seen throughout the world and throughout this book. Should government attempt to promote the general will, or should it protect the rights of each individual to advance his or her specific will? To the extent there is a trade-off between the two, how should it be balanced? If government limits itself only to the protection of individual rights, what about the benefits that could accrue to members of society through collective action, but that will not be supplied individually? On the other hand, how can political institutions know the general will, and how can they advance it without falling victim to the human failings seen elsewhere in society? Not only does much of modern political philosophy trace back to this debate, but an entirely new but related discipline, economics, emerged at this time, offering new tools to better understand these and other important questions.

Adam Smith and the Birth of Modern Economics

The founder of economics is generally considered to be Adam Smith (1723–1790), another Enlightenment philosopher best known for his two great works, *The Theory of Moral Sentiments* (1758) and *An Inquiry into the Nature and Causes of the Wealth of Nations* (1776). In addition to setting the agenda for economic thinking, these companion books also form part of the philosophical foundation for today's classical liberalism. Smith does not set out to establish a separate discipline of economics. Rather, in his system of thought there is an inextricable link between questions about the best political order and questions about economic life. No matter what modern political philosophers think of Smith, this link between politics and economics is essentially taken for granted today.

From an early age, Smith was educated to think of the relationships between individual morality, social rules, and public welfare. Once he begins writing his two great books, he spends many pages discussing how customs, traditions, and other social norms make it easier for people of disparate backgrounds and motivation to cooperate peacefully and productively. His life's work aims to build a system of philosophical and economic thought where a society's formal and informal rules (its history, its culture, its government) determine whether people interact sociably or violently. The capacity to cooperate, in short, depends on the rules of the game.

Smith poses the classic question: What is good, or virtuous? He finds that virtue derives from that which individuals desired to approve—approbation is the key word here—and their ability to sympathize with situations in which others find themselves. Smith does not quite offer the utilitarian philosophy of his friend, Hume, though the similarities are remarkable.

Like Hobbes, Smith views individuals as fundamentally equal by nature, though like Locke he has a decidedly more optimistic view of individuals' abilities to cooperate without the use of force. In this respect, he also differs dramatically from Rousseau. Indeed, it is Smith's view of the benefits of social cooperation that so distinguishes his political philosophy. The concept of the "invisible hand"—familiar even to critics who have never read Smith—first appears in the *Theory of Moral Sentiments*. Smith argues that individuals produce value for others in the course of pursuing their own selfish ends, always within a set of rules that protects the rights of each member of the society. While it is in *The Wealth of Nations* that Smith describes how this value creation is enhanced through, for example, comparative advantage and the division of labor, it is clear that he views the concept of the invisible hand—an unintended consequence of individual self-interest—to be an important element of social cooperation. This message was entirely new to eighteenth-century readers, who viewed wealth in terms of gold and silver coins, not the ability to produce valuable goods and services. Linking this new concept of wealth to social cooperation meant ideas about how people interact were more important than ever.

Smith fuses political and economic thought in a way that had not been achieved before him. *The Wealth of Nations* shows again the link that Smith draws between the economic and political realms. The last section of this book addresses the "duty" of the sovereign, which Smith divides into three parts. First, the government should protect society from violence by foreign threats (for example, invasion). Second, the government should protect every member of society from violence or oppression by internal threats (such as crime by other members of society). Third, the government should erect and maintain those public institutions that are advantageous to society but that would not be maintained if the expense had to be borne by only one or a few members.

Smith's view that government should remain limited flows directly as an implication of his philosophical-economic system of thought. The capacity to cooperate depends on the rules of the game. These three functions for government, supported by social conventions outside of government, come the closest to the ideal set of rules that would allow a people to cooperate voluntarily toward mutual and social gain. The invisible hand works best under these rules.

The American Framers

While Adam Smith was polishing the prose in *Wealth*, Thomas Jefferson and the American revolutionaries were writing the Declaration of Independence. Both great works were published in 1776, and both were steeped in Enlightenment ideas. While critical to establishing the core principles of the fledgling United States, the political structure of this newly independent nation was established by the U.S. Constitution, ratified in 1789. In the two-year period between a constitutional convention and the document's ratification, a number of important essays, today know as *The Federalist Papers*, were published by Alexander Hamilton, James Madison, and John Jay. The American Framers were grappling with Cicero's question about how to define a republic, not in theory but in real and often bloody practice.

The Federalist Papers are an attempt to convince the citizens of New York to adopt the new constitution that had been drafted in 1787. It is important to remember that the Constitution, revered (if not always respected) in the United States today, was not universally appreciated at first. On leaving the Constitutional Convention, Benjamin Franklin answered a woman who asked what had been created with the quip, "A republic, if you can keep it." Opponents of the new Constitution genuinely worried that, rather than creating a republic, it would create a strong, perhaps tyrannical, central government. In this, the skeptics were simply favoring the Greek experience, as well as Montesquieu's argument that republican government worked only with small countries. Large countries, the skeptics feared, risked becoming tyrannical due to the authority needed to control them.

The Federalist Papers respond to this concern with a model for a specific type of republic designed for a geographically large country made up of diverse interests. This model of government is not a direct democracy because the citizens do not individually vote to approve or disapprove specific laws. Rather, citizens elect representatives to make such decisions on their behalf. The concept of a republic as presented in *The Federalist Papers* is, therefore, one of representative democracy.

In this view of government, the influence of Locke and Montesquieu is clear, especially the concept of separation of powers. The authors of *The Federalist Papers* argue for executive, judicial, and legislative functions that are not carried out by the same people and with at least some protection against abuse of a minority group—the tyranny of the majority. The Constitution contains a clear separation of powers, as well as other limitations on a potentially overreaching central government. The Tenth Amendment of the Constitution, for example, clarifies that the "powers not delegated to the United States by the Constitution, nor prohibited by it to the States, are reserved to the States respectively, or to the people." In an economic sense, these provisions raise the cost of converting the power of government into tyranny. The early political history of the United States, with limited government and a clear separation of powers, closely tracks this model. And while the modern United States has a central government that is expansive compared to its early history, it also is true that, relative to most any other country on the planet, the United States continues to enjoy one of the governments with the clearest separation of powers because its institutions enshrined the principle of property rights.

Marxism: Class Interest Meets the Social Contract

Karl Marx (1818–1883) is famously quoted for having observed early in his career that "philosophers have only interpreted the world in various ways; the point however is to change it." He meant it. Few philosophers in history have changed the world so dramatically. The Soviet Union, the People's Republic of China, Cuba, and countless wars and revolutions have been driven by his ideas and desire to change the world.

So pervasive is Marx's influence that, in many countries across the world today, calling someone a Marxist has meaning, whether in a favorable connotation or not. But while a speaker may know whether the label is an insult or not, relatively few know what Marx really said.

Surprisingly to those who have never read him, Marx has great respect for the productive forces of a capitalist (he calls it bourgeois) society, to which he attributes the nineteenth century's unprecedented advances in agriculture, manufacturing, transportation, communications, and more. Marx is as much an historian as an economist, and he sees history through a particular lens. That perspective borrows heavily from Hegel's theory of the dialectic, in which social change occurs through a discontinuous rather than smooth process.

Per Hegel, social change involves periods of thesis (in which a key idea emerges), followed by antithesis (in which a contrary or opposing idea comes forth) and then synthesis (the resolution of the conflict between thesis and antithesis, which in turn forms a new thesis). But this battle of ideas is, to Marx, too far removed from the real world. It is too idealistic. Marx insists that ideas are the products of the real, material world around us, which influences those ideas. In so arguing, he thus introduces materialism to Hegel's dialectic. This mix of the dialectic with materialism would be called dialectical material-ism by later proponents, such as Frederick Engels and Vladimir Lenin, who played a rather pivotal role in the emergence of the Soviet Union.

Applying dialectical materialism to the study of history, and taking a good look at the plight of the workers around him, Marx concludes that "the history of all hitherto existing society is the history of class struggles." Spe-cifically, the struggle is that of the workers (proletariat) against the capitalists.

Marx's critique of capitalism remains popular among "occupiers" and other revolutionaries today, as it has been for over a century. Yet even as few understand the extent to which he sees capitalism as a necessary step in history and an improvement over what came before it, Marx sees history as a natural progression from slavery in the Greek, Egyptian, and Roman so-cieties, to feudalism in Medieval Europe, to capitalism in his own time. But while capitalism is an improvement, exploitation remains and in fact is a de-fining characteristic of this stage. Socialism comes after capitalism collapses. And why does capitalism collapse?

Marx argues that capitalism will collapse because it is a system in which capitalists exploit the workers. His understanding of this exploitation derives from a concept adhered to by classical economists called the labor theory of value. While economic theory would later completely discredit the labor theory of value (as we'll see in Chapter 3), Marx has quite good company in his day because both Adam Smith and David Ricardo partly subscribe to this theory. According to the theory, the value of a good is determined directly by the amount of labor needed to produce it. The clever reader may ask how this is so when goods are produced by a combination of labor and capital. Simple, replies Marx. Capital goods such as machines and equipment have a value that reflects the amount of labor used to produce them. A car, for example, has a value exactly equal to the labor used to produce all of its intri-cate parts and their assembly. One counts the labor not only of the assemblers but also the labor of those who built the machines used to assemble the car, those who built the factory in which the car was assembled, and so on.

According to Marx, because the value of a good is exactly equal to the amount of labor used to produce it, if workers were paid the full value of what they produce, then they would receive 100 percent of the price paid for any good. Because workers do not receive the full value of what they pro-duce, they are exploited. The capitalist receives a portion of this value cre-ated by the worker, what Marx calls the surplus value. Further, as technology advances, new capital makes it possible to pay workers a smaller amount of the value they create, which in turn further impoverishes the workers and sows the seeds of a future revolution.

Most modern economists dispense with the labor theory of value, recognizing several reasons that Marx, along with Smith and Ricardo, are wrong about it. First, labor is not a homogenous factor; some workers are highly productive and others less so. To appreciate this, flip over your iPhone and notice the words "Designed by Apple in California and assembled in China." There is significant variation in *human capital* (which, as we'll see in Chapter 5, is what economists today call skills, training, and education) among the assembler, designer, engineer, and many others involved in producing a good. Further, Marx ignores the role of less-obvious contributors to the production of a valuable good. Take the middleman, for example. Bankers provide financing, with a commercial loan that allows a company to build a plant and produce something now rather than wait until it has the funds to do so later, or with a mortgage that allows a family to buy a house now rather than wait until it has saved an amount equal to the entire value of the home. Similarly overlooked by Marx, advertisers provide information to potential customers, while good managers provide organization and thus help avoid wasted effort by workers.

Most notably, Marx ignores the role of the entrepreneur, who searches for and responds to unmet needs in the market. Workers do not magically know what to produce or where to send it. The entrepreneur, in trying to fulfill consumers' needs as conveyed by prices in the market, directs labor and capital and all resources to where they are most needed. Communist economies would ignore this lesson to their peril in the twentieth century. In the approach we develop in this book, a form of entrepreneurship—what we call political entrepreneurship—is the key driver of political change.

In short, post-Marxist economics shows that the labor theory of value offers an incomplete account of the market value of a good or service, as well as its cost of production. Labor alone tells us nothing about value because supply is only one-half of the equation and thus insufficient to determine the value of anything. Like many economists and others prior to the late nineteenth century, Marx fails to understand that the value of a good or service is determined, as Alfred Marshall aptly demonstrates, by both supply *and* demand. Marshall's contribution is part of what is known in economics as the Marginalist Revolution. This intellectual "revolution" is a devastating critique of one of the key tenets of Marxism. But one can safely bet that few soldiers in the Bolshevik Revolution (led by Lenin) or on the side of the communists in the Chinese Civil War (led by Mao) were aware of the Marginalist Revolution.

That battle of ideas had already been fought and won, and the communist revolutionaries were on the losing side; they just didn't know it.

The American Progressives:
From Individual Rights to Public Interest

While technical errors would shatter Marx's economics, they hardly gave pause to reformers wanting to implement egalitarian ideas. These reformers, known as the American Progressives, changed the landscape of politics and economics at such fundamental levels that their influence can hardly be overstated.

Progressivism is not an entirely unified movement. There is significant dissent among Progressive thinkers, activists, and political figures, and significant variation in the degree to which important figures of the time can be called Progressives. There is no single philosopher who encapsulates the key arguments of the movement—no Karl Marx, no Adam Smith, no Aquinas or Aristotle. Rather, important contributors to Progressive thought include presidents, Supreme Court justices, economists, social reformers in a number of areas, novelists, teachers, and many more. There is also significant variation in the degree to which important figures of the time can be called Progressives.

The Progressives reached their pinnacle during the decades around the turn of the twentieth century, from about the 1880s to about the 1930s. Yet the intellectual roots of Progressivism trace backward through the history of ideas to the economics of Karl Marx, to the social experiment of the American founding, to Enlightenment coffee shops and debates about the relations between individuals and society, to Rousseau and Hobbes, and to the ideas of direct democracy in the School of Athens. From their peak in the early 1900s, the ideas of Progressives achieved institutional changes that continue to shape human affairs in profound ways.

We can say only a few words about this vast topic. Our focus will be to substantiate a simple claim. Progressive ideas have permeated several areas of life, and under favorable political conditions these ideas have become instilled in shared institutions, both formal and informal, so that their effects are still easily visible today.

Conditions leading up to the turn of the twentieth century were ripe for Progressive ideas. Darwin's revolution of the biological sciences was being vigorously adapted to many areas of human life. And life, to the Progressives, was brimming with social ills that reforms could abate. The need was desperate. Widespread hardships had crept into Americans' living standards as life became industrialized and urbanized. Mass migration separated families and intensified racial and ethnic tensions. Unsanitary slums and workplaces spread illness into epidemics, leaving widows and orphans unable to provide for themselves. With low labor productivity and the one-factory labor market, masses of people barely subsisted despite working long hours each day in miserable and unsafe conditions, a condition that was dramatized most famously in Upton Sinclair's *The Jungle* (1906). Children of impoverished families were put to work instead of given proper schooling (as were many in the earlier agrarian period). And real or perceived increases in income inequality emerged, as portrayed most famously by Thorstein Veblen's *The Theory of the Leisure Class* (1899). For Progressives, it was the worst of times.

The Progressives believe that the good society was not only conceivable in thought but achievable in practice, through the enlightened application of science and civic virtue to human institutions. Sinclair personally sent a copy of his book to President Theodore Roosevelt. Not coincidentally, the Pure Food and Drug Act was enacted that same year, requiring ingredient labels and setting the stage for the safety and efficacy requirements of today's Food and Drug Administration.

The Progressives influenced a wide range of public life. New labor regulations included the eight-hour workday, the banning of child labor, workers' compensation programs, minimum wage laws, and protections of labor unions' activity and strikes. New business regulations would control manufacturing operations. Antitrust statutes were enacted to divest monopolies and punish business practices deemed to be anticompetitive. Prohibitions on alcohol and marijuana were promoted. Environmental conservation was sought through the designation of national parks and land reclamation programs. And governments were called on to provide services like health care (the first national health care plan appeared in Theodore Roosevelt's 1912 presidential campaign platform).

A hallmark of Progressive thought was the priority on efficiency in social organizations including governments, businesses, schools, charities, and more. Frederick Winslow Taylor, for example, pioneered the field of scientific management, which revolutionized the organization of business and manufacturing. An engineer by training, Taylor won the first U.S. doubles tennis championship at the age of twenty-five using a racquet of his own design. He viewed the world as a series of mechanical relationships and saw enormous and needless waste in the industrial operations of his age. Taylor's basic objective was to hone manufacturing to ensure that a given set of inputs could produce the greatest possible quantity of output. By analyzing manufacturing—that is, breaking the process into individual steps and measuring its progress—Taylor's scientific management sought to maximize the productivity of labor. In Chapter 3 we will meet the great twentieth-century economist, Paul A. Samuelson, whose approach to economics strongly paralleled Taylor's approach to management.

Taylor was not very political. However, his same scientific approach was carried into public life during the Progressive era. The power of scientific knowledge made it feasible for governments and private aid societies to implement policies with precision. They required measurement, standardization, municipal administration, and efficient use of resources in all public fields, from education to social services to government administration to disaster aid. They abhorred corruption in public life, preached temperance in private life, and strove for greater equality in political-economic life.

There were major obstacles, both constitutional and philosophical. But Progressive ideas eventually began to occupy our shared institutions, both formal and perhaps especially informal. The footprints of Progressive thinking are all around our modern day.

For example, several constitutional amendments have their origins in Progressive ideas, including progressive income taxation (Sixteenth Amendment), direct election of U.S. senators (Seventeenth Amendment), and alcohol prohibition (Eighteenth Amendment). Late in the nineteenth century, twenty-four states introduced direct democracy institutions, including referendum, recall, and citizen initiative.

In education, college entrance exams have their roots in the 1905 Binet-Simon scale, which became the Army's Alpha Beta testing program. Researchers at Stanford University, led by Louis Terman, developed the Intelligence Quotient Test, which is the basis for modern standardized testing.

It's also during this time that political language gets inverted in America. So a "liberal" in the United States is someone on the left, but in most of the world it's someone who is on the right.

Before concluding, we do want to say a few words about yellow school busses. We mentioned the Progressive priority on standards. Early on, around 1839, Horace Mann began advocating and founding government schools after touring schools in Germany (Prussia) and being very impressed. Mann's influence would expand in the late nineteenth century, under the lead of the education philosopher, John Dewey. Instituting Dewey's ideas, government schooling was transformed into a professional industry in the late nineteenth century. In 1887, Columbia University founded Teachers College, to teach teachers how to implement standardized, measurable delivery of education for the betterment of the public good and democracy. In 1905 the Carnegie Foundation for the Advancement of Teaching was founded to study the way teachers were being taught. Frank W. Cyr was a graduate of Teachers College and an education reformer. In April 1939, Cyr received a grant from the Rockefeller Foundation to organize a weeklong conference on standardizing bus colors. Around the table were educators, state-level politicians, and manufacturers of busses and paints. The result was forty-four standards for school bus design, including the standard designated color "National School Bus Chrome," more commonly known as School Bus Yellow.

And finally, the Progressive influence can be felt in the era also in the transformation of political and economic inquiry into separate professions. The American Economic Association was founded in 1886, and the American Political Science Association was founded in 1905. Both quickly took control over their respective graduate curricula. Interestingly, political "science" largely continued the path of philosophical inquiry that we've begun in this chapter, but economics became more scientific, more concerned with inputs and outputs in the style of Frederick Taylor. Taylor's maximizing approach and input-output mode of thinking would become a natural fit for economic theory in the twentieth century. Already Taylor's work implied a theory of wages by which workers should be compensated according to their productivity. "Pay the worker, not the job" was the mantra of scientific management. As we'll see in the next chapter, this is barely a stone's throw from the conclusions that economic models would soon support.

In sum, the Progressives took firm stances on the main questions we have posed in this chapter. The role and function of government are to promote the general welfare, not merely to protect the rights of individuals. Indeed, only by advancing the public interest is government truly able to keep individuals free from the inability to advance their own wills. Through the scientifically enlightened expertise of its leaders, combined with an electorate whose civic virtues are cultivated in public schools, political discourse will find the path of the public interest. By amending the federal constitution, government would be empowered to act accordingly. And by eliminating corruption in government, political leaders would resist temptations to use their new powers in self-serving ways. Finally, with the dawn of mathematical economics in the twentieth century, the Progressives would have on their side formal "proofs" of the need for government regulation in the name of the public interest.

3

Economists Join the Battle of Political Ideas

For a modern "mixed economy" in the post-Keynesian era, fiscal and monetary
policy can definitely prevent chronic slumps, can offset automation or under-
consumption, can insure that resources find paying work opportunities.
—Paul A. Samuelson, *The New York Times* (1970)[1]

The . . . approach that I suggest places "the theory of markets" and not the
"theory of resource allocation" at center stage . . . The same basic data
are central to the allocation approach and the exchange approach. But the
interpretation of these data, and even the very questions that we ask of them,
will depend critically on the reference system within which we operate.
—James M. Buchanan, *What Should Economists Do?* (1964)[2]

It was the summer of 1985 in northern Virginia. A young, accomplished
economist held pen to paper and gazed off his back screened porch onto Fair-
fax County's lush rolling hills. In a few months' time he would fly to Dallas
to deliver his presidential address to the fifty-fifth meeting of the Southern
Economic Association, the oldest of the "regional" economics societies in
the United States. His audience would be a room filled with hundreds of his
fellow economists. Most of them would be the speaker's senior, and all of
them would be wondering what he might have to say. Patting the head of his
snoozing dog, sipping his sweet tea, and watching the wind in the trees, the

young Robert D. Tollison pondered the same. He looked down at his yellow pad and wrote, "Economics is economics."[3]

Knowing the speaker as a leading scholar of the public choice school of thought, the economists in Dallas may have anticipated a lecture on mercantilism, that protectionist system of international trade, or a theory of legislation, or another subject of his past work. As it turned out, Tollison didn't talk about any of these topics that day. Instead, he talked about *them*, his audience, the economic thinkers in the room.

Bob Tollison has spent his career challenging economic theory to explain not only markets and governments but a range of human experience, too. He has written piles of studies on novel topics like the geographical patterns of Civil War mortality rates, the productivity of basketball players, the formulaic structure of pop music, the evolution of the English language, the racial integration of pro baseball, and more. On this occasion in Dallas, he would push economic theory in yet another direction, this time by bringing it closer to home. Under the title, "Economists as the Subject of Economic Inquiry," Tollison's presidential address turned the lens of economic theory onto the production of economic theory. "Economics is economics," he said. "The economist cannot take a measure of the world without obeying its postulates."

There is a deep parallel between Tollison's approach toward economists and Lionel Robbins's approach toward philosophers, which we discussed at the start of Chapter 2. The production of ideas, whether philosophy or economics, is an economic enterprise—both in terms of providing alternatives to consumers *and* in terms of their having to compete with other producers.

In his Dallas address, for example, Tollison is preoccupied with analyzing economists as *Homo scientificus*—as rationally self-interested individuals who can be modeled exactly like consumers and firms. Tollison shifts the lens of economic theory onto the producers of economic theory; the basic economic tool kit can be used to understand the creation of ideas in economics, just as it can be used to explain the production of basketball games, potatoes, even public policies. Punctuating things, Tollison surmises: "The economist is a rational, maximizing individual, subject to the predictions of economic science." As one implication, he predicts, we should expect the supply of economic ideas to be high in situations that offer low costs of innovation, and vice versa.

Certain biographical sketches of some great economists seem to obey Tollison's postulate. For example, the Victorian economist Alfred Marshall invented the concept known as price elasticity of demand—a brilliant stroke of creative genius—while on an extended convalescent vacation on the coast in southern Italy. The cost of creative production is low while sunning oneself on the roof at Palermo. On the other hand, Adam Smith all but quit writing once he took on the responsibilities as commissioner of the Scottish customs office, just two years after publishing *The Wealth of Nations*. The immediate lesson is that time constraints matter. The broader moral is that examining biography offers much understanding about the creation and dissemination of ideas.

We can parlay Tollison's rational thinker approach into a view of economics itself as exchange. Individual economists might very well adhere to the tenets of the rational individual model. As a group, economists compete with each other in the marketplace of ideas. Aside from a handful of fundamentals on which all competent economists agree, there is wide and deep dissent on the rest. Take, for example, our first motivating question from Chapter 1: Why do democracies generate policies that are wasteful and unjust? A majority of economists likely would not care to study or comment on justice. And while most do occasion themselves with the issues of waste, there is dissent there as well. The old joke is, you could line up all the economists in the world, and they still would not reach a conclusion.

In the marketplace of economic ideas, scholars are in the *business* of crafting arguments, techniques, theorems, policy recommendations, and so forth, all in the hope of exchanging their craft for the currency of readership, praise, influence, and ultimately some prominent place in the body of economic scholarship. Economists act like idea entrepreneurs, identifying niches of unexplored opportunity and areas where innovative work is most needed. Seeking audiences and like-minded thinkers, scholars select themselves into groups and schools of thought. Over time, as with all crowds, schools of thought and areas of inquiry come into and out of fashion. And so, the history of economics, like that of political philosophy, is one of certain ideas being picked up and systematically adapted into orthodoxy, while other ideas get left behind with only the lonely hope of being rediscovered by future wandering scholars.

As modern economic thought roared into the twentieth century, the battleground of economic ideas shifted ever more toward government policy and the public interest. Two competing schools of thought emerged: welfare economics and public choice. With the great Paul Samuelson as its figurehead, welfare economics advanced theories of market failure and enlightened government intervention. It construed the basic economic problem as one of *allocation*—how society can allocate its scarce resources so as to best serve the public interest. In stark contrast, public choice theory, with James Buchanan as Samuelson's counterpart, advanced theories not of market failure, but of government failure. Buchanan argued that the fundamental economic question is not allocation but *exchange*. Viewing politics as exchange, public choice theory would show cracks in the thinking that enlightened public policy can achieve a sort of Nirvana in human affairs. Interestingly, both the welfare and public choice schools of thought spawned directly from the model of neoclassical economics that took shape between 1870 and 1950, and both trace their lineage directly to the seat of Adam Smith. Yet the competing schools couldn't be more different from each other in the advice they would lend to those who grip the levers of economic policy.

This chapter and the next tell the story of these two opposing paradigms in the economics of politics. Samuelson and Buchanan are not the only players, of course. Each side is joined by towering figures and more Nobel Prizes than a two-handed economist could count on all his or her fingers. This tale involves intrigue and drama. There is rational self-interest, as predicted by Bob Tollison. And more to the point, at stake are answers to our first and second motivating questions from Chapter 1. As the philosophers in Chapter 2 give us sound ways to think about *justice* and *good political rules*, the welfare economists in this chapter afford us a *standard for waste*—namely, economic efficiency. In Chapter 4, public choice theory will provide an account of why democracies might generate policies that diminish economic efficiency. The next chapter also will help us get to our second motivating question about why those failed policies might endure even though their failures are well known and even though seemingly better alternatives are waiting in the wings.

The Marginal Revolution and the Rise of Allocation Economics

By the 1850s and 1860s the marketplace of economic theory had gone flat. Towering figures were lacking. And revolution was in the air. The first revolutionary shots were fired in 1871, even though guns were loaded in the decades before. The dramatic account maintains that three brilliant minds—William Stanley Jevons, Leon Walras, and Carl Menger—working in separate countries and from radically different perspectives simultaneously and independently discovered the concept of marginalism. Economic theory would forever be changed.

At the heart of marginalism is the idea that market value is determined not only by cost of production but also by diminishing returns to consumers. Prices for goods and services don't correspond to the total value of all those goods in existence but instead to the value of the *next unit* of that good (the marginal unit). A commodity's price is set by the value of the last buyer and last seller—the *marginal* traders. Workers are paid according to the incremental value that their labor adds to the firm. Diamonds are dear and water is cheap because the latter is relatively abundant. In these and many ways, marginalism solved deep paradoxes that now seem as obvious as the force of gravity but at the time were revolutionary.

This new foundation started modern economic thought on the voyage it continues today. But there are radical differences even among Jevons, Menger, and Walras. The most important difference is the extent of mathematical exposition. Menger and Jevons use little math and were widely read at the time—although Jevons was not well received and never did attract much of a following. Menger, by contrast, was influential and drew a following among several economists who came to be known as the Austrian school of economics, including Ludwig von Mises (1881–1973), author of the quintessentially Austrian text, *Human Action: A Treatise on Economics*, and Friedrich Hayek, whom we'll discuss later in this chapter. Austrians like Menger, Mises, and Hayek believe that economic life is too complex to be modeled with mathematical formulas and equations. By contrast, Walras is highly mathematical and, in retrospect, overly ambitious for the time. In the words of the prominent historian of thought, Mark Blaug, Walras was "monstrously neglected" because he set out to "write down and solve the first multi-equational model of general equilibrium in all markets [which was] enough to scare off most of his contemporary readers."[4] Yet despite his initial failure, Walras ultimately triumphs as future scholars pick up his method and gradually fix his system in place as a cornerstone.

The marginal revolution led to a new economics that rested on three bedrock principles: (1) methodological individualism; (2) rational choice; and (3) equilibrium. These foundations deserve our close attention because they are the foundations of both neoclassical welfare economics and public choice theory. Understanding how these schools differ begins with understanding their shared intellectual heritage and illustrating the power of neoclassical reasoning.

While the characters are interesting and the battles important, all this talk of math and equilibrium might not sound so gripping. But, as we said, there is intrigue and drama ahead. We lace it with tales of red wine, German beer, corn ethanol, old movies, and the latest fashions—all told by a parrot.

The Neoclassical Edifice

What is neoclassical economics? At some level, one could train a parrot to be a good neoclassical economist. Why did the price of gasoline triple between 1998 and 2008? Supply and demand. Why will Silicon Valley firms sell millions of electronic goods this year? Supply and demand. What will determine the housing market over the next couple of decades? Supply and demand. Okay, you get it. But talk is cheap (because its supply exceeds its demand), and our parrot's answers hold only superficially. We can peel back the parrot's refrain to appreciate at a deeper level *why* its answer is always correct.

In the neoclassical economics that grew out of the marginal revolution, there is no talking about markets without first talking about individuals. The first bedrock principle is *methodological individualism*. This means that societies and classes don't make choices; only individuals do. What we observe as social patterns and group outcomes is actually the aggregation of individual choices. Each individual consumer, for example, chooses his or her groceries and clothes, decides where to live, and all the rest, in a particular combination that he or she likes best. When everybody goes about his or her day making decisions both big and small, the total sum of each person's choices is what we observe at some aggregated level like markets and society.

Aside from individual-level analysis, what really distinguishes neoclassical economics is how the individual is modeled. Under the second bedrock principle, known as *rational choice*, individuals maximize their goals subject to the constraints of living in a world where anything that's valuable is scarce. For consumers and workers, the objective is utility. For firms, it's profits. As workers, individuals like to have income and leisure (what David Hume calls the pursuit of life's conveniences), but they are constrained by their own productivity and prevailing wages in the labor market. As consumers, individuals get more utility from consuming more and better food, housing, clothing, transportation, gifts, and entertainment. Yet consumers are constrained because these goods can be had only by paying their market prices. As savers, people want low risk and high reward. But you know how that goes. Facing inherent tradeoffs and hard resource constraints, rational individuals end up choosing some compromise of stuff they like and that they can afford. A head of household, for example, will adjust his work effort and his family's consumption bundle to get the most out of his consumption budget, relative to prevailing prices. Similarly, a business firm will adjust its mix of labor, capital, and other inputs to produce its wares at the lowest possible cost.

How can you tell if a consumer reaches the maximum utility? This is where we turn to marginal thinking and the third bedrock principle, *equilibrium*. The consumer spreads scarce budget dollars over a variety of goods, and the trick is to get the most satisfaction out of the next dollar spent. Across the range of goods in a consumer's bundle, she chooses to add a bit more or less of each one by comparing its price per unit to the marginal utility she gets from it. Because utility is subjective, she is the only one who can make these calculations. So if the price of a movie ticket is less than the utility of going to the movies, and if there's no other way to get more fun out of the dollars spent, then a rational consumer will go to the movies that night. But if she's already gone to the movies twice this week, she might not enjoy going a third time enough to make the movie ticket worth it. Instead, she might stay home and watch an old movie, or maybe she will save money instead of going out one more time. The more general idea is that rational consumers look for ways to adjust their consumption so that the next dollar spent goes toward the marginal unit of whichever good produces the biggest gain. The consumer adjusts quantities on every margin to equate the price paid with the satisfaction received on all goods. Once the consumer has exhausted all opportunities to make those kinds of adjustments, and once she has spent her entire budget, then she reaches equilibrium. The consumer is in perfect balance. Utility is as great as it could possibly be. There is no better way.

Until something changes, that is. In the early 1990s some studies reported that moderate consumption of alcohol, particularly red wine, offered significant health benefits. Demand for red wine went through the roof, creating tidy profits for those who already had made investments in wineries. Changing incomes and prices also can shift the rational individual's equilibrium choice. If your grocer runs a sale on your favorite cheese, you buy a big block of it. If it's been a cold winter and heating bills are up, you might tighten the entertainment budget. When new electronic gadgets come out, you might hear your friends say, "I'm gonna wait until prices come down." Rational choosers adjust to prices. Income dynamics count, too. For example, as incomes rise from high to higher, consumers begin to demand more luxury items and status goods. Or, as incomes rise from low to medium, demand for energy increases, as any North American can attest who has followed gas prices since the economic emergence of India and China.

It's a big advantage that the rational individual model integrates individual consumption, labor, and savings decisions. After all, consumers and workers are the same individuals. In the integrated model, the size of a person's consumption budget depends on how hard she works in the labor market. If a middle-age couple without a trust fund likes wearing new fashions and drinking old wines, then we could surmise that they have a high taste for income over leisure, that they're highly productive workers who get paid well, and that's how they meet their desires.

Marshall's Partial Equilibrium

While history attributes the marginal revolution to Menger, Jevons, and Walras, by the end of the nineteenth century it was Alfred Marshall (1842–1924) who became the leading figure in economics. In the family tree of economists, Marshall is the trunk, where the many roots of modern economics meet many branches away from a center point. Marshall dominated for about three decades, starting at around 1890. Part of his success came from being very careful in his reasoning and thorough in supporting every claim. He laid everything out for his readers. He also took a middle ground when it came to using math, which assured him an audience among many economists unfamiliar with newer methods.

At the heart of Marshall's work is the supply and demand model. Prior to the marginal revolution, classical economics explained the market value of a good by its cost of production. This essentially was the view of both Adam Smith and Karl Marx. Menger, Jevons, and Walras say price is determined by marginal utility, and Jevons especially overemphasizes the consumer as the sole determinant of price. A great synthesizer, Marshall was the first to clearly show that both supply and demand are needed to explain market prices. His famous analogy is a pair of scissors. One does not say it is the upper or lower blade of the scissors that cuts the paper; the two blades cut together. Marshall further shows that it is the marginal buyer and the marginal seller who determine price because these individuals will be the last to strike a new deal or the first to kill an existing one if adjustments are needed.

Marshall kindly makes the supply-demand model easy to use. Let's suppose there is a surplus of beef on the market. In Marshall's terms, we'd say the supply of beef exceeds its demand at current prices. Competition gives sellers an incentive to reduce their asking prices. As the price of beef consequently goes down, rational buyers adjust their consumption to include more beef. At what point does the price stop its decline? At the price where sellers can sell the amount that buyers want to buy, which is the equilibrium price. The key to this coordination is the freedom to exchange at any price agreed to by a buyer and a seller.

If instead we started out with a shortage of beef, the same process would unfold but in the opposite price direction. Buyers would not be able to get all they want to buy at current prices. So buyers with a strong enough preference for beef (the *marginal* buyers) will start to bid up the price. At each higher price, sellers put more on the market and buyers want less, so the shortage begins to disappear, one steak at a time. The price per steak keeps rising until it equates the amount buyers want to buy and the amount sellers want to sell.

Marshall prefers to look at one market at a time and their relations to each other. He fights against the general equilibrium approach of Leon Walras, arguing that it is too unrealistic and too elaborate in its assumptions. Under Marshall's influence, the profession would neglect general equilibrium modeling, leaving Walras in a temporary backwater. It would take an outsider, not a Cambridge colleague of Marshall's, to resuscitate the Walrasian technique.

Pareto's Brief Yet Fertile Love Affair with Economics

Vilfredo Pareto (1848–1923) was an engineer by training who switched to economics after discovering Walras. He later became frustrated with economics and switched again to sociology, where he wrote his most famous work, *The Mind and Society* (1935 in English). Pareto was a study in contrasts. A staunch antisocialist his entire career, he criticized aristocratic governments but rejected democracy. He was born of Italian nobility but lived modestly until the death of his parents, when he married a Russian girl and lived an aristocratic lifestyle in the Austrian mountains.

Pareto's approach to engineering prepared him well for discovering Walras. Unlike most economists of the time, Pareto wasn't put off by the quantitative nature of Walras's *Elements*. And, he would go on to advance general equilibrium modeling in ways that Walras did not.

Pareto's major dispute with economic theory is the way economists used the concept of "utility." Pareto knew that people were prone to make decisions that added to their satisfaction but were nonetheless not in their best interest. Drawing heavily on his reading of Aristotle, Pareto painstakingly works out a substitute concept, which he calls "ophelimity" and by which he essentially intends to mean "well-being." Unfortunately for Pareto, other economists would not pick up this idea, and the steady march of utility into the core of economic theory continued. This dispute was no small part of Pareto's eventual disenchantment with economics and departure for sociology.

If Pareto were alive in 2007, he would have been intensely interested in the fact that beer prices were spiking in Bavaria. Germans drink more beer per capita than anyone besides the Czechs and the Irish. There are something like 1,300 breweries in Germany brewing over 5,000 labels, and they all use basically the same ingredients: water, yeast, hops, and grain. In 2007 German brewers couldn't find enough of their favorite grain, barley, as market forces drove its price up 40 percent in just two years.[5] Brewers passed on the cost, and beer prices at Munich's annual Oktoberfest reached an all-time high of $10.70 per liter.

What caused this surge in beer prices in Bavaria? The barley shortage was created when corn prices spiked and farmers converted their fields from barley to corn. Corn prices were driven up by a new source of demand, oil companies refining corn into ethanol. Even though ethanol can be refined more cheaply out of sugar, U.S. refiners wanted corn because it was favored by government subsidy. Starting in January 2005, the U.S. government began paying forty-five cents per gallon to companies for blending ethanol fuel with gasoline. Farmers cut into forestland and converted fields to corn, yet demand grew even faster. Even the price of tortillas in Mexico spiked in 2007, as corn was diverted from feeding Mexicans to feeding U.S. ethanol plants. Pareto would have loved studying the effects of the blenders' subsidy and using it to show the interconnectedness of markets.

General equilibrium looks simultaneously at all persons and all markets in the economy. The idea is that all economic activity can be linked through individuals as they participate in different sorts of markets and in different capacities like consumers and entrepreneurs in goods markets, savers and investors in capital markets, and firms and workers in labor markets. General equilibrium models reach equilibrium when market prices throughout the economy adjust so that demand equals supply in every market. Each individual in the economy is at optimal rest in labor, capital, and goods markets. Each firm maximizes profit by adjusting combinations of labor and capital to minimize cost of production.

Imagine standing on the bank of a large pond. The surface of the pond gets disturbed by wind and by critters moving around close to the surface. But if the wind stops and all the critters arrive at their destinations for the time being, then the surface of the pond will become perfectly still. This is like general equilibrium. When all markets come into simultaneous equilibrium, the entire economy will come to an ordered rest. Any change in the system acts like a movement in the pond. Thus, when the new study announces the health benefits of wine, its effects ripple like waves of energy throughout all related parts of the economic system. Consumers spend more on wine and less elsewhere; winery owners make more money while other producers do less well; and so on. In response to this one ripple, prices and quantities adjust throughout the economy until new equilibrium points are again reached by each individual and in each market, and the entire system again comes into rest.

Pareto's brief love affair with economics was extremely fertile. By about 1960 economists had worked out most of the particulars in general equilibrium theory. It wasn't built in a day. There was no fell swoop that ushered in the new framework and made classical economics passé. There was no central authority directing economists to study particular subjects and problems. Rather, there were dozens and hundreds of minds working on individual parts of the problem in different but overlapping times and places. Individual scholars competed like entrepreneurs in the market for ideas—looking for niches, unexplored areas, and new ways of examining things. Policy-minded economists would soon be quick to deploy the new theory into policy matters and the proper role of government.

The Rise of Market Failure Economics

Suppose you walk over to your local Starbucks for a *venti* of your favorite blend. You say hello and place your order. You swipe your card, and in a few moments the barista presents you with your caffeinated treat. At this point, something kind of interesting happens. You both say, "Thank you." That's right. You *both* say thank you. Now, there's no doubting that you two are polite people, but this ordinary event reminds us that voluntary exchange has extraordinary implications. When two people freely agree to exchange, it is mutually beneficial and therefore promotes the public interest. You valued the coffee more than the money, and Starbucks valued the money more than the coffee. This makes voluntary exchange very attractive, and rationally self-interested people will tend to unearth these win–win opportunities. Therefore, absent hindrances to trade (like weak property rights or low confidence in contracts) all mutually beneficial trades will take place, all resources end up in the hands of their highest-value users, and the system of free market exchange is efficient.

Suppose instead that you get a letter in the mail from your local economic development authority. They want to buy your home, and they're offering fair market value. As the letter explains, there are plans for a new mixed-use development, and your lot is included in the plans. Do you want to sell? If you're like a lot of people, the answer is no. You may have lived in your house a very long time. You may have had no intention of selling, now or anytime in the future. And even if it were on the market, no one could pay enough to offset all the ways that you're attached to your house. In other words, there's no "For Sale" sign on your lawn because your subjective value is greater than market value.

On the other hand, your subjective value could be nothing special, and you might still have a reason to hold out. You could be *strategically* holding out, trying to dig more than a fair price out of the developer's deep pockets. This will make you unpopular with your neighbors if they've already sold, and it is also less than economically efficient. It is as though you wield monopoly power because the project only goes through if you sell. Yet monopoly is bad for social welfare, so this makes your decision to be a holdout a market failure. And here's the rub: Under the rules of voluntary exchange you have the right to refuse to sell, but if you exercise that right as a strategy then the development might not go through and resources fail to be allocated to highest-valued uses.

In the coffee scenario, the market was efficient, and therefore so is a policy of laissez-faire. But in the latter scenario, some form of government intervention could substitute for voluntary exchange and improve matters. For example, depending on your state's eminent domain law, the city could declare that the development serves a public purpose (creating jobs, growing the tax base). This gives power to the development authority to force you to sell so long as you're paid fair market value. In the end your property goes to the developer, and government intervention has achieved a more efficient allocation of resources than market exchange could muster.

These opposing scenarios capture the crux of neoclassical welfare economics. Do scarce goods like money, coffee, real estate, and so forth find their way to their highest-valued uses? If so, then this allocation is deemed to be "efficient" in an economic sense. If not, then government intervention would be required to restore efficiency and truly maximize the public interest.

In a watershed 1954 paper, Kenneth Arrow (born 1921, Nobel Prize 1972) and Gerard Debreau (born 1921, Nobel Prize 1983) prove that competitive markets in general equilibrium—like a perfectly still pond—guarantee efficient resource allocation throughout the economy. Known as the Fundamental Welfare Theorem, the idea embodies Adam Smith's invisible hand while using modern, mathematical economics. If people trust that property rights will be respected and contracts will be honored, and if people are free to exchange in goods, labor, and capital markets, then Arrow's equations show that market prices will direct people's choices to make sure that goods and services get produced at the lowest cost and are then allocated for greatest marginal value.

The catch is that the model needs to make very restrictive assumptions to solve for the system of supply and demand equations throughout the economy. For example, people are assumed to have perfect information about prices in all markets; this is so they can recognize price disparities and act on them to move markets toward general equilibrium. General equilibrium models also assume identical goods across all markets, which is okay for commodities like wheat and oil but hardly applies in a world with many diverse products. Also, consumer preferences and business cost structures are assumed to take on very specific mathematical properties so they are easy to manipulate using calculus. These restrictive assumptions naturally invited examination of their exceptions. And soon the proponents of government intervention would be the same scholars who studied most closely how actual markets might deviate from the "perfectly" competitive ideal.

Arthur Pigou and Externalities

Arthur Cecil Pigou (1877–1959) was Marshall's successor at Cambridge University, where Pigou lectured in economics from 1901 until World War II. A champion of Alfred Marshall, Pigou is the first to deploy the supply-demand model to build a general argument for the role of government in the economy. His early books, *Wealth and Welfare* (1912) and *Economics of Welfare* (1920), mark the founding of neoclassical welfare economics. Paving wide ground for government intervention, the latter was described as "virtually a blueprint for the welfare state."[6]

Pigou's key contribution is the idea that government intervention is necessary to correct *externality* problems. The term *externality* is a flexible one, referring to areas of economic life where there are spillover costs or benefits on other people. Traffic congestion is an example of an external cost that drivers create for each other. Immunizing your children means their classmates are less likely to get sick, an example of an external benefit for others. In externality situations, some resources may be allocated inefficiently. For example, whoever bears the brunt of external costs has less to spend or save in other parts of the economy, or whoever enjoys the external benefit pays less than the efficient compensation for the enjoyment. These little disturbances cause ripples throughout the economy, and the invisible hand doesn't work as well, making it harder to convert rational self-interest into social harmony. In short, externalities are market failures that require government intervention: Taxes or subsidies on the people creating the externalities compels them to act as though they bear the external cost or benefit themselves. Having internalized the externality, government intervention surgically removes inefficiency from the market and restores an efficient allocation of resources.

Pigou's essential idea has been remarkably influential, and we can still see it in our midst today. If you were to pay the market price for a gallon of gas and drive from home to work in the morning, the benefits of the exchange are enjoyed entirely and uniquely by you: You get to work. But the costs would not be entirely accounted for by your own costs. By adding another car to the road, you contribute to increased air pollution and traffic congestion. By paying only the market price for gas, you don't have the incentive to conserve on gas according to its full social costs. As a result, more than the efficient quantity of gas is refined, distributed, and burned. Pigou says a tax on driving would cause you to internalize the costs of pollution and congestion into your rational choice calculations, and fewer gallons of gas would therefore be sold on the market.

Pigou's ideas have influenced economics and policy in enduring ways. In 2006 the Harvard economist Greg Mankiw issued an open letter to join what he dubbed the Pigou Club, "the elite group of pundits and policy wonks with the good sense to advocate higher Pigovian taxes."[7] Mankiw's Club proposes a $1 per gallon tax phased in over ten years. His top reasons are the environment and road congestion, saying we need to internalize the external costs we're imposing on each other. "A higher gas tax would give us all the incentive to do just that," he says.

Pigou fell ill in 1927, and health issues increasingly took their toll on his lectures and writing. In 1933 he published *Theory of Unemployment*, which was notoriously thrashed as the best example of the worst that classical economics was capable of. With this shift, the window was open for a new thought leader in economics.

Contenders from Cambridge, the Austrian school, and the newly founded London School of Economics were all stepping up to the plate. For the first time, serious competition was emerging from the United States as well. For decades American economists had made important contributions, had published at the top levels, and had turned out high numbers of doctoral students from American universities. By the early 1940s, according to the historian of thought Henry Spiegel, "American economics had come into its own, but it had in the process produced no towering figure comparable in stature to the great classics, no Marx, Jevons, Walras, or Keynes."[8]

That was about to change. And Pigou's welfare economics was about to come along for the ride.

Paul Samuelson and Public Goods

Paul Anthony Samuelson (1915–2010, Nobel Prize 1970) was a great generalist during a time of great specialization in economics. He made pathbreaking contributions to virtually every area of economic theory. He was not only a top theorist but also an unapologetic advocate of government regulation, and, at least until 1989, his undergraduate textbook taught that Soviet central planning was more efficient and more productive than Western market economies.[9] In addition to perfecting neoclassical welfare economics, and providing an economic justification for any number of government regulations, Samuelson recommended automatic stabilizers like unemployment insurance that would build in spending increases during economic downturns and automatic cuts during booms.[10] As this chapter's opening quotation makes clear, Paul Samuelson believed that public policy could faithfully and competently correct all the imperfections of the market.

And Samuelson's voice mattered. He was so formidable a scholar that, after he presented his doctoral dissertation at Harvard in 1938, his advisors supposedly asked each other if *they* had passed. In 1970 he became the first American and second person ever to win the Sveriges Riksbank Prize in Economic Sciences in Memory of Alfred Nobel. Samuelson was also the most successful economics textbook author of all time. First published in 1948, his *Economics* would eventually run through nineteen editions over the span of fifty years, and it was the only economics book studied by millions of college students for generations around the world. "The Samuelson prose," said *The New York Times* in 1969, "apparently sings as brightly in Punjabi and Swahili as it does in English."[11]

Even Paul Samuelson's family tree looks like intellectual royalty, with prominent economists branching in all directions. His brother Robert Summers and sister-in-law Anita Summers are both well-regarded professors at the University of Pennsylvania, and his nephew Larry Summers was president of Harvard and later a top economic advisor to President Obama.

Despite his presence in policy discussions, Samuelson considered his true place to be in the academy. When summing up his contributions to economics, *The New York Times* called him "the economic theorist's economic theorist."[12] From his earliest publications, he methodically lays down important theoretical contributions. His early works focus on perfecting the rational individual model discussed earlier, as well as international trade, and especially welfare economics. In the mathematical lineage of Walras and Pareto, his papers brought calculus and differential equations to bear on questions that economists had grappled with for generations. One by one, Samuelson finds all the loose ends in economic theory and nails them down with a mathematical proof. And from these proofs he draws his policy conclusions.

His major contribution to the economics of government intervention doesn't arrive until sixteen years after his Harvard dissertation defense. With two monumental papers in 1954 and 1955, Samuelson lays out his argument that government needs to provide public goods to achieve efficiency in the economy. He uses a general equilibrium model, but not all goods in all markets are identical. Like Pigou, Samuelson seeks to model goods that are not entirely private—goods that have spillover effects or shared costs and common value across many people. Samuelson calls them collective consumption goods, "in the sense that each individual's consumption of such a good leads to no subtraction from any other individual's consumption of that good. . ."[13] For private goods like clothing and food, markets work fine as rational buyers and sellers reach equilibrium and allocate resources efficiently. But the markets for collective consumption goods fall short. In those markets, buyers free ride on each other, and suppliers don't have enough incentive to produce. Goods like national defense are underproduced by free markets.

When the Nobel committee described Samuelson's award, they spoke of unification. There was no more "this school of thought." There was one economics. It was the economics of general equilibrium, market failure, and government intervention to promote the public interest.

Adam Smith famously argues that government should assume only three duties—protection against foreign aggressors, protection against domestic aggressors, and provision of goods that will not be provided in the market. Samuelson's model ensconces these ideas for the role of government into the elegant proofs of neoclassical economic theory. Practical men, as Keynes calls policymakers, have been unwittingly applying Samuelson's theoretical proofs to the real world ever since.

The Rise of Keynesian Macroeconomics

It is about time we come to John Maynard Keynes (1883–1946). A towering figure in economics, Keynes was an entrepreneur of ideas who ultimately influenced everyone's views about what government should and should not do.

The world was ready to hear what Keynes had to say in 1936, the year he published his most famous book, *The General Theory of Employment, Interest, and Money*. Much of it seems like common sense today. But Keynes has to spend much of his book promoting a more expansive view of classical economics.

Keynes had an expansive view of just about everything, including his ability to influence ideas and policy. He once remarked that, if public opinion were to be influenced by an idea that later was found to be in error, it would be his responsibility to change public opinion again. To his credit, he was not adverse to presenting more than one opinion or changing his position when the circumstances or facts recommended it. But his famous ability to argue two sides of an issue also brought him consternation from a few political leaders, one of whom commented that if you were to ask two economists for an opinion you would get two opinions, unless Keynes were one of the economists, in which case you'd get three. He even took both sides in love, not terribly unusual among the intellectuals of his circles in that day. As a young scholar Keynes had male lovers, including the writer and critic Lytton Strachey. But, like Pareto, he later in life married a Russian woman, the ballerina Lydia Lopokova.

One of Keynes earliest works, *The Economic Consequences of the Peace*, was published at the end of World War I and shows a mind grasping politics and economics as an integrated whole. Here, Keynes argues that the severe reparations imposed on the losers of the war would sow the seeds of economic and social turmoil in those societies. He was right. In the 1920s, hyperinflation in Germany wreaked economic turmoil, while in the 1930s Hitler and the Nazis provided the social turmoil.

But Keynes is most famous for his theories on governments' fiscal and monetary policies, especially the need for an activist approach to counter economic downturns. Such downturns are not, according to Keynes, as readily self-correcting as was argued by the classical economists.

Keynes instead argues that total demand, not supply, is the most important component of the economy, and demand is driven by consumption spending. Because a penny saved is a penny not spent, too much savings can actually be bad for the short-term economy. Keynes calls this the paradox of thrift. The conclusion is that, at least in depressed economic conditions, a low propensity to save and a high propensity to consume are desirable.

From here, Keynes derives his famous *multiplier*. According to Keynes, if a society has a propensity to save one-tenth of its income, then the multiplier is one divided by one-tenth, which equals ten. If the propensity to save were one-twentieth of income, then the multiplier is twenty (that is, 1/0.05). Thus, a low propensity to save means a large multiplier, and a large multiplier means that government spending to "prime the pump" of the economy has a much greater effect. In other words, a large multiplier means that additional spending by government on roads, ports, and generally anything that is "shovel ready" (in the modern parlance), will generate additional income for workers, who then spend a large portion of their additional income on more clothes, cars, and other goods, and the suppliers of these items in turn see their incomes rise, which prompts spending on their part. In contrast, a smaller multiplier means governments have to spend even more to get an economy out of a slump.

Keynes argues that government should not, however, always be trying to raise consumer demand. Rather, government should spend more in an economic downturn, even if this entails running a deficit, and spend less in good economic times, when the budget should be in surplus. Nor should government take the more drastic step of owning the means of production. Indeed, Keynes is thoroughly unimpressed with Marx and communism. Rather, he thinks his ideas are critical to saving capitalism, not undermining it.

Scholars still debate the extent to which Keynes's recipe for promoting aggregate demand stimulated economies in the 1930s, but it certainly stimulated the demand for economic advice. President Franklin Delano Roosevelt was influenced by Keynes, as were most U.S. presidents indirectly for decades after the Great Depression. Eventually, in the 1970s, President Richard Nixon declared, "We are all Keynesians now." In the 1980s and 1990s, Keynesianism died down somewhat. Policymakers focused on supply-side policies to increase productivity rather than manage aggregate consumption. But demand-side stimulus came roaring back in the midst of the 2008 economic downturn, and one country after another enacted large government spending projects in the spirit of Keynes. Even so, the responsibility for government to manage unemployment, inflation, and economic stability never waned.

The Pigou-Keynes-Samuelson Paradigm

With Pigou, Keynes, and Samuelson, the invisible hand would have its counterfoil. Granted, self-regulating competition works well in conditions that resemble Ken Arrow's perfectly competitive general equilibrium model. But externalities create costs and benefits that are not accounted for in any free market. And lots of things that people value aren't supplied very well in markets because people share in their consumption, like national defense and clean air. On top of these individual market failures, the system as a whole is unstable and is given to wide cycles of boom, bust, and depression. In the name of the public interest, as measured by economic efficiency and stable macroeconomic growth, government intervention is necessary to correct market failures and smooth out the business cycle. The new economics had finally solved the age-old question that we took up in Chapter 2. To achieve the good society, government should surgically correct for the failings of the market. No more, no less.

From today's point of view, we can see the Pigou-Keynes-Samuelson paradigm anchoring current policy debates. The debates over taxes on energy and unhealthy foods all come down to Pigou. Proposals for government to subsidize journalism and green jobs and other "public goods" are derived from Samuelson. And fiscal stimulus packages come straight out of Keynes.

The consequences of these ideas are in our midst, but they have not gone unchallenged in the marketplace of ideas. There has been dissent, both in the moment and much later. Three thinkers in particular—eventual Nobel Prize–winners all—offer three distinct perspectives that nonetheless share a common foundation of construing the basic economic problem as exchange rather than allocation.

Seeds of the Counterrevolution
Hayek's Challenge

Along with Ludwig von Mises, Hayek (1899–1992, Nobel Prize 1974) was the leader of the Austrian school in the middle part of the twentieth century. Hayek parts ways with neoclassical economics from the very core. He is a methodological individualist of the Menger and Mises sort rather than the Walras and Pareto sort. This means that the individual that Hayek models doesn't merely maximize utility but is the entrepreneur driving economic change. The market is a dynamic discovery procedure, not a static equilibrium at rest. And even if policymakers could devote themselves to maximizing efficiency, no more and no less, they don't have the requisite knowledge to calculate the right course of action. For Hayek, there is something deeply fictional about the Pigou-Keynes-Samuelson paradigm.

In all his written works in economics, psychology, political theory and more, Hayek always emphasizes the role of knowledge in the economy and society. From the perspective of the information age and the rise of the knowledge economy, Hayek's notion might seem obvious. But in the middle part of the twentieth century he stood virtually alone. A neoclassical economist might refer to information such as whether a used car is a lemon, what are the costs of various production runs, or how many workers are employed by sector and age. Hayek argues that these data offer a somewhat fictional account of what they're supposed to be measuring, and there is far more economic knowledge in the economy that can never be measured.

In Hayek's worldview, economic knowledge exists in dispersed bits and pieces throughout the economy, in fleeting opportunities that emerge at particular times and places, that are known by few people, and that disappear quickly. Valuable knowledge winds its way throughout the corners of society and all the nooks and crannies of the economy. Knowledge is also tacit, difficult to explain, and even more difficult to aggregate. When people act on economic knowledge, often times it's without explicit intention or even conscious plan. No one can have access to all the information in an economy at once, but no one needs to, either. Everyday actions like people changing jobs, buying a new suit, saving more for the future, buying durable goods, buying real estate, and so on are coordinated by the relevant prices in each scenario.

Hayek's view of economic knowledge supports a biological rather than mechanical view of the economy. To Samuelson, the economy might appear as an intricate, mechanical clock or a combustion engine. But to Hayek the economy is organic, with many ephemeral economies emerging and dying all the time, like a coral reef or rain forest. This fundamentally different view of the economy casts grave doubt on the vision of Keynes and Samuelson to centrally plan economic life. Hayek's wordy papers differ dramatically from Samuelson's elegant equations nestled in a minimal amount of prose. More fundamentally, Hayek's approach to economic analysis focuses on exchange—the interaction of two parties trying to satisfy their respective needs. This approach differs dramatically from economic analysis that focuses on allocating goods to their best uses. The allocation problem is impossible to solve because no person or central authority can conceivably possess the knowledge of every person's benefit from every good at every moment in time. But Hayek goes further: Framing economic analysis as an allocation problem distracts economists from the true economic problem. Like countless survival opportunities for the many species in a rain forest, profit opportunities in an economy constantly emerge and attract people who are alert to them. A single, watchful eye from above would have to be omniscient if it were to recommend all the best courses of action for each species in the rain forest, or each individual in a market, at all points in time.

Hayek is clearly uncomfortable with concentrating too much authority into the hands of any entity—a government agency, a religious institution, a political party, or even a majority of the people. Without access to economic knowledge as it emerges in real time, no single person, business, or government could ever possess all the information needed to solve for perfect allocation of resources. On the contrary, Hayek's theory supports relying more heavily on dispersed plans, by all the individuals, households, and firms interacting with each other in the economy. The challenge for economics is to understand how knowledge is created, transmitted, and destroyed in an economy, how ordinary people organize their activities around the economic knowledge that they (not a central authority) possess, and how dispersed activities can become coordinated into beneficial social orders. Like a school of fish darting this way and that, each individual fish responds to signals that tell it when and how to act. In an organic economy, Hayek says, the system of market prices provides the signals for how individual people should act to meet their specific needs:

> We must look at the price system as such a mechanism for communicating information if we want to understand its real function . . . The most significant fact about this system is the economy of knowledge with which it operates, or how little the individual participants need to know in order to be able to take the right action. (Hayek, 1945, pp. 526–527)

A central plan, therefore, is not only impossible; it is unnecessary. A market economy can handle the basic economic problem if it is based on freely negotiated prices for exchange—and by implication, property rights for those who are doing the exchanging.

By framing the economic problem as exchange instead of allocation, Hayek argues that we can better understand economic life and therefore feel confident in abandoning the allure of central planning. Like the Scottish Enlightenment philosophers, Hayek attributes order not to centralized human design but to the spontaneous coordination of dispersed human actions, organized through competitive market exchange to promote the good.

Hayek's political theory is a direct consequence of his market theory. When a population allows for increasing government interventions in the economy, it risks opening the floodgates to government interventions in other areas as well. In the limit this can set in motion a process that moves towards totalitarianism. "To be controlled in our economic pursuits is to be controlled in everything," Hayek warns us. Interventions that begin as corrections of market failure, or aggregate demand management, spill over into noneconomic realms of ordinary life. History points to episodes of intervention that have snowballed into totalitarian regimes. Hayek witnessed firsthand how the economic troubles of the early 1920s unfolded into global war in the late 1930s. Having migrated to London, he found many intellectuals advocating the same economic policies of the national socialism that he thought he'd abandoned in Germany. Hayek wrote *The Road to Serfdom* (1944) to warn the public that the dangers of socialism are incipient, and he founded the Mont Pelerin Society in 1948 to invigorate his fellow scholars and their ideas in opposition to socialism.[14]

In all his social theory, the important question to Hayek is *how* the relevant knowledge needed for people to coordinate plans gets transmitted and what rules are needed to allow that information to be transmitted. The rules of government do not allow for very effective communication of economic knowledge, a feature that is needed to reach a rational economic order, to use Hayek's words, or to serve the public interest in the language of welfare economics. Society benefits from the division of knowledge that emerges under a system of market prices supported by sound rules of property and contract.

To Hayek, the advance of civilizations does not come from the quality of its leaders and their ability to design the best society but from the quality of its rules and their ability to evolve and improve as individuals learn. Too often leaders are overcome by a fatal conceit, Hayek argues in a book with the same name. The conceit is to assume we can design solutions, rather than to respect the complex processes by which solutions evolve. On economic regulation, on money, on stimulating consumer demand in the economy, on full-blown central planning, Hayek's challenge is to recognize the market as a space for coordinating behavior toward beneficial ends. Competition is the process by which economic knowledge is discovered. Regulators do not have a means of capturing the information they need to plan at any given time or plan ahead by forecasting economic models. The externality problem cannot be solved except by allowing market competition to solve it. A market failure is an incentive for entrepreneurial action—a profit opportunity—not a justification for intervention.

Coase's Dirty Hands

Ronald Coase (born 1910, Nobel Prize 1991) was raised in suburban London among a family of athletes, but he had weak legs as a boy and preferred bookish pursuits instead. He excelled academically and at age eighteen began studies toward a Bachelor of Commerce degree at the London School of Economics. Coase arrived at LSE in the fall of 1929. While he wasn't pursuing a degree in economics, some of his professors were economists. And in his second year he was introduced to Adam Smith's theory of competition. Coase became fascinated by the invisible hand and the body of work it spawned. He mastered economics by reading all the neoclassicals and more. He abandoned plans for a career in law, and LSE instead sent him to the United States for a semester to tour businesses, plants, laboratories, and other production facilities. Coase studied the process of production and exchange, read scores of legal cases, and conducted interviews with men of practice, not theory. It was a very different approach.

Coase's most famous works are "The Nature of the Firm" (1937) and "The Problem of Social Cost" (1960), two wordy, detailed, and extremely fertile papers. These papers created entirely new lines of research and fundamentally changed the path of scholarship in business, the environment, economics, and law. Not even Milton Friedman or Paul Samuelson had a publication that has been cited even half as many times as either "The Nature of the Firm" or "The Problem of Social Cost."[15]

Coase's method of studying economics is an unconventional one. He investigates the real world first and uses the patterns he observes to form theories. He says that to truly analyze the effectiveness of market and government institutions requires getting one's hands dirty with real-world details. When asked how he developed his theory of the firm, for example, Coase said he went out and asked businesses what they do. There are no mathematical models in Coase's work. There are just gritty evidence and detailed explanations. He was never indoctrinated into the orthodox economics of allocation, and he uses that to his advantage: "Not being trained to think in a certain way, I hadn't been trained not to think in a certain way, and therefore I was free to tackle the problems . . . At that time, the only place you could find discussions of real problems were in the law cases, because they weren't in the economics literature."[16]

Contrasted with the Pigou-Keynes-Samuelson paradigm, Coase's study of legal and historical detail portrays a very different picture of market failure and government intervention. Coase studies a variety of obscure but important stories in the area of nuisance law. His papers are riddled with characters from different periods and walks of life. There are railroads and farmers, doctors and confectioners, beekeepers and orchardists, smokestacks, hog farms, cattle ranches, and fallow fields. There are even rabbits.

First, Coase says, every externality is reciprocal by nature. Suppose you're stuck in traffic and so am I. We both want to be in a lane where only one car can fit. Who creates this externality, and who is the victim? We both do, and we both are. In Pigou's system an externality is viewed as one party harming another. On the contrary, in Coase's stories an externality is of mutual responsibility. The sparks from a passing train would do no damage to crops if the farmer would set his growing area back a few more feet. A confectioner's grinding machinery wouldn't disturb the doctor's consultations if the doctor's office were not located next door. The hog farm's stench and drainage wouldn't matter much if the neighboring property didn't have a house on it. In each case, curtailing the activity to avoid harm to the "victim" necessarily means harming the perpetrator.

The problem is reciprocal in nature. As a consequence, not all externalities are undesirable. That thirty minutes in traffic is a cost, for sure, because it could be time well spent relative to the alternatives (unfortunately, an empty freeway during rush hour isn't a relevant alternative). Even if the externality is undesirable, reciprocity means that either side can avoid the externality. The doctor's office could postpone visiting with clients and therefore be undisturbed by the confectioner's grinding noises. An obvious question is, if either side could avoid the externality, then which side *should* avoid it? Coase points out that economic efficiency is served only when the avoider is the person who can avoid at lower cost. Thus, a general rule comes into view: If an externality is undesirable, then liability should be assigned to the party who is the least cost avoider. If it costs the railroad less to install a spark arrester than the costs of paying for crop damages, then the railroad has a clear choice.

In separate work, Coase also challenges the theory and facts supporting Samuelson's public good argument. The seventeenth-century lighthouses along coastal England are a favorite example of economists from John Stuart Mill to Paul Samuelson. Before the marine-chronometer enabled precise on-ship calculations of longitude in 1759, rocky coastlines were a deadly and costly menace.[17] In Samuelson's framework, a lighthouse beacon is of immense value, but unfortunately it is also collective in consumption. One ship can follow the beacon to safe passage and not limit another ship's ability also to pass safely. With vessels free riding, no purveyor of lighthouses could make ends meet. Therefore, taxation and government expenditure are necessary to create the value that lighthouses provide.

On the contrary, Coase argues that lighthouses were in fact provided through voluntary exchange. Coase uncovers documents detailing the finance, construction, and operation of lighthouses during the period. People who financed lighthouses looked for and found ways to charge their customers. By contracting with nearby ports the purveyors of lighthouses could collect fees from docking ships.

Coase's revisionist history of lighthouses itself has been revised somewhat, as subsequent scholars have shown that purely private lighthouses did not survive very long, and successful ones acquired rights from the Crown to collect fees from ships.[18] Even so, these facts don't undermine Coase's argument against Samuelson, that market failure is not sufficient justification for government intervention. Many externalities are desirable in the sense that they are byproducts of valuable economic activity. And even undesirable externalities often go away through voluntary cooperation. There is neither an automatic nor general necessity for government to correct market failures.

And there is no guarantee that government intervention will improve efficiency. "Furthermore," Coase writes, "there is no reason to suppose that the . . . regulations, made by a fallible administration subject to political pressures and operating without any competitive check, will necessarily always be those which increase the efficiency with which the economic system operates."[19] Coase's "fallible administrators" echoes Hayek's knowledge problem, and his "political pressures" directly anticipates public choice theory. Perhaps this is no small coincidence. In the late 1950s, while researching all those nuisance cases, Coase worked down the hall from James Buchanan and Gordon Tullock at the University of Virginia.

Buchanan's Three-Pronged Hay Fork

Throughout his career of over six decades, James McGill Buchanan (born 1919, Nobel Prize 1986) was a maverick economist who always dared his students and colleagues to be different. Because he was trained in the Chicago neoclassical tradition and patriarch of the Virginia public choice school, Buchanan's work steadily brings new depth and insight to questions that most conventional economists take for granted.

Born into agricultural poverty in south Tennessee, Buchanan worked his way through state college by milking dairy cows twice a day for four years. He was the top student during his time at Middle Tennessee State College, and his memoirs admit some gratification that "the country boy more than held his own against the boys and girls from the towns." Buchanan's plans to attend Columbia University were derailed when he was drafted in 1941 and spent four years as a Navy operations officer at Pacific fleet headquarters. While at officer training school in New York City in the summer of 1941, Buchanan was "subjected to overt discrimination" that favored "products of eastern-establishment universities." These humble origins and outsider experiences, Buchanan would later write, surely explain much of the professional path he would eventually take.[20]

Two channels of influence were especially formative during Buchanan's doctoral studies at Chicago. The first was his professor, Frank H. Knight (1898–1972). The second was his independent discovery and translation of some early work by the influential Swedish economist, Knut Wicksell (1851–1926).

Stepping onto the University of Chicago campus that fall of 1945, Buchanan knew that he was like most other students—intellectually bright and politically socialist. Yet ideology was not the forefront of his intellectual interests, and his political views were not yet well formed. After a mere six weeks in Frank Knight's price theory class, Buchanan says he was "converted by the power of ideas, by an understanding of the model of the market."[21] At Chicago, Jim Buchanan was made into a neoclassical economist—with a twist. Buchanan saw in Knight an unfailing penchant to question anything, to take nothing as sacred. He was inculcated with Knight's openness to all ideas while recognizing that most ideas in circulation hold up poorly to scrutiny. From Buchanan's first papers in public finance theory, between 1949 and 1951, we see a mind testing the limits of economics and calling on his colleagues to push back those limits. He was a maverick scholar right out of the gate.

Buchanan's second major influence while in graduate school was his lucky discovery of Knut Wicksell. While browsing the stacks at Chicago's Harper Library, Buchanan found Wicksell's 1896 doctoral thesis:

> Wicksell laid out before me a set of ideas that seemed to correspond precisely with those that I had already in my head, ideas that I could not have expressed and would not have dared to express in the public-finance mind-set of the time. Wicksell told us that if economists really want to apply the test of efficiency to the public sector, only the rule of unanimity for collective choice offers the procedural guarantee.[22]

That is, true efficiency is achieved only if *everyone* is satisfied with the proposed outcomes and their respective payoffs. Otherwise someone or some group, often a minority of the population, is harmed.

Knut Wicksell knew a thing or two about being in the minority. Late-nineteenth-century Sweden was socially conservative and traditional, and Wicksell was neither. He married outside the state church, taking a common-law wife instead. He withheld swearing loyalty to the king and went to jail because of it. To solve various social problems, he advocated birth control a century before it was no longer a taboo topic. And Wicksell made money writing for popular outlets about individuals against the establishment. If Dale Carnegie were advising turn-of-the-century Swedes how to win friends and influence people, Wicksell's would not be his preferred formula.

Wicksell was unpopular in society, but he was a major influence on economists. Claiming Wicksell as direct influence are John Maynard Keynes, Ludwig von Mises, Paul Samuelson, and James Buchanan. And two of his students, Gunnar Myrdal and Bertil Ohlin, went on to win a Nobel Prize in economics. Though not as conspicuous as Marshall, Wicksell makes a formidable claim as the trunk of economists' family tree.

But the book that Buchanan found, Wicksell's *Finanztheoretische Untersuchungen* (Theory of Public Finance), was not discussed by other economists.

Buchanan read it in its original German, and he later describes the experience as being like scales falling from his eyes. Buchanan knew immediately that this would be the set of ideas he would work with, and he was determined to translate Wicksell's forgotten book for the English-speaking world.

Wicksell's argument in this book is a critique of majority rule, in terms of both justice and efficiency. He is one of the first economists whose work called for constraining majority rule by imposing supermajority voting requirements. One safeguard against majority tyranny is to raise the cost of obtaining a majority. It is one thing to find a 51 percent majority voting to take others' property because of their skin color or the sound of their surnames. It would be much more costly to carry out the injustice if the vote required a two-thirds or three-fourths majority instead. It also means fewer people will be in the minority to be harmed by the measure.

Pushed to its logical conclusion, if the issue is protecting individual rights, then Wicksell suggests a unanimity rule. Most societies take murder charges seriously, and one way to do that is to require a unanimous vote by twelve jurors to convict. But it takes little imagination to see the tradeoff. If all 100 members of your parent-teacher association or homeowners' association must agree on every matter, then nothing will get done. A strict unanimity rule essentially gives veto power to each and every voter. Under the influences of Knight and Wicksell, and arming himself with a three-pronged fork of fundamental arguments—a hay fork, if you will—Buchanan gradually and systematically shakes the foundations of welfare economics.

The first prong of Buchanan's hay fork is a 1962 article titled "Externality," coauthored with his University of Virginia colleague, William Stubblebine. They argue that the concept of externality had never been carefully defined, and they narrow the scope of Pigou's concept. A "technological" externality is very close to what Pigou has in mind: A factory pollutes a river, another driver crowds the roads, a neighbor plants flowerbeds in the front yard. In contrast, a "pecuniary" externality is denominated in market prices. For example, a new physician opens a practice in a one-doctor town, thus reducing the prices the incumbent doctor can charge. The price reduction is not a policy-relevant externality because the loss to the incumbent doctor is exactly offset by gains to patients who pay lower, more competitive prices. Indeed, as Coase might add, for centuries common-law courts have ruled that competition is not a tort. Buchanan and Stubblebine also distinguish between marginal and inframarginal externalities. The idea here is that externalities are byproducts of valuable economic activity, so a little pollution can be a good thing. To be more precise, an inframarginal externality is one that does not alter the prices and quantities that markets would reach in equilibrium. At the end of the day, only technological and marginal externalities can reduce the efficiency of the market. But pecuniary and inframarginal externalities are policy irrelevant and do not justify government intervention.

With the second prong, Buchanan attacks Samuelson's public good theory. In 1965 Buchanan publishes a paper with the seemingly harmless title, "An Economic Theory of Clubs."[23] As Coase explains how Pigou's externalities can be solved efficiently through private exchange, so Buchanan's theory of clubs explains how Samuelson's collective consumption goods can be supplied through voluntary groups, or clubs. Buchanan points out many examples of seemingly "public" goods being supplied everyday through subdivisions, professional associations, neighborhood cooperatives, trailer parks, and much more. Just as important, clubs are voluntary; therefore individuals can choose the ones they wish to join and thus choose the amount of "public" goods they enjoy and for which they pay. It is not *necessary* for the state to handle public goods. There are many shades of degree that make it difficult to pin down the exact circumstances when intervention could improve on voluntary production of collective-consumption goods.

And with the third prong of his fork, Buchanan cofounds public choice theory, which beckons Chapter 4 and the answer to our first motivating question. Public choice theory emerges on the principle that economics should have a uniform approach to the study of human affairs, rather than one set of theories for politics and another set for commerce. On this principle, public choice models would analyze how people make decisions in government and whether policymakers have the right incentives to use the powers of government to restore economic efficiency, no more, no less. Or, instead, do they have the incentive to use their powers for other purposes? Against the market failure theories of Pigou-Keynes-Samuelson, public choice would pose theories of government failure as well.

Ultimately, Hayek, Coase, and Buchanan are but three of the exchange economists who would challenge the allocation economists over what government should and should not do. Hayek argues that policymakers don't have the knowledge to plan the allocation of resources, and Coase shows us detailed examples of private parties working to eliminate market failure where doing so is worth the cost. Buchanan complements these arguments by essentially saying that even if policymakers were fully informed and therefore capable of central planning, they still cannot be relied on to correct market failures and nothing more. A government once empowered to restore economic efficiency often will use its powers of taxation, regulation, spending, and all other forms of coercion to pursue shortsighted, misguided, and ultimately inefficient outcomes. As we will see in the next chapter, the public choice argument also fundamentally critiques Keynesian stabilization policies.

Setting the Stage for Public Choice Theory

With the rise of neoclassical welfare economics, we are halfway to being able to answer our first motivating question. Economic theory has matured to the point that it could pinpoint even the most minor deviations from the socially optimal use of resources. With every increase in the scope of market failure also grew the scope of government intervention that was justified—so long as the intervening government was willing and able to correct market inefficiencies, no more, no less.

The great virtue of welfare economics was its ability to settle practical questions of economic policy by clearly demonstrating their effects on social welfare. Should governments levy taxes to build roads? Would there be too little education of youngsters without public schools? Should we put a tax on pollution and subsidize research and development? For the first time in history, the twentieth century saw economists treating these age-old questions like scientific matters. The new welfare economists could help define the "public interest" by proving (at least in theory) when voluntary exchange would not suffice and government intervention would be needed to correct market failures.

Yet for all its precision, the great vice of the new welfare economics was to crowd out politics and philosophy. Prior to the 1950s, economics focused only on two subjects: consumers (that is, households) and firms. There was no room in the new scientific economics for proper analysis of things like voting and policymaking. Why? Because there were no mathematical models for it—at least not yet. Economists at mid-century were preoccupied with the pure theory of households and firms and busy themselves with proving equilibrium and devising optimal conditions for allocating scarce resources. Interestingly, the main problem was that many of those optimal conditions included very specific policy choices, like taxing polluters, subsidizing education, and deficit spending during recessions. But the people making these policy choices—the madmen in authority—are not part of the economic model. There was no consideration of the politicians in Washington, the regulators in Sacramento, the voters in Schenectady, and so on. *Their* decisions were not factored into the precise calculations of the effects of their choices on social welfare. For the most part, welfare economics treated as irrelevant whether policymakers would have sufficient purpose and skill to enact just those exact policies that are prescribed by the new economic models, even though it has been treated as vital that they do so to maximize social welfare.

By the middle of the century, the table had been set for adding a new wing onto the neoclassical edifice, one that the economic analysis of politics would call home. Public choice is the study of government as practiced by imperfect individuals, with human goals and aspirations, operating under recognized rules of the game and figuring out how to work together through compromise and exchange. Public choice is revolutionary because it turns the new lens of economic theory onto the political process itself. It is counterrevolutionary because it poses a challenge to proponents of market failure: Government failure is plausible, too.

4

Public Choice

How We Choose Bad Policies and Get Stuck with Them, or Not

The diversity in the faculties of men, from which the right of property originate,
are not less an insuperable obstacle to uniformity of interests . . . Those who hold
and those who are without property have ever formed distinct interests in society.
Those who are creditors, and those who are debtors, fall under a like discrimination.
A landed interest, a manufacturing interest, a mercantile interest, a moneyed
interest, with many lesser interests, grow up of necessity in civilized nations, and
divide them into different classes, actuated by different sentiments and views.
—James Madison, *Federalist #10*

The U.S. federal government protects domestic sugar growers from competition through a combination of subsidized loan programs, price supports,
and import controls called the "sugar program." Each year, the Department of Agriculture (USDA) sets a number for total sugar production in the
economy. It then divides the work between cane and beet farmers. Having
negotiated a minimum price with Congress in advance, the farmers are guaranteed a market for their crop. Domestic sugar prices are generally between
two and three times higher than the global average, so the policy would
seem to have its intended effect of supporting domestic sugar growers.

Yet USDA regulators cannot control the program from imposing un-
planned, unintended consequences on the rest of society. And understanding
all effects of a policy—both the beneficial and the harmful—is the essence

of neoclassical welfare economics. Thus, when we look more broadly, we see that, according to the Government Accountability Office (GAO), the sugar program costs U.S. consumers almost $2 billion a year, and it harms producers in sectors like food and candy that buy sugar as an input. Over the decades of the program's life, those sectors have steadily laid off thousands of workers while moving operations overseas. The program also closes the world's wealthiest market to sugar growers in poor countries, especially in the Caribbean, worsening poverty and unemployment in the places where economic development is needed most. In short, the sugar program is a net loser; it harms domestic consumers and poor foreign farmers to benefit relatively well-to-do workers and stockholders in America's concentrated sugar industry. It is wasteful and unjust.[1]

The unintended consequences of government policy do more than raise the cost of a candy bar. Consider sick people who need a kidney or liver transplant. In 2011, over 100,000 patients were on the vital organ waiting list in the United States. About a quarter of those patients will get matched with donors and receive a transplant. Another quarter will be removed from the list within a year of getting on it. Relatively few patients stay on the list more than two years. "Removed" could mean the person gets better and goes home. It could mean they got worse and couldn't survive an operation. Or it could mean that they simply died waiting. According to the United Network for Organ Sharing (UNOS), 81,822 people died waiting between 1995 and 2007.[2] A branch of the Department of Health and Human Services, UNOS describes the problem in the language of supply and demand: "This large waiting list is in part due to the cumulative effect of the imbalance between supply of organs and demand (need) for organs over past years."[3] For some organs, the demand is not very high. But for kidneys, livers, and pancreata—which combined make up 97 percent of the list—demand is growing faster than supply. So the waiting list grows, waiting times get longer, and more people die waiting. Despite this injustice, economists have estimated the price for kidneys that would eliminate the shortage. It's approximately $15,000.[4] In other words, if donors could be paid something like the value of an economy car, then the supply of kidneys would catch up, and there would be no more waiting and dying. Of course, it doesn't matter what price would emerge on the market. There is no market because it is illegal for donors to be compensated under the 1984 National Organ Transplant Act.

We suggest sugar and vital organs as examples of wasteful and unjust policies. There are other examples. We talk about some of them in this book. In this chapter, we suggest a set of ideas that can account for and explain these and many other failed policies from government. This set of ideas is known as public choice theory. The basic message is that, just as markets may fail to allocate resources according to some theoretical ideal, so may government fail to achieve what we hope to get from it. In short, society cannot easily empower government to correct market failure without those powers also being used for other, perhaps very costly, purposes as well. By examining politics and democracy, public choice theory found that the processes lend themselves to programs that concentrate benefits on a relative few in society while the costs of the transfers are borne by many diffuse groups of people. There is no question that certain U.S. sugar growers benefit from the sugar program, and many hospitals and organ procurement organizations benefit from the ban on donor compensation. But the whole point about neoclassical welfare theory is to count the welfare of *all* groups in society, not just a privileged few.

Policies that are net losers for society—benefitting some while imposing even greater harm on others—aren't supposed to occur under the Pigou-Keynes-Samuelson paradigm. It's not supposed to work like this. Instead, as benevolent and omniscient public servants, policymakers are supposed to care about economic efficiency and use their discretion only to grow the size of the social pie, not to privilege certain groups in society. Perhaps neoclassical welfare theory just doesn't explain politics very well. Yet, as we saw in Chapter 3, perhaps this is unfair to the Pigou-Keynes-Samuelson paradigm because it was never an *attempt* to explain democratic politics. It merely assumed that government would capably fulfill the market corrections that economists would recommend. The experience of history, plus a little common sense, would suggest there are some problems with that point of view—all of which brings us back to our three motivating questions from Chapter 1:

1. Why do democracies generate policies that are wasteful and unjust?
2. Why do such failed policies persist over long periods, even when they are known to be socially wasteful and even when better policies exist?
3. Why do some wasteful policies get repealed (for example, airline rate and route regulation), while others endure (such as sugar subsidies and tariffs)?

In the public choice view that took shape from the 1950s to the 1990s, all these wasteful policies are the routine products of ordinary democratic politics. Rather than pursuing efficiency as the public interest model suggests, policymakers strike deals (they *exchange*), creating concentrated benefits while dispersing the costs widely. Because these policies restrict market competition, they cause resources to be allocated inefficiently, thus harming losers more than helping winners. Another way of saying this is that political exchange transfers wealth between groups in society, from amorphous groups like consumers to concentrated groups like certain labor unions, industries, and other organized interests. Furthermore, once the policies are in place, there is a vested interest attached to the continuation of the policies. So, as we'll see in this chapter, public choice theory builds on the last two chapters to pose answers to our first and second motivating questions. We see much more clearly why government sometimes produces unjust or inefficient policies and then maintains them. Yet because public choice emphasizes *equilibrium* in politics, just as neoclassical theory does in markets, the school of thought evolved in ways that made it relatively incapable of answering our third question. To understand political change, we must go beyond the main message of public choice theory, that "incentives matter" in politics, and introduce the influence of ideas—which is our subject for Chapter 5.

The Public Choice Revolution

When James Buchanan won the Nobel Prize in 1986, the usual press inquiries followed. Each fall the Nobel committee announces six prizes over several weeks, and reporters get into full-blown geek mode, knowing they'll have to quickly write informative summaries of complex science for the general public. When Paul Samuelson won the economics Prize in 1970, the *New York Times* asked whether it was even possible to explain his work to readers and insisted that Samuelson would say no, not possible.[5] The paper nonetheless found it possible to convey Samuelson's philosophy of government intervention, and it went on to describe him as "the Hollywood image of a Cambridge professor." Other Nobel Laureates are easy to write about because they already have a public image when they win the prize, like Paul Krugman in 2008 and Milton Friedman in 1976. But this Buchanan character—he didn't fit the mold.

The Nobel committee's official notice recognized Buchanan for "a synthesis of the theories of political and economic decision-making (public choice)."[6] When Buchanan was asked by his local paper, *The Washington Post*, to explain "exactly what public choice is,"[7] Buchanan said public choice is studying politics with the tools that economists use to study markets. Public choice treats voting, lobbying, regulating, and all other political decisions as made by self-interested individual people, working within agreed-upon rules. The *Post*'s reporter was nonplussed. Well, isn't that just common sense, the paper asked? And why would the Swedes award common sense with a Nobel Prize? Perhaps recognizing a language barrier, Buchanan agreed, saying it probably wasn't much more than common sense. But he reminded his interviewer that most economists didn't see it that way.[8] Unsatisfied, *The Post* ran a guest column ten days after Buchanan's prize. "What it all boils out to is that Buchanan's economics represents a particular ideology: leave the economy alone and everything will be all right."[9] A *New York Times* op-ed of exemplary candor upped the ante: "To put it bluntly, the Nobel Committee's choice is far more a testimonial to the fashionable popularity of conservative politics in the United States and elsewhere than a tribute to Mr. Buchanan's rather modest achievements."[10]

The Nobel committee fired back. Its selection chairman later told the *Post*, "That's stupid, that we think about people's political opinions. It's a very superficial interpretation. No, no, we're not that simple-minded."[11] Nonetheless, the spin continued even at the heights of the profession. The previous year's Nobel Laureate in economics, Samuelson's colleague at MIT, Franco Modigliani, told the *Times* that "Dr. Buchanan says very emphatically that the government should get out, and this fits very nicely with the Swedish view right now."[12]

This was how the establishment of the time received the news of Buchanan's Nobel Prize. What got them so riled up?

Foundations of Public Choice Theory

Buchanan says that public choice theory begins with three presuppositions about politics: (1) methodological individualism; (2) rational choice; and (3) politics-as-exchange. The first two assumptions are the same starting points that we encountered in the last chapter with neoclassical economics. We've used the metaphor about shifting the lens of economic theory onto non-market situations, namely politics. The way public choice did this was to model people in politics as rational-choice individuals engaging in political exchange, as voters, parties, politicians, bureaucrats, regulators, and other political decisionmakers. Over the next few pages, we'll "unpack" Buchanan's three suppositions to see what they mean and how they form the foundation of our understanding of political change.

Rational Individuals Exchanging in Politics

The best discussion of methodological individualism in politics is in the book most often identified with public choice theory, *The Calculus of Consent* (1962) by Buchanan and his cofounder of public choice theory, Gordon Tullock (born 1922).

In the early chapters of *Calculus of Consent*, Buchanan and Tullock defend the approach to politics as the collective action of rationally self-interested individuals. They talk about many of the philosophers we met in Chapter 2 and how at least since the time of the Scholastics the human individual has been the primary unit of inquiry. They talk about what factors cause people to hold government in high or low esteem. And they talk about how the rules of politics shape the incentives of those people at the center of the political game:

> The Scholastic philosophers looked upon the tradesman, the merchant, and the moneylender in much the same way that many modern intellectuals look upon the political pressure group. Adam Smith and those associated with the movement he represented were partially successful in convincing the public at large that, within the limits of certain general rules of action, the self-seeking activities of the merchant and moneylender tend to further the general interests of everyone in the community. An acceptable theory of collective choice can perhaps do something similar in pointing the way toward those rules for collective choice-making, the constitution, under which the activities of political tradesmen can be similarly reconciled with the interests of all members of the social group.[13]

Rational self-interest motivates the butcher, the brewer, and the baker as well as the politician, the voter, and the bureaucrat. In other words, public choice begins by adopting a symmetric stance between markets and governments: People are assumed to be rationally self-interested in both settings. Only with this consistency, with this symmetric treatment, can economic science truly compare how government and market institutions perform.

But why *also* presuppose that rational individuals *exchange* in politics? Because in both the market and in politics, as Mick Jagger reminds us, you can't always get what you want. Adam Smith says that in the market, rational individuals—the butcher, the brewer, the baker, as well as consumers—pursue their own interests and find ways to cooperate via exchange. At least, that's what happens when there are effective rules, such as those that protect property and allow the price system to work without interference.

Buchanan and Tullock are reminding us that something similar happens in politics. The butcher, the brewer, and the baker, as well as consumers, have different political interests. These and many more groups of what Buchanan and Tullock call "political tradesmen" have different things they want from government. In a political market based on a democratic-republican form of government, people work together to make decisions about how to allocate resources. They set tax rates, approve construction projects, hire first responders, educate children, and so on. They engage in political trade. And they do so from different sets of interests. Notice in this chapter's opening quotation the many lines of political interest that James Madison sketches for us. Buchanan and Tullock also remind us that in both market and political exchange, the public interest is on the line. So it is important to establish appropriate rules of exchange in both settings, markets and governments. For example, most people are not happy with the political rule set known as dictatorship because no one gets what he or she wants except for the dictator. Most intuitively prefer something like democracy, with all of the good and bad that this arrangement entails.

Early work by Tullock sets the tone for looking at majority rule in a representative democracy. His papers show how majority rule quickly turns into logrolling—that ancient act of political back-scratching also known as vote trading.[14] In many political bodies, decisions about spending on public goods are put up for a vote, with a simple majority deciding the issue and with taxes to pay for that spending levied on everyone in the community. Oftentimes, no one group has enough votes to get what they want by themselves. That is, there simply aren't enough butchers to vote for their preferences and win a majority without the help of either the brewers or the bakers. Here is where logrolling comes in. It allows the butchers to get the spending they want, albeit at the cost of supporting something the brewers want. The benefit of this type of political exchange is that more people get what they want. The cost is that there is more spending than the majority desires, at least if the majority could evaluate each issue individually, without policies bundled by coalitions.

Tullock's logrolling analysis is therefore an economic response to Paul Samuelson's public goods argument. It is one thing to point out that markets fail to produce certain types of collective goods. It is another thing to analyze how a democratic republic would step in and supply those goods. Tullock argues that rational people will engage in logrolling, forming coalitions and blocks when voting under a majority rule. Unfortunately for Paul Samuelson, nothing guarantees that the outcome of this political process will come close to what economic theory would say is efficient.

The contrast between Tullock and the welfare economists can also be viewed in terms of externality. Like Pigou arguing that market transactions create externalities and market failure (too few public goods), Tullock shows that logrolling through voting also creates externalities and government failure (too many public goods). The externality in this case is called a *fiscal* externality, and it takes the form of too much spending on government services, which ultimately must be paid for through taxes. (This is why legislatures often spend beyond their means, even when the politicians who work there claim to be fiscally prudent. It also helps explain why President Reagan oversaw deficits while negotiating with Congress for the policies he wanted.) In short, against this public interest standard called economic efficiency, Tullock shows that government failure is at least as plausible as market failure. And so the tip of the public choice iceberg comes into view.

When early public choice scholars shifted the lens of economics onto politics, what they found was a theoretical explanation for the messy downsides of democracy. As German Chancellor Otto von Bismarck said, "Laws are like sausage. It is better not to see them being made." Perhaps public choice riled up so many people for having the gall to show how sausage is made.

Voters

When Gordon Tullock taught at George Mason University in the 1980s, "Tullock votes" was rumored to have adorned the economics department bathroom wall. The graffito (which is false, by the way) pays homage to Tullock's argument that a wealth-maximizing agent will never choose to vote. Think about that for a minute. The way a rational agent decides whether to vote (like anything else) is to compare the expected benefits to the expected costs. Known as Tullock's voting paradox, the idea is that the costs of voting exceed its benefits in all but the rarest of circumstances. Thus the act of voting is itself irrational, which raises the question: What kind of system is it that relies on the judgments of irrational people? This is the kind of stark reasoning that irked many traditionalists and solidified Tullock's iconoclastic status, winning him many fans. Tullock and others have much more to say about voters. As we'll see, the voter is the most controversial figure in public choice theory.

Majority Rule with Rational Voters

While the public choice school of thought gained real momentum in the mid-1950s, some early papers pioneered the economic study of voting, treating voters almost exactly like neoclassical consumers. A 1943 paper by an economist named Howard Bowen is a pioneer in the twentieth century (French economists had studied the mathematics of voting in the early nineteenth century).[15] Bowen's paper "The Interpretation of Voting in the Allocation of Resources" was published while Bowen was leaving a successful career as an economics professor for a new career as a tax economist on Capitol Hill. In Bowen's model, the government is a supplier of some valuable good, such as national defense or homeland security. Voters differ in how much value they place on the public good, but everyone winds up with the same quantity because it's a nonrival good. To model things, we pretend that something as complicated as homeland security can be collapsed into a single variable; perhaps it's dollars of spending or the number of homeland security officers.

Each of Bowen's consumer-voters is also a taxpayer. The tax is like a flat tax on income, so each voter pays a "tax price" that increases with his or her own income and with the number of homeland security officers. Each individual's ideal number of officers is where the increase in income taxes (the marginal cost to the voter) just equals the marginal benefit of the added security. Because income and preferences vary, voters' ideal points for officers also will vary. And because we have collapsed everything into one variable, it is easy to line up all taxpayers according to their ideal policies, as in Figure 4.1.

Suppose we have five voters. Each has an ideal quantity of a public good, such as homeland security officers hired per 1,000 people. Person A wants one officer, person B wants two, person C wants four, D wants five, and E wants thirteen. How will this vote turn out? With these types of models, it helps to think of voting as occurring head-to-head between two choices,

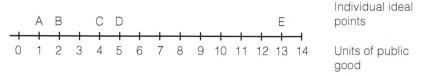

Figure 4.1 Voters as consumers of public goods (for example, homeland security officers per 1,000 population).

like a round-robin tournament in sports. For starters, if these folks were voting whether to increase from zero units to one unit, then this move would win a unanimous vote. Next, if we vote whether to move from one to two, everyone except Voter A will vote yes, and the measure wins four to one. Similarly, moving from two to three will win yes votes from C, D, and E, bumping Voter B off her ideal point.

As we increase from three units, the voting coalitions get interesting. Moving from three to four wins by a three to two vote, with Voters A and B losing to the C, D, and E majority. But on the vote from four to five, the majority changes sides with A, B, and C teaming up to keep the quantity at four and Voters D and E now on the losing side. Any quantity above five will similarly lose to four. And that's how this vote will go.

It's no coincidence that Voter C is on the winning side in all head-to-head votes. She is the median voter. This means that there is an equal number of voters wanting a position to the left on the spectrum of possible positions (those wanting fewer officers) as there are voters wanting a position to the right (those wanting more officers). As a general rule, in any situation resembling Figure 4.1 the outcome will arrive at whatever quantity the median voter prefers. This is called the Median Voter Theorem.

The median voter was first seriously studied by a Scottish economist named Duncan Black (1908–1991). Half a century after Wicksell, Black sets out to demonstrate the usefulness of majority rule as a political institution. He succeeds in part, but not exactly as he intends. Black finds that majority rule works well, but only under limited circumstances, when two very specific conditions hold. First, voters decide on a single issue at a time, like the number of officers to hire. And, second, each voter has "single-peaked" preferences over the issue. "Single-peaked" means there's one position on the number line that is ideal to each voter, and movements away from that point in either direction are progressively worse. When these conditions hold, Black shows, then the Median Voter Theorem holds.

Every four years the U.S. presidential elections present a nice example of the Median Voter Theorem. During the primaries, the successful candidate has to appeal to the party base while inspiring confidence that he or she can beat what the other party has to offer in the general election. Once nominated, that same candidate now must reach the median of the entire electorate, not just the party. This explains why presidential candidates run to the center after the primaries. The same goes for any office elected under two-party primaries, including Congress and the state legislatures.

A fundamental question is whether the median voter's preferred outcome, such as the quantity of homeland security officers, represents an efficient outcome. In other words, does majority rule allocate resources optimally through the political process in the same way that the Fundamental Welfare Theorem proves that markets allocate resources optimally through the economic process? This is one of the core questions that welfare economists began taking up in the 1950s. Soon it would become apparent that the answer is no. The same Kenneth Arrow who gives us the Fundamental Welfare Theorem of markets also proves another theorem about voting. Arrow's voting theorem says there is no method of voting that is even *theoretically* ideal. To prove this, Arrow has to entertain a more complicated model than our simple number line. First, Arrow's model lets multiple issues be voted on at once. Next, he develops certain reasonable conditions that an ideal voting process ought to meet. In simplified form, the conditions are:

1. The voting system must represent the wishes of multiple voters. No single voter can dictate the outcome.

2. The voting system must represent all preferences of the voters and rank them for the society as a whole.

3. The voting system must rank preferences among a subset of all options just as it would if all options were considered. Thus, if voters prefer A to B and B to C, then the voting rule must have B win over C even if A is not an option.

4. The voting system must rank group and individual preferences identically when there is unanimous agreement. Thus, if everyone in the group prefers A to B, then the system must rank A over B.

Arrow concludes that no voting system can satisfy all four of these reasonable criteria. Hence the name: Arrow's Impossibility Theorem. For an economist trying to suggest democratic rules that improve social outcomes, this is a pretty pessimistic result.

Several other problems with majority voting were exposed, as a flood of scholars became attracted to the mathematics of voting. Stability became a major issue. Outside the familiar confines of Black's two conditions—single-issue, single-peaked preferences—models show that majority rule voting is prone to shifting coalitions and wild swings from one election to the next. This point has been intensely debated because scholars despise models that lack determinate solutions and also because it suggests that governments are volatile relative to markets. But a fair comparison would say that market exchange depends on institutions like property and contract, so perhaps the stability of political exchange also depends on institutions. For example, if it's agreed that instability in voting is socially undesirable, then one way to counter instability is to be very careful about what items actually come up for votes. This explains why political traders use committee structures to spread agenda-setting and gate-keeping powers. Another counter is to make sure the votes are there beforehand, which explains why political traders make regular use of logrolling and why party leaders appropriately called "whips" are appointed to line up the rank-and-file votes ahead of time. Simple majority rule is unstable (when Black's two conditions don't hold), but institutional structure can suppress that instability and induce equilibrium in voting.[16]

Another issue arises because voting assigns equal weights to voter preferences, except under logrolling, as Tullock points out. In other words, majority rule voting has been shown to ignore the intensity of voters' preferences. In Figure 4.1, a statistician might call voter E an "outlier." In politics he would be an "extremist." But in economics, Voter E's subjective value matters as much as anyone's value does, and the theory used to measure social welfare must count it. Voter E is like the homeowner who sincerely (rather than strategically) doesn't want to sell out to the new development. The city council imposes the interests of the majority by forcing out the homeowner with eminent domain. Like Knut Wicksell, a consummate outlier and extremist in the eyes of some, an ousted homeowner will likely come to adopt strong opinions about majority tyranny.

Rational Ignorance

Duncan Black didn't initially succeed in the marketplace of economic ideas. Because he was an outsider looking in, Black's work was initially undervalued by the mainstream of the profession. Working from remote outposts, he had difficulty getting his work published and gaining interest from his fellow economists. It helped that Ronald Coase was a friendly connection, and William Riker (another major figure in early public choice) wrote favorably of Black's work. But for some time, the median voter model would brew in fairly small circles. Then Black's idea was picked up.

A newly minted Stanford PhD economist named Anthony Downs (born 1930) made the median voter model a core part of his doctoral dissertation, which was then published as the landmark 1957 book, *An Economic Theory of Democracy*. Downs's dissertation advisor at Stanford was none other than Kenneth Arrow.

As an undergraduate, Downs successfully ran for student body president at Carleton College. While serving, he discovered that most of the student body didn't know or care about the job he did as president. Downs saw his classmates paying as much attention to student body politics as it was in their interest to do so and no more. Downs knew his classmates were making rational choices with their time and knew they weren't the only ones. Across the board, Downs surmised, voters economize on information costs and wind up being rationally ignorant about the functions of government, what kinds of jobs their representatives are doing, and even who is in power. Throughout his career, Downs would anchor all his analysis of politics to the assumption that voters are rationally ignorant. He would not be the only one.

Perhaps ignorance isn't personally costly in politics, but it is in markets. As in the case of Tullock's farmers, consequences are more individual in markets, more shared in politics. To illustrate, let's say you are buying a new car or smartphone. This thing that you wind up buying will be with you almost every day of your life for the next couple of years and perhaps longer. You have the incentive to educate yourself on all the available features, think about how important certain features are to you, and familiarize yourself with how everything is priced. You'll probably shop around a little bit, check out *Consumer Reports* and some online user reviews, and maybe sleep on it.

Suppose instead that you're going to the voting booth. The consequences of choosing poorly at the voting booth don't fall directly on each voter. They get shared with all other citizens. People thus have less of an incentive to make the right decisions in politics than they do in markets. So they have little incentive to diminish their ignorance about much of what happens in politics. Even if people do inform themselves dearly about politics, their vote still only counts as much as someone who is completely oblivious. And we are back to the Tullock voting paradox.

Downs motivated generations of scholars, mostly in political science, to find out what voters know. A vast amount of evidence overwhelmingly confirms that voters know very little about government. People are just as given to wild conspiracy theories as to reasonable explanations for government. Majorities of voters incorrectly answer questions about the basic organization of government. Most cannot even name their representatives aside from the president and perhaps one senator.

Voters are even less informed about the effects of policies and seem to take stated intentions on face value. For example, observe what happens in the days following a damaging earthquake, tornado, or hurricane. Many states have antigouging laws, which legally prevent sellers from increasing their asking prices on ice, plywood, batteries, portable generators, and so forth. The intent of an antigouging law is easy to understand: The legislature is protecting people from getting ripped off. The effects, however, almost never work out that way.

Antigouging laws actually make it *harder* for disaster victims to find ice and plywood at all, much less at prices deemed exorbitant. After Hurricane Fran in 1996, for example, almost a million people in Raleigh, N.C., were without electricity and badly needed ice. In response, four men from a town about 100 miles away paid $1.75 each for 500 bags of ice, trucked them into the disaster area that was Raleigh, and started selling to willing but complaining buyers at about $8 per bag. The police showed up, discovered the state's antigouging law was being violated, and hauled away the four men *and* the remaining bags of ice. You might think the people standing in line would scream, "Hey, bring back the ice!" But instead they cheered.[17]

In short, people can be cognitively biased. Behavioral psychologists tell us that people naturally find ways to conserve on brainpower. For example, we all have "anchoring" and "availability" biases that affect the way we interpret novel circumstances. When disaster victims know that the price is $1.75 under normal conditions, people default to $1.75 as their perceived appropriate price, even though supply and demand conditions are radically changed during the disaster. So, whether locals cheer or boo depends on which of two narratives people believe: Is $8 a fair price for providing a badly needed service, or is it an exorbitant price that takes advantage of the situation?

In the supply-demand model, $8 is the price that motivates sellers to take on the added effort, expense, and risk of supplying ice to disaster victims living in another state, and $8 is the price that buyers are willing to pay because their food, baby formula, insulin, and other vital items are spoiling by the minute in their powerless refrigerators. As Alfred Marshall taught us over a century ago, when supply decreases and demand increases, prices will go up. On the other hand, the "gouging" narrative says that $8 is the price charged by greedy, opportunistic sellers whose attempts to rip off the public must be stopped, even if that means no ice is made available. Unless people have studied the supply-demand model, the gouging narrative will be more cognitively available, and people will anchor to it when they see the police hauling away the bad guys. And so they cheer.

These cognitive biases often mutually reinforce rational ignorance. The supply-demand reasoning is opaque; it takes mental effort and a willingness to think in terms of general rather than their own individual interest. In contrast, the gouging narrative is vivid; it is easily grasped and satisfies a cognitively available sense of fairness. Just as rationally ignorant voters have little incentive to gather and evaluate information about politics, cognitively biased voters support antigouging laws because it is easier to see them as a good idea.[18]

People hold similarly erroneous views on trade restrictions, minimum wage laws, occupational licensing laws, and scores of other market interventions. By "erroneous," we mean that the policies people support fail to achieve what most supporters think they achieve and in fact do great harm. These beliefs affect how political parties take shape, how interest groups acquire influence, and how politicians ultimately respond to voters and vice versa. When voters don't understand the basic structure and functions of government, much less the causes and consequences of policies enacted by government, it is both easy and common for voters to support wasteful and unjust policies. It seems a whole theory of politics could rest on Downs's idea.

Political Parties

In simplest terms, political parties are coalitions that seek control over the policy levers that set the political rules of the game, to accomplish their specific goals, and to advance their particular interests. In Downs's uncertain political world, political parties are a way to communicate ideological and policy stances between voters and politicians.

It's a lot of work for the average voter to come up with an opinion on exactly what government should do, how to resolve all those messy questions about what to regulate and what to leave to the market, how to spend tax dollars in one area compared to another, and so on. Most of us have better things to do.

If you want someone who would vote as you would vote or someone you can count on to "do the right thing" (as you conceive it) in Congress, and if the costs of monitoring the most basic political activities is high, what do parties do to help? They provide inexpensive signals on how political candidates think, otherwise known as their ideology.

Party affiliation helps politicians, too, including the benefits of branding for voters, and an easy way for a politician to do that is to be a "proud Democrat" or a "proud Republican." This is simply the mirror image of the benefit to voters—lowering information costs. In addition, party affiliation allows a politician to be part of a coalition that can jointly produce political benefits.

Finally, political parties can be a convenient means for politicians to limit competition (we didn't say it was good for the voters). For example, in the United States, the vast majority of the members of Congress belong to either the Democratic or the Republican Party. While this usually guarantees two fairly different ideologies in a given race, it also makes it hard for a third point of view to emerge.

Interest Groups

In the passage from *Federalist #10* quoted at the chapter opening, James Madison articulates how people in a geographically representative republic naturally fall into groups of common sentiments and views. However, being of common sentiments is not the same as being of common interests. If you and I are both landed interests (say, sugar farmers) or manufacturing interests (say, steel mill owners), then we both would benefit from interventions that protect us from competition. Yet it would be in my interest to enjoy the benefits of protectionism while letting you pick up the political tab for convincing policymakers to provide the protection. Lobbyists are not cheap. Intervention is a nonrival good to us, which we share equally with other sugar farmers or steel mills. And just like Samuelson's public good problem, there is a free rider problem that every interest group needs to solve to be politically relevant.

Mancur Olson (1932–1998) was a public choice pioneer whose work suggests that much of politics comes down to which interests groups are good at solving free rider problems. His most famous book is *The Logic of Collective Action* (1965), where the starting point for analysis is to ask: How big is the group? An industry with four firms will find it easier to monitor and punish free riding than will an industry with 4,000 firms. Furthermore, there is more at stake for each individual in small groups (a political favor worth $4,000 to the four-firm industry will get split into $1,000 chunks instead of $1 bits). So Olson predicts, all else being equal, that smaller groups will be more politically relevant than larger groups.

A second criterion for collective action is the uniformity of interests. An industry of four firms that make widgets and widgets only is one thing. A four-firm industry where each firm makes widgets and 100 other goods is another. The latter group won't be as motivated to lobby for protection from imported widgets, for example.

Third, even if groups are relatively small and cohesive so that free riding isn't a big problem, a group must still incur startup costs to lobbying. Here

Olson distinguishes between groups that are already formed for nonpolitical purposes, like private clubs, and groups that share a common political interest but are not preformed. Olson argues that already formed groups will be more politically relevant as a byproduct of the fact that they were already formed for other purposes.

And, fourth, Olson develops a theory of voluntary public goods based on the concept of "selective incentives." A *selective* incentive is a way to reward contributing members but not free riders, to encourage individuals to supply the public goods they care about. Selective incentives take all forms, like group discounts at major retailers, magazine subscriptions, logoed swag, or group insurance premiums. Groups vary in their effectiveness of applying selective incentives, and so groups vary in their ability to get members to voluntarily contribute.

Putting all this together, Olson describes politics as adhering to a logic of concentrated benefits and diffuse costs. Wealth will be redistributed from groups that can reduce free riding only at high cost, toward those groups that are able to reduce free riding at lower costs. Government favors will be acquired by small, cohesive groups that were already formed and can effectively use selective incentives. The cost of government favors will be borne by large, disparate groups that are not already formed outside politics and therefore cannot easily apply selective incentives to members. Typically the most important factor is group size. Thus, Olson describes interest-group politics as the "exploitation of the great by the small."

Mancur Olson never writes about the U.S. sugar program, but it's a clear illustration of the logic of collective action driven by rationally ignorant consumer-voters and rationally self-interested policymakers. Sugar farmers are a small, cohesive group. According to a 2006 study by the U.S. Department of Commerce, there are about 61,000 full-time equivalent workers in growing and harvesting sugar. By contrast, almost a million people work in sugar-using industries like food, breakfast cereal, and chocolates. And even though the aggregate cost of the program to consumers is anything but small at $2 billion, if one spreads this cost over 300 million Americans, the average cost per consumer is less than $7 per year. This is why you don't see "Citizens against High Sugar Prices"; the costs of consumers organizing outweigh the benefits of lower-priced sugar. Meantime, according to the Center for Responsive Politics, a watchdog group that tracks money in politics, sugar growers spend tens of millions of dollars each year lobbying regulators and contributing to political campaigns.

Olson studies the pernicious effects of concentrated interests accumulating greater political clout over time. In his second most famous book, *The Rise and Decline of Nations* (1982), Olson observes that revolutions and significant upheavals can destroy some of these special interests, which may create opportunities to limit future inefficient, wealth-destroying transfers within economies. He cites as examples the experience of Germany and Japan following World War II, with political institutions being dramatically rebuilt, followed by the opportunity for economic growth as fewer special interests were in place, at least at first.

In short, Mancur Olson's theory of collective action helps us understand why it is that some interests are well represented and others are not, and he hints at some of the implications of this for political change.

Rent Seeking

The investment of valuable resources into activities that are counterproductive is what economists call "rent seeking." Theft is a particularly vivid example. So is much of politics.

If you have ever been a victim of identity theft or a computer virus, you have personal experience with the socials costs of rent seeking. Hackers invest time, money, and resources into mastering the ability to disrupt and steal other people's property. And when people invest in becoming better thieves, there is a net loss in the economy because this effort could have been directed at producing something that creates value for others. On the defense side of things, all sorts of resources go into stopping hackers. But it's arguably all a waste, because antimalware products would have zero value were it not for hackers.

Theft is the opposite of mutually beneficial exchange. It is not a mere transfer from the victim to the one doing the stealing. In theft, the loss to the victim is greater than the gain to the thief because the thief has to deduct the time and effort he or she put into being a good thief from the bottom line. In politics, interest groups compete to win sway over the levers of policy. The cost of the policy to society is greater than the gain to the winning interest group, because the winner must deduct the lobbying costs that were sunk into becoming the winner in the first place. In both arenas, theft and politics, people invest resources into activities that are counterproductive.

Gordon Tullock first raises these issues in his most famous paper, a nine-page explosion of ideas entitled "The Welfare Costs of Tariffs, Monopolies, and Theft." In this paper Tullock responds to the predominant view in the profession at the time that there didn't seem to be much waste involved when government sets up monopolies and tariffs because the consumers' loss was assumed to be the same as the producers' gain. This troubles Tullock, partly because he seems to think it is the unique duty of the economics profession to point out that, indeed, government monopolies and tariffs are costly on net. Otherwise we might return to the protected and poor days that motivated Adam Smith to argue against mercantilism. "The classical economists were not concerning themselves with trifles when they argued against tariffs," Tullock insists in this paper.[19]

Tullock sets out to show that the predominant view is nonsense. Government tariffs and monopoly are enormously costly in practice, and the predominant view exists only because of flawed measurements that understate these costs. There are, Tullock shows, several categories of socially wasteful behavior that are encouraged by government interventions but that are not being accounted for by the work of economists.

In the case of tariffs, for example, economists predominantly recognized that it is wasteful to require goods to be made by high-cost producers. They just argued that the magnitude of this waste was small. Having spent nearly two decades working in various bureaucracies across America and Asia, Tullock merely observes that governments tend not to take steps like imposing tariffs on their own:

> They have to be lobbied or pressured into doing so by the expenditure of resources in political activity. One would anticipate that the domestic producers would invest resources in lobbying for the tariff until the marginal return on the last dollar so spent was equal to its likely return producing the transfer. There might also be other interests trying to prevent the transfer and putting resources into influencing the government in the other direction. These expenditures, which may simply offset each other to some extent, are purely wasteful from the standpoint of society as a whole; they are spent not in increasing wealth, but in attempts to transfer or resist transfer of wealth.[20]

Tullock makes a parallel argument for monopoly, and the argument extends out to all regulations that limit competition: tariffs, quotas, price controls, entry controls like occupational licensing, and all other seemingly well-intentioned policies that draw applause from people like Raleigh denizens after a hurricane. In all these instances, some political decision alters the rules of the economic game in such a way as to create an opportunity to redistribute wealth. Tariffs, for example, redistribute wealth away from consumers (a dispersed, large group) to the protected industry (a concentrated, small group). Rational people will compete to have their industry protected in this way. And Tullock's basic point is that the resources consumed in that sort of competition are a social waste, so economists need to count these costs when measuring the welfare losses of government policies.

Tullock struggled to get his most famous paper published. By his own account, it was rejected at all the major journals where he usually published his articles. Finally an obscure (at the time) journal, the *Western Economic Journal*, agreed to publish it, and a new way of looking at the world came about. Interestingly, Tullock actually never used the phrase "rent seeking" in this first piece. It is not until seven years later, in the prestigious *American Economic Review*, that World Bank economist Anne Krueger dubs Tullock's concept "rent seeking." The name stuck, and the rest is intellectual history.

Also interestingly, some economists invested their scholarly resources into coming up with a better name for Tullock's concept, one that presumably would be adopted as the standard term and therefore associated with their name. The Columbia economist Jagdish Bhagwati termed it "directly unproductive profit-seeking," or DUP, in 1982. A bit later the New York University economist William Baumol called it simply "unproductive entrepreneurship." As we'll see in the housing bubble case study in Chapter 6, when unproductive entrepreneurship becomes systemic it can take a heavy toll. On Tullock's side, his colleagues in Virginia also spent a good deal of their time in defense of Tullock's claim. Robert Tollison, for example, in 1981 published a lengthy paper called simply "Rent Seeking: A Survey," to document the lineage of Tullock's idea. As we heard from Tollison in Chapter 3, economists are maximizing agents. And apparently there is rent seeking in the marketplace of ideas, too.

Rent seeking is often thought to be synonymous with lobbying politicians, but clearly that is only a slice of the broader concept. Rent seeking is investment in unproductive activity, whether in theft or in politics or elsewhere. Ultimately, the rules of the game encourage people to compete in socially destructive or socially beneficial ways. The constructive message of public choice is that, by introducing good rules for politics, society can achieve better outcomes, less waste, and improved justice. Otherwise, societies with significant amounts of rent seeking tend to use scarce resources in ways that do not create net benefits, which leads to depletion rather than growth over time. Societies that use their resources more productively have rules that promote cooperation *and* competition. In other words, the right rules help promote Adam Smith's model, in which the pursuit of private interest leads to the public interest.

Politicians

What do politicians want? To begin, we assume politicians wish to be politicians. In doing so they seek to advance the well-being of themselves and their families and friends, just like the rest of us. And like the rest of us, they have their own views on how the world would be a better place. But if politicians want to do anything, they have to get elected—and then reelected. To do that requires beating the next guy before the voters.

If you are a politician, it is easier to please voters if your ideology nicely lines up with the majority views of the electorate. For example, if you are a fiscal and social conservative, life is much easier if you represent a district with similarly minded voters as compared to, say, a politically liberal district in San Francisco. Similarly, if you believe aid to U.S. agricultural interests (such as ethanol subsidies or the sugar program) hurts consumers at home and impoverishes farmers abroad who otherwise would sell to us, you probably should not be a farm state senator. In this way, politicians who believe that farmers need subsidies are most likely to represent farmers who want subsidies.

In short, if you and your constituents have very similar ideologies, not only do they get what they want—someone who thinks just like them—but it is much easier to vote your own preferences once in office. That's a good thing because, as we know, it is rational for voters to be ignorant of many policies. They are counting on you.

But from the perspective of the economic well-being of your society, this also presents a challenge. If you are a politician, and you know that voters are rationally ignorant and cognitively biased, what should you do when voters get it wrong? One option is to simply accept the erroneous views of the public and give your support to the policies they want. A different strategy would be to support the policies that *you* want. So a basic question is: Do politicians support policies favored by the median voter or their own preferred positions? In broad terms the job of a politician is like any other job. You produce something, you get paid. If you don't do your job very well, you get fired.

In the public choice approach—in the world of rational ignorance, rationally self-interested policymakers, and concentrated benefits and diffuse costs—the job of politicians is to broker wealth transfers between groups in society. For example, as a politician, you may support a defense contract or a farm subsidy that would directly benefit only a small fraction of the voters in your district. So why do it? The answer, of course, brings us back to Mancur Olson's concentrated benefits and dispersed costs. The many who will not benefit may not care very much, and they probably won't even know about it. The few who benefit will be keenly aware of your support, and they likely will help get you reelected. And if you can get reelected, you can go on to do great things for everyone else in the district, help advance world peace, or further some other lofty goal. The benefits of helping the rent-seekers are high, and the costs are few. In short, as a politician (and as a rational human being) you respond to incentives. Those incentives may change over time as a consequence of the many individual ideas, beliefs, and attitudes held by the electorate, and the many special interests that make you keenly aware of the concentrated benefits that you may be able to bestow on them, in return for political support, of course.

The Economics of Regulation
Capture

George Stigler (1911–1991, Nobel Prize 1982) is the Nobel Laureate who did more than any other scholar to fuse public choice into the mainstream orthodoxy of economic thinking. A fixture at the University of Chicago during the second half of the twentieth century, Stigler was rivaled only by Milton Friedman as the face of Chicago during their day. Awarded the Nobel Prize for his work in industry and regulation studies, Stigler was a great synthesizer, a great theorist, and perhaps an even greater igniter of controversy. He coined the term "Coase theorem," despite the fact that Ronald Coase himself never claimed to prove anything. He once argued that only active scholars can be good teachers, yet he condemned intellectual hubris. Reviewing Samuelson's *Foundations* in 1949, Stigler does little to conceal his distaste for that particular form of intellectual elitism. "He dismisses translations into words as 'mental gymnastics of a peculiarly depraved type.' I disagree. There is no depravity, nor is there virtue, in telling other competent economists things in a language they all can understand—there is simply responsibility to the canons of scholarship."[21]

From the beginning of his publishing career in 1937, Stigler shared Downs's intent on understanding the effects of information costs on economic and political behavior. He wrote fine technical papers as well as historical essays on long-neglected economists. In the 1960s he began to turn more attention to such regulatory issues as electricity, trucking, labor, and securities. Culminating in a landmark 1971 paper, "The Theory of Economic Regulation," Stigler applies public choice theory to the executive branch, specifically to the people making the decisions that regulated these industries. Stigler's paper forges a theory of regulation that would become the antithesis of the Pigou-Keynes-Samuelson public interest model.[22]

According to Stigler, regulatory agencies tend to get captured by the very industries they regulate. Regulators, like the rest of us, respond to costs and benefits in their decisions. Voters are rationally ignorant. By contrast, the regulated businesses have every incentive to know the regulators who oversee their business. In practice, they tend to know the regulators quite well, along with their spouses, their children, their favorite restaurants, their golf scores, and more. Bribes and junkets are monitored, but to have the information needed to do their jobs, government regulators do have to meet with those they regulate, and they need some way of sorting the legitimate concerns from tall tales. With all this contact, relationships form between the regulators and the regulated.

Stigler poses an explanation for regulation based on supply and demand. Politicians and regulators have access, through political exchange among their colleagues in representative bodies, to a supply of wealth that could be transferred to a worthy group in society that is willing to pay the right political price. Firms are willing to pay up to a certain amount for regulations that limit their competition. They'll hire the best lawyers who will make the best arguments. They'll rent office space close to government buildings and host events with good food and lots of wine. And they'll put the best spin that public relations can muster. Being an influential interest group exacts a heavy price. Regulators will be responsive to the "price" paid, even though the regulator may not be its recipient. Nonetheless, the regulation passes, competition is stifled, firm profits go up, and consumer welfare goes down.

For all these reasons and more, interest groups and their government benefactors want to attract very little attention to their political exchange deals. Thus, they package favors in ways that will resonate with rationally ignorant voters and will keep other interests at bay. Stigler explains his point as follows:

> Let us consider a problem posed by the oil import quota system: why does not the powerful industry which obtained this expensive program instead choose direct cash subsidies from the public treasury? The "protection of the public" theory of regulation must say that the choice of import quotas is dictated by the concern of the federal government for an adequate domestic supply of petroleum in the event of war—a remark calculated to elicit uproarious laughter at the Petroleum Club.[23]

The strategic oil reserve is a good enough story for rationally ignorant voters. And the import quota rather than cash subsidy keeps the benefits concentrated on a few businesses without attracting other businesses from suddenly developing the urge to enter the oil business.

In light of Downs's rational ignorance, Olson's logic of collective action, and Tullock's theory of rent seeking, Stigler's account of regulatory capture is a plausible one. His account also extends to other industries besides just energy and to other interest groups besides business. Stigler offers additional examples, such as the Civil Aeronautics Board, which had not approved a single new interstate air carrier in its history, and the Federal Deposit Insurance Corporation, which had reduced the rate of entry into commercial banking by 60 percent. In Chapter 6 we'll see in great detail how these tidy arrangements between regulator and industry play out.

Government entry regulations are popular in part because of what they are supposed to do, namely protect consumers from incompetence. People don't want any idiot providing delicate services. Brain surgeons and airline pilots come to mind. Then again, the state of Florida licenses interior designers, and Washington, D.C., requires tour guides to be licensed before showing visitors around. Where is the line between consumer protection and supply restriction? Rationally ignorant voters aren't likely to know, but we might ask teachers' unions, because Paul Krugman, a Nobel Laureate in economics, cannot legally teach economics at your local public high school without a license, and forget about Maya Angelou leading your teen's creative writing class. There are concentrated interests, and there are dispersed groups from whom small wealth transfers are politically available.

The Interest Group Theory of Government

Stigler's theory can be mistaken for a caricature of government agents hopelessly captured by special interests. While he does talk about some of the limitations that policymakers face, it wasn't until later that this was built into the model. Stigler's student Sam Peltzman (born 1940) builds a model of the policymaker's rational calculations—balancing marginal political gains of a policy decision against its marginal political costs to the policymaker. And Peltzman integrates the interest group explanation of the demand for wealth transfers into his new model. In equilibrium, the policymaker will not simply grant the wishes of concentrated interests. Rather, he or she will weigh the relative political sway of groups supplying the wealth for transfer against the clout of groups demanding the wealth transfer. The winners come down to Olson's theory of collective action—which groups can better organize for political action. And it's mostly a social waste, according to Tullock's rent-seeking theory.[24]

Peltzman applies the public choice framework to areas of regulation that aren't typically thought of as economic regulation. For example, he studies the Food and Drug Administration. Regulators there have the incentive to prevent incidents with approved drugs. They are less concerned if thousands get sicker and die as new treatments go through the lengthy safety and efficacy approval works. Peltzman also studies the effects of public safety regulations on people's behavior, for example seat belt laws. Seat belts make people safer in the event of an accident, but this added safety makes people drive slightly riskier, adding to more accidents. Peltzman finds that the two effects just about cancel each other out, thus concluding the number of lives saved because of seat belt campaigns was pretty small. In other words, Peltzman pushes the frontier of Stigler's approach into new areas of regulation, areas not typically thought of to be *economic* regulation. He makes Stigler's theory more general, from "a theory of economic regulation" to "an economic theory of regulation."

In the early 1980s the interest group approach was pushed even further to encompass all of government activity, not just regulation of markets and public safety. Robert McCormick and Robert Tollison's book *Politicians, Legislation, and the Economy* (1981) treats policymakers as brokers of wealth transfers. Building on the simple observation that virtually any action taken by a government will involve winners and losers, McCormick and Tollison reason that the winners in any government action would be those same groups that are so effective in Olson's theory of interest groups. When pushed far enough, every group in society (each one of Madison's "distinct interests" from this chapter's opening quotation) can be treated as having some economic cost of influencing legislation. Those with very high costs in politics will be the groups "supplying" the wealth for transfer to those other groups in society with much lower political costs. As a clearinghouse for wealth transfers, it is the legislature's job to match demanders of wealth transfers with those who supply them (we didn't say they were *willing* suppliers, or even aware). So sugar subsidies and import tariffs benefit domestic beet and cane growers, and the war on drugs benefits the worldviews of socially conservative voters. In other words, the interest group model applies not only to Stigler's theory of economic regulation and Peltzman's economic theory of regulation but to virtually all actions that any government undertakes.

Answering Question #1:

Why Democracies May Generate Unjust and Wasteful Policies

When we view politics through the lens of economic theory, a realistic picture of government comes into focus. Politics is a form of exchange, as Jim Buchanan teaches in his famous article, "What Should Economists Do?" Rationally self-interested people want public policies that benefit them and reflect their attitudes, beliefs, and ideas. But voters are rationally ignorant, and competition in political markets creates social losses in the form of rent seeking. Therefore public policies fall into the grip of special interests, and government becomes a game of balancing the relative influence that interest groups have over policymakers. As a result, public policies are not directed at eliminating waste or ensuring justice. Rather, they have the effect of transferring wealth from large, unorganized groups of people to small groups that have invested in political influence. And, in doing so, they often turn out to be wasteful and unjust in the process.

Transitional Gains Trap

If you're a homeowner, then you're familiar with the mortgage interest deduction. In fact, it is an important part of your financial life. It reduces your taxable income, and it supports the market value of your home. It also entices people to overinvest in housing by effectively taxing nonhousing investments more heavily. Hayek would say it distorts relative prices and prevents prices from reflecting people's true time preferences. Tullock would add that this rent seeking is socially wasteful, in part because people invest too little in other areas, namely business and research. With less business investment in the economy over time, less capital is used in production, and this in turn decreases labor productivity. In the end, wages and incomes are smaller than they would be in the absence of the mortgage interest deduction. Economists at the Government Accountability Office estimate the effect is anything but trivial. These distortions ripple throughout the economy and subtract as much as 1 percent from GDP, currently about $140 billion, every year.[25]

If it's such a wasteful policy, then why doesn't Congress repeal it? This, of course, is a version of our second motivating question. The interest group theory of government explains why democracies enact inefficient policies, but it doesn't necessarily answer the question as to why bad policies persist over time. To address our second motivating question, we once again turn our attention to Gordon Tullock.

Answering Question 2:
Why Democracies May Get Stuck with Bad Policies

Gordon Tullock's most underrated paper is his 1975 article, "The Transitional Gains Trap." As he does with his original paper on rent seeking, here Tullock begins with a simple observation. On the one hand there are a large number of industries that enjoy the benefits of government protectionism in some way or another. Yet, on the other hand, these industries don't appear to be any more or less profitable than the unregulated ones. "This raises the question of why these special privileges do not seem to do much good," says Tullock in the introduction.[26] And Tullock further extends the interest group theory into an explanation for political stasis.

As Stigler reminds us, political favors to industry rarely come in cash form. Instead, the right to the favor is tied to ownership of some resource. To get the mortgage interest deduction you have to buy a house. To practice law you have to get a law degree and pass the bar. To drive a taxi in New York you have to purchase a taxi medallion. When people get a hold on those assets early in the life of a program, their market prices have not adjusted yet. But the policy artificially increases demand for the assets that are tied to the favor. And the prices for those assets increase as a result. So law school gets very expensive, home prices shoot up, and taxi medallions start selling for big money. In October 2011, two medallions sold for $1 million each.[27] In short, the value of the political favor gets capitalized into the assets attached to the political favor. And people end up paying dearly from the beginning for the right to the political favor.

So Tullock's first point is that the gains to steering policy in one's favor are transitional. His second point is that policy gets trapped. As a result of gains being transitional, people who want to enter these industries must pay significant up-front costs. Once those costs are incurred, a repeal of the program will reduce demand for the assets they've invested in. Prices will plunge. This is why homeowners across America would scream at the sound of politicians threatening to repeal the mortgage interest deduction. And this is why any cab driver who paid six or even *seven* figures for a medallion has a lot at stake in the status quo. Even if people aren't making huge profits under the political privilege, they'll protect their investments by lobbying against the repeal of these inefficient policies. In fact, fully rational economic agents will spend up to the amount of the skin they have in the game.

More broadly, Tullock suggests that things in politics can't easily be reversed. Merely identifying a wasteful policy is not enough to repeal that policy. Protected firms may not earn high profits due to the policy being in place, but they would suffer huge losses by its repeal. Once market forces capitalize the value of a public policy into the assets tied to that policy, then a strong set of interests becomes vested in that new status quo. These vested interests will oppose reform or repeal and in most cases will be a more potent political force than other groups seeking to roll back the bad policies. Presidents Kennedy and Reagan both sought to eliminate the sugar program, but they were unable to mount the political pressure to break the status quo coalition. So public choice theory explains why democracies may produce wasteful and unjust policies and why we get stuck with those policies.

The Mystery of Deregulation

And then a funny thing happened: Deregulation! Just as public choice theory seemed to be mounting a comprehensive case that inefficient regulations were both inevitable and irreversible, history took the most curious of turns. Starting in the 1970s there was widespread deregulation of markets. In one industry after another, policymakers found occasion to decrease the role of bureaucracy and rely instead on greater competition. According to Brookings Institution economist Clifford Winston, deregulation occurred most intensively in transportation (especially airlines, railroads, and trucking), television, phone service, banking, brokerage, and energy. Winston reports that, in 1977, fully regulated industries accounted for 17 percent of GNP, but in 1988 that share had dropped to 6.6 percent of GNP.[28]

Deregulation was a surprise to some, especially to public choice theorists. From rational voters and parties to the logic of collective action, from capture theory on through to the transitional gains trap, public choice predicted the opposite of deregulation. Public choice predicted that inefficient regulations would persist in equilibrium.

Struggling with Question 3: Ideas, Not Just Incentives, Are Needed

Public choice theory gives us a clear picture of institutions and incentives in politics. But because public choice emphasizes the vested interests side of political change, it assigns relatively little role to the power of ideas in politics. And because public choice is an outgrowth of neoclassical economics it also tends to emphasize equilibrium over process. Interest groups compete for the rights to influence public policy, which concentrates benefits on well-defined and politically powerful groups while diffusing the costs on ill-defined and politically weak groups. And policy gets stuck in this outcome. Period. But to get a clear picture of political change means introducing a bigger role for ideas, in particular how ideas and interests do battle over shaping institutions. To incorporate ideas, we will have to build even further and go beyond traditional public choice approaches.

Legacy of Public Choice

Like many revolutions, public choice began with a simple idea. According to economic theory, we should assume that politicians, bureaucrats, and voters are rational, maximizing individuals just as we assume that consumers, households, and firms are. That's for starters anyway. As the implications of this point began to be explored, a group of scholars formed, and a school of thought emerged. As theory and evidence began to mount, public choice scholars systematically filled the void left by the earlier, romantic view of government found in neoclassical welfare economics.

Public choice is both normative and positive. It's one thing to ponder "the good" and come up with ways for government to achieve whatever we think is "the good." It's another thing to recognize that collective action is not as simple and clean as it appears on the chalkboards of Pigou, Keynes, and Samuelson. In the real world, when it comes to implementing public-interest policy prescriptions, the process suffers interference from the rational self-interest of the actual people making decisions in government. Self-interest gets in the way of our chalkboard wishes and public interest dreams, so if public choice theory holds a normative lesson it is to adjust our expectations downward as to what government is able to accomplish—and perhaps to view government in an entirely different way normatively, not as a noble pursuit of the good but as an ordinary enterprise of exchange by way of redistributing wealth in society.

But public choice shouldn't be taken only as a counsel of despair, that governments fail, period. It should be viewed as a research program, an approach to doing social science, one that offers both a realistic account of order within politics and a hopeful course for reforming institutions in socially beneficial ways.

5

How Ideas Matter for Political Change

Ideas, unless outward circumstances conspire with them, have in general no
very rapid or immediate efficacy in human affairs; and the most favourable
outward circumstances may pass by, or remain inoperative, for want of
ideas suitable to the conjuncture. But when the right circumstances and
the right ideas meet, the effect is seldom slow in manifesting itself.
—John Stuart Mill, *Edinburgh Review* (1845)[1]

Maggie, Mart, and the Madmen

It happened with Lenin rousing the crowds in Russia. It happened with Mao
driving China into the Cultural Revolution and Great Leap Forward. It happened with Che Guevara's motorcycle ride across Latin America, looking
for fights and finding Castro's revolution in Cuba. It is happening today in
Venezuela and Bolivia, where presidents proclaim a "new" revolution in the
names of Simón Bolívar and the last Incan emperor, Atahualpa. All these
revolutionaries espouse an ideology known as socialism—the same ideology that transformed a third of humanity during the twentieth century. It's
an ideology that took life from the pen of Karl Marx, sitting in a library in
London, writing books. Ideas have had their consequences.

On the other side of the revolution spectrum, people have advanced the
ideas of economic freedom and prosperity. In 1975 an emerging leader of En-

gland's struggling Conservative Party, Margaret Thatcher, famously slammed a book on the table in front of her colleagues. "This is what we believe," she declared. The book was Friedrich Hayek's *The Constitution of Liberty* (1960), which helped shape many of the policies that Ms. Thatcher would later pursue as prime minister. Less than a generation later, when the Berlin Wall fell, post-Soviet Estonia removed trade barriers, introduced a low flat tax, and saw its economy flourish. The Estonian prime minister, Mart Laar, was a historian by profession. Years later Mr. Laar reflected, "I had read only one book on economics—Milton [and Rose] Friedman's *Free to Choose* . . . I simply introduced it in Estonia, despite warnings from Estonian economists that it could not be done. They said it was as impossible as walking on water. We did it: we just walked on the water because we did not know that it was impossible."[2]

While not all revolutionaries walk on water, all great revolutions are rooted in ideas. Keynes no doubt has something similar in mind when he pens his famous passage about "academic scribblers" and the battle between ideas and vested interests:

> . . . the ideas of economists and philosophers, both when they are right and when they are wrong, are more powerful than is commonly understood. Indeed, the world is ruled by little else. Practical men, who believe themselves to be quite exempt from any intellectual influences, are usually the slaves of some defunct economist. Madmen in authority, who hear voices in the air, are distilling their frenzy from some academic scribbler of a few years back. I am sure that the power of vested interests is vastly exaggerated compared with the gradual encroachment of ideas. Not, indeed, immediately, but after a certain interval . . . [S]oon or late, it is ideas, not vested interests, which are dangerous for good or evil.[3]

Keynes's passage encapsulates a rich process by which even the most abstract ideas may come to have real-world consequences. From its quiet beginnings as an academic scribble, to its subtle absorption into popular belief, to its implementation by madmen walking on water, a mere idea has the power to change the world. Yet Keynes says little about *how* we move from the ivory tower of ideas to the average person's opinions and from opinions to influence current events. It is Keynes's intellectual adversary, Friedrich Hayek, who peers into the Keynesian capsule.

In a 1949 *University of Chicago Law Review* article, "The Intellectuals and Socialism," Hayek describes how ivory tower ideas descend to have an influence on public opinion. Hayek begins by making a sharp distinction between "scholars" and "intellectuals." Scholars are experts and original thinkers in specific subject areas. Intellectuals, on the other hand, are figures in society, neither original thinkers nor decisionmakers, who habitually stray from one subject to the next. This broad class of people comments on a range of weighty issues, presenting each to the general public as either good or bad ideas. Calling them "professional second hand dealers in ideas," Hayek says the intellectual class acts like a sieve between scholars and public opinion:

> The [intellectual] class does not consist of only journalists, teachers, ministers, lecturers, publicists, radio commentators, writers of fiction, cartoonists, and artists all of whom may be masters of the technique of conveying ideas but are usually amateurs so far as the substance of what they convey is concerned . . . There is little that the ordinary man of today learns about events or ideas except through the medium of this class and outside our special fields of work we are in this respect almost all ordinary men, dependent for our information and instruction on those who make it their job to keep abreast of opinion. It is the intellectuals in this sense who decide what views and opinions are to reach us, which facts are important enough to be told to us, and in what form and from what angle they are to be presented. Whether we shall ever learn of the results of the work of the expert and the original thinker depends mainly on their decision.[4]

While "second hand dealers" may not be the most dignified of monikers, Hayek doesn't necessarily use it as a term of abuse. Nor does he suppose that the "intellectuals" harbor ill motives or act selfishly; in fact, elsewhere in the essay he likens them more to philosophers than to politicians. Nonetheless, Hayek's tone is an irritated one. In a particularly feisty passage, he complains: "Even though [the intellectuals'] knowledge may often be superficial and their intelligence limited, this does not alter the fact that it is their judgment which mainly determines the views on which society will act in the not too distant future."

Hayek argues that there is pathology among the intellectual class, a pernicious bias in how they select the ideas they favor. In the mid-twentieth century, surrounded by technological progress, the intellectuals were biased toward the application of hard science methods to design human institutions. They therefore supported government central planning of economies. This trend is deplorable in Hayek's worldview. He derisively terms it "scientism" and teaches the dangers of its intellectual overreach. Hayek writes of the rationalism developed by Descartes (whom we met in Chapter 2) and how its mistaken leap from physical science to human affairs encourages reformers to design that which they and others could not truly understand.

Nonetheless, to most people in the middle of the twentieth century, the logic seemed airtight. If humans could control their physical world to make life better, then shouldn't the next achievement be to control human society through centralized economic planning? The intellectuals of decades past had embraced this logic and gone to work to convince the masses, which soon placed vested interests at the mercy of the ideas that would usher in socialist central planning for a third of the world's population. We can see why Hayek might be angry. He believes that well-intentioned intellectuals are dooming the world with their bias toward scientism. Meanwhile good ideas—namely his own classical liberalism—lie dusty on the shelf.

As we observed in Chapter 1, both the Keynes and Hayek passages imply top-down processes, from the abstract heights of academia outward and down to public opinion. Keynes's academic scribblers are equivalent to Hayek's scholars—they are the innovators of big ideas with the potential to change the world. It is Hayek's intellectuals who filter the abstract into the ordinary, in a process that he says will involve "many further relays." Over time, perhaps several generations, the course of public opinion creates opportunities for "madmen in authority" to implement the very ideas of the "academic scribblers" whom the "intellectual" class chose to ordain. Both Keynes and Hayek seem to echo Mill from this chapter's opening quotation. When the circumstances are right, the ideas of elites, which by a point in time had soaked into people's collective beliefs, will hold sway over public affairs—but only if their ideas overcome the interests of the status quo.

Writing in 1936, Keynes's mention of vested interests anticipates the development of public choice analysis that would soon follow. It is not a complete theory of political economy—nowhere else in *The General Theory* does Keynes discuss vested interests, and he offers no analysis that would approach Tullock's transitional gains trap, for example. Rather, the perspectives offered by Keynes and Hayek make clear that, prior to the development of public choice analysis, at least a few thinkers were concerned about the effects ideas have on outcomes in a society and the vested interests they must overcome.

Nor is the link between ideas and interests merely academic, as underscored by recent and sometimes violent revolutions in the Arab Spring that have overthrown long-standing governments. Even when there are no revolutions unfolding before our eyes, the interplay of ideas and interests still unfolds on a routine basis, with the daily increments to the roles and functions of governments. In other words, political change comes about—violently or peacefully, quickly or slowly—and all too often it is difficult to pin down exactly why it comes about, much less when. So again, we return to our three motivating questions for understanding the process of political change:

1. Why do democracies generate policies that are wasteful and unjust?
2. Why do such failed policies persist over long periods, even when they are known be socially wasteful and even when better policies exist?
3. Why do some wasteful policies get repealed (for example, airline rate and route regulation), while others endure (for example, sugar subsidies and tariffs)?

Given that public choice theory doesn't offer a neatly packaged answer to question 3, this chapter develops a framework to understand political change as entrepreneurial action that alters the interplay of ideas and interests in shaping social institutions. To keep things as simple as possible, we anchor our framework to one of Hayek's earliest economic theories, his theory of capital investment and economic development.[5]

The Relationship between Ideas and Institutions

All else being equal, given the choice, most people would want to live in a rich society instead of a poor one. Material wealth is not every person's ultimate goal, but wealth and especially the circumstances that create wealth are directly tied to many of the good things in life that people want. At the very least, we would want to avoid poverty, where we'd have little choice but to work our children, deplete common pool resources, and worse.

To create wealth, people must first produce goods or services that others value, and people are more productive when they work with more and better capital. For example, U.S. workers don't specialize in manufacturing as much as they did in the past, yet their productivity is very high. Like other similarly wealthy societies, the United States has invested significant amounts of capital per worker, especially capital in the form of valuable knowledge. The well-educated and well-paid scientists and engineers who design new drugs, better computers, and smartphones are just one example. As we suggested in Chapter 2, flip over your iPhone and notice the small print: "Designed by Apple in California, assembled in China."

In the 1990s, a particularly prosperous decade, U.S. worker productivity increased dramatically. A 2001 study by the McKinsey Global Institute looked into what caused this "productivity miracle" in the U.S. economy. It turns out that some large percent of the aggregate productivity gains during this period originated in the retail sector. The study spends a lot of time talking about Walmart, especially its growing distribution network and the various economies of scale that the company had to invent for itself in order to sustain its rapid, comprehensive expansion. Walmart was busily innovating new distribution and marketing processes like warehouse and purchasing logistics, electronic data interchange, and wireless bar code scanning. Competition in the sector soon made these easily transportable innovations standard for any retail operation of significant scale, essentially forcing the entire sector to become more efficient. The innovations also migrated vertically from retailers to wholesalers, especially in industries like pharmaceuticals. These improvements raised labor productivity in retail and distribution so much that it became visible in the aggregate data for the economy as a whole.

The interesting thing about all these innovations is that none of them was directly valuable to consumers. Each was only valuable by making the retailer more efficient, thereby reducing costs and enabling it to pass these savings to its customers in the form of lower prices. The term for this is *roundaboutness*. Consumer value gets created by a *roundabout* process in which investment in higher-order goods such as distribution and network technology lowers prices and increases options for consumers. In short, better capital makes labor more productive, which creates more value for all of us as consumers.

Walmart's inventory-tracking gizmos are what Carl Menger, a seminal figure of Austrian economics, would call "higher-order" goods, while consumer goods are things we directly enjoy like food, housing, transportation, and leisure. In other words, higher-order goods are things that help us acquire the consumer goods we really want, and thus they create value roundaboutly.

One of Hayek's early works develops Menger's categories into a model of capital accumulation. Figure 5.1 shows a simplified version of Hayek's model. Consumer goods are situated at the base of the triangle. Capital comes in a variety of forms, from simple tools to more complex and abstract higher-order capital goods.

For example, even poor economies have final goods and some amount of capital goods. In agrarian societies, a farmer might plant and harvest with an ox-drawn plow and simple hand tools. With meager capital, it should come as no surprise to find that this farmer is not very productive. In such a society, the triangle is not very tall (there is little capital and little roundaboutness), nor is it very wide (there are few consumer goods). In contrast, in a high-capital

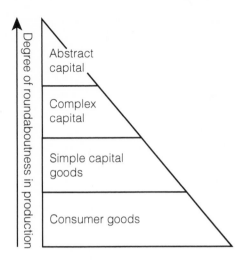

Figure 5.1 Capital in economic development.

economy the same farmer might use tractors with global positioning systems (GPS) and yield a hundred times more food at lower average cost.

It's not just the amount of capital but its *composition* that Hayek's theory emphasizes. An advanced economy will have more complex and diverse forms of capital. The tractor, for example, has to be manufactured with machine tools in a factory. Whoever made those machine tools invested in even more roundabout capital. And the machine tools and factories were made possible by design and engineering principles, a type of knowledge-based capital that is still more roundabout.

The economic benefits of using more varied capital speak for themselves. In 1800 about 95 percent of the U.S. labor force worked in agriculture, while in 2000 it was less than 1 percent. The other 99 percent were not unemployed; most of them were busy providing other valuable goods and services. Put in terms of Hayek's model, in such a society the triangle is much taller (there is more capital and more roundaboutness), and the base of this triangle is much wider (there are many more goods and services).

Returning to our Walmart example, we might think of forklifts and hand trucks as belonging in the area of the Hayekian triangle labeled "Simple capital goods." But handheld scanners and smart conveyers would be more complex, higher-order forms of capital. And the software that lets the scanner run the inventory system is an even higher-order, even more complex capital good that would go in the area labeled "Abstract capital."

The dimensions of the Hayekian triangle are interesting. Notice that the vertical dimension in Figure 5.1 is labeled as the "Degree of roundabout-ness in production." More roundabout production is synonymous with more investment in higher-order capital. As entrepreneurs invest and accumulate capital, you might visualize that increased investment as a vertical stretching of the triangle, making production more roundabout. As the capital invest-ment raises productivity in the economy, this in turn creates growth in con-sumer value, as if the triangle were being stretched horizontally so that its base covers greater distance and the area representing consumer value is greater.

The operative question, then, is: How does an economy increase in-vestment in higher-order capital goods? In other words, what carrots and sticks—what *incentives*—do entrepreneurs have when considering those very investment deals that raise labor productivity and living standards?

This brings us back to Chapter 1 and Danny Biasone's basketball shot clock. The way people play the game depends on how the rules of the game are set up and honored. If people aren't sure that their contracts will be hon-ored in a few years, or if they fear that the dollars with which they will be re-paid in the future will be worthless, then economic activity will suffer. But in an advanced economy like that of the United States, entrepreneurs generally have good incentives to develop new, efficient ways of doing things because formal and informal rules support innovation, entrepreneurship, and com-merce. In turn, competitive markets give Walmart the incentive to implement these innovations into their routine operations. These incentives to innovate and implement exist in large part because of a legal system that protects prop-erty rights, honors contracts, and maintains a sound currency, which in turn give people sure footing when striking deals over long periods of time.[6]

In other words, individuals have an incentive to invest in capital when the right institutions are in place. The institutions themselves are not as vis-ible as a new machine or factory, but they play a similarly critical role in the creation of wealth. Economists have long recognized the importance of institutions, and, more recently, they have sought to estimate it empirically.

In 2006 a group of economists at the World Bank published a 188-page study titled, "Where Is the Wealth of Nations?" The study attempts to mea-sure "intangible capital" by country. Natural capital consists of a country's forests, fields, waterways, and similar resources. Produced capital is more what Hayek had in mind, things like machinery, infrastructure, communi-cations, and other things that would count as higher-order capital goods in Figure 5.1. According to the World Bank study, intangible capital includes the human capital that people have accumulated as well as "social capital, that is, the degree of trust among people in a society," and a number of "governance elements that boost the productivity of the economy." The study concludes that wealth increases with an efficient judicial system, well-defined property rights, and accountable government.[7]

Hayek calls sound institutional arrangements—in particular the protection of property rights and enforcement of contracts—the rule of law. By restraining governments from arbitrary property takings and contract reversals, he argues, the rule of law makes investment more efficient and less risky, which in turn facilitates economic growth. A recent study by Paul Mahoney looks closely at thirty-three years of economic growth patterns in 102 countries. Following Hayek, Mahoney reasons that the rule of law is stronger in English common law countries than in French civil code countries. As compared to the more constructivist French civil law, Hayek argues, common law is more organic, emerging over time in response to the needs of a people, and building on the precedent (and knowledge) of previous rules. Hayek's theory finds much support in Mahoney's regression results, which show the thirty-eight common law countries having significantly better economic growth than the sixty-four civil code countries, even after controlling for important variables like education for human capital and investment for physical capital.[8]

So it is not just physical capital that matters; it is also the formal and informal institutions that support economic activity. If so, then the next question is: What makes a society predisposed to establishing sound institutions? To begin thinking about the social forces that shape institutions, we take our first cue from the Victorian historian Lord Acton, who in 1877 writes:

> The history of institutions is often a history of deception and illusions; for their
> virtue depends on the ideas that produce and on the spirit that preserves them,
> and the form may remain unaltered when the substance has passed away.[9]

Acton suggests that institutions and ideas are intertwined with one another. Ideas can be the impetus for institutional change. On the other hand, ideas can also be constraints on institutional change, or "the spirit that preserves" the status quo. In either sense, ideas and institutions are closely bound up in each other.

Of all the Nobel Prize winners in economics, the 1993 laureate Douglass C. North (born 1920) most closely takes up Lord Acton's suggestion. North is the scholar who innovated the rules-of-the game concept of institutions. In his Nobel address, North writes, "Institutions form the incentive structure of a society and the political and economic institutions, in consequence, are the underlying determinant of economic performance."[10] In more recent work, North turns to the question of what forms institutions. He has been exploring cultural, historical, and other human factors that seem to propel societies toward adopting particular rules over others. He homes in on ideas, in particular how individual cognitive processes organize the information that makes up our real world, in all its messiness, and how individual beliefs spread into collective beliefs. In a slender 2005 book, North speculates about that world: "Successful economic development will occur when the belief system that has evolved has created a 'favorable' artifactual structure . . . "[11] In this sense, North parallels Hayek, who argues that institutions in support of the rule of law emerged where belief systems placed a high value on individual liberty, namely by the spread of the English common law system.

One formal institution that mutually reinforces the rule of law is the federal separation of powers, such as that seen in the U.S. system. North and his frequent coauthor, Barry Weingast, analyze federalism as a "market-preserving institution." The idea is that a well-functioning separation of powers helps to prevent policies that deter economic development by undermining security of property and contract or by politicizing the currency.

In turn, they argue that market-preserving institutions have their roots in society's shared beliefs about innovation and commercial life. In a landmark 1989 paper, North and Weingast argue that England's seventeenth-century civil war jolted prevailing belief systems in English society, shifting them to be more wary of authoritarian structure and likewise more welcoming of market institutions like property and contract. This spurred the emergence of stock exchanges and other financial intermediaries, thus giving gradual rise to England's lead in history's most important period of capital investment, the Industrial Revolution.

The Industrial Revolution is alive and well in cutting-edge research on the power of ideas. Joel Mokyr's important book *The Enlightened Economy* (2010) traces the remarkable growth of England's economy between 1700 and 1850 to earlier innovations—not just in technology and machinery but also in ideas and institutions. Mokyr argues that the Enlightenment sowed into the shared beliefs of Britons the ambitions of progress, the achievements of science, and the virtues of commerce. With these ideas to swaddle market institutions, England became a cradle of the Industrial Revolution and reaped the reward of becoming the place where capitalist invention was itself invented.

Deirdre McCloskey's recent works argue that the line between ideas and economic development is more direct than even North, Mokyr, or others allow. In volume two of a planned six-volume treatise, McCloskey's *Bourgeois*

Dignity (2011) deconstructs and ultimately rejects the theory that institutional change was the proximate cause of the Industrial Revolution. Institutions of property predate the era, McCloskey argues, so if institutions were a sufficient explanation then we'd have seen the Industrial Revolution emerge much sooner. But there was, according to McCloskey's research, a surge in certain beliefs and attitudes about the right time. A review of documents from the era reveals increasing discussion of and attention to such things as "temperance, courage, justice, faith, hope, and love."[12] For McCloskey, the story of economic development is one of virtue and vice, not of institutions and mere incentives. In Chapter 2 we were reminded by the School of Athens that individual morality is the foundation of political philosophy. Today's economic historians are building a parallel argument, pointing out that individual virtues are also the foundation of a market society.

And here, like elsewhere, the new economic histories are rediscovering the work of Adam Smith. In his *Lectures on Jurisprudence*, for example, Smith argues that individuals naturally desire to participate in society at the level of ideas. In fact, he says that our natural propensity to participate in commercial life—to "truck, barter, and exchange"—is rooted more deeply in our desire to participate in a social life based on civil discourse and shared beliefs: "The real foundation of [the division of labor] is that principle to persuade which so much prevails in human nature."[13] In short, the division of labor is a natural propensity because humans naturally want to cooperate with each other, and this cooperation makes both parties better off.

Ideas as Higher-Order Capital Goods

At first glance, all this interaction appears to be incredibly complicated. Apparently, if we want to understand political change, then we have to account for a lot of complex things in society, including the ideas of academic scribblers, formal and informal institutions in that society, the shared beliefs and attitudes of ordinary people, and all the various ways that ideas and institutions shape incentives for people to be for or against the status quo. That's a lot to handle.

Figure 5.2 organizes everything into a simple adaptation of Hayek's capital model. The triangle shows the nexus of ideas, institutions, and incentives that generate social and political outcomes in a society. At the base of the triangle is the state of affairs. Are we a prosperous society? Are we a free and virtuous society? As we have been discussing, these are intertwined ques-

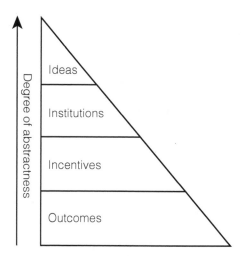

Figure 5.2 Ideas and institutions as higher forms of capital.

tions. The triangle situates incentives as proximate causes of outcomes in society, which reflects the bedrock principle, taught in almost every economics textbook, that incentives determine people's decisions. But what shapes people's incentives? The triangle shows that incentives in turn depend on the interplay of institutions and ideas. The adapted Hayekian triangle helps reduce the complexity of the problem and lets us consider all the various questions about political change within an integrated whole.

In short, ideas are a type of higher-order capital in society. Like a society that is poor in capital and therefore produces little consumer value, a society that is poor in ideas and institutions will have bad incentives and therefore few of the desirable outcomes that people want.

It's also intuitive to think of institutions as depending on the climate of ideas. Per Mokyr and McCloskey, societies are predisposed to establishing sound institutions when shared beliefs in society extol information sharing, innovation, entrepreneurship, and commercial life in general.

Nonetheless, the nexus of ideas, institutions, and incentives is not the entire story. Does all the "action" originate within the ideas section of the triangle? If so, is the flow of ideas a one-way street from elites down to the masses? Of course not. Figure 5.2 is not meant to suggest that the interplay of ideas, institutions, and incentives is linear. There is observable feedback between and within the areas of the triangle. Nor are academic scribblers the only source of ideas in society because there is much bottom-up input into people's shared beliefs. Finally, the ideas of academic scribblers are not produced in a vacuum but within a social context at a particular time and place.

Consider, for example, Karl Marx. He sat in a library and wrote about the alienation of workers as a consequence of the division of labor. But the location of the library and the time of his writing matter greatly. Marx wrote from London in the middle of the nineteenth century, in the cradle of the Industrial Revolution. The social upheaval associated with this era was real. One could walk the streets of London and see poor factory workers. Never mind that these impoverished masses were transplants from an even more impoverished countryside; the suffering was nonetheless new and very real, and as a result there was a receptive audience for radical ideas about social organization. Had Marx lived instead in the nonindustrialized societies of twelfth-century Italy or fifteenth-century Spain, his theory of alienation likely would not have been so well received.

But for thinking about political change, this Hayekian structure gets us asking the right kinds of questions. At the base of the triangle, we treat political outcomes as public choice theory does, as the product of exchange among rationally self-interested people who respond to incentives. It's the rules of the political game that deserve our focus, not politicians' personalities or party affiliations. At the level of institutions and ideas, what matters is the confluence of top-down and bottom-up beliefs and ideas. Most importantly, we focus on the agents of change, those entrepreneurs of ideas and new institutions who find the "loose spots" in Figure 5.2 and exact political change: John Maynard Keynes, Karl Marx, all those whose ideas conspire with outward circumstances.

The Complex Formation of Individual Beliefs: Bottom Up and Top Down

Circumstances matter. We start life as a bundle of genes, prewired with a bundle of strengths and weaknesses and inclinations. Next, we spend a couple of decades soaking in the ideas, attitudes, and experiences of youth. Then we go vote. As complex and intricately woven characters, we choose our madmen in authority.

What views bear on the shape of government when a person, young or old, casts a vote? Each person's beliefs take shape under circumstances that vary by time and place, by culture and convention, and by a number of personal factors unique to individuals. The diversity of individual experiences maps onto the variety of ways that individual beliefs emerge, are nurtured, promoted, and ultimately adopted or rejected.

For example, talk to your elders who lived through the Great Depression. Ask them about the things that matter in life. They'll probably mention patriotism, survival, the honor of a day's paid work, and good government. For a different perspective, talk to people who grew up behind the Iron Curtain, in Soviet bloc Eastern Europe. You may hear them talk of their parents working in jobs picked for them by the Party or how they quickly learned to watch over their shoulder for the secret police, knowing that the world might never consist of more than the four walls assigned to them by the housing authority. You'll get a different set of beliefs about the proper role and function of government.

When an academic scribbler comes up with a new idea, it has to resonate well with widely shared beliefs, which in turn must overcome the vested interests at the table. Many forces come together to explain political change, even though it may seem like coincidence of time and place.

The Importance of History

Five years after "The Intellectuals and Socialism," Hayek organized a collection of essays about history, called *Capitalism and the Historians* (1954). At the heart of this book is the question: How do ordinary people acquire their conceptions of history?

> Although in the indirect and circuitous process by which new political ideas reach the general public the historian holds a key position, even he operates chiefly through many further relays. It is only at several removes that the picture which he provides becomes general property; it is via the novel and the newspaper, the cinema and political speeches, and ultimately the school and common talk that the ordinary person acquires his conceptions of history. But in the end even those who never read a book and probably have never heard the names of the historians whose views have influenced them come to see the past through their spectacles.[14]

This passage has strong parallels with the passage we quoted earlier. Hayek's "second hand dealers" from before are now his "many further relays." What's more, the anchor to historical record lets us see the process Hayek describes unfolding in our own experience, in our modern world. Consider, for example, how most of us view World War II. Having a father or grandfather who fought in it provides an inside view. For a more expansive, less personal view, there are impressive histories, like H. P. Wilmott's *The Great Crusade* and John Keegan's *The Second World War*. Yet even high-minded readers are also bound to take in historical novels like Herman Wouk's romantic saga *The Winds of War* and journalistic accounts like Tom Brokaw's *The Greatest Generation*. And for almost anyone who reached adulthood before the end of the twentieth century, it's not possible to think of wartime North Africa without visualizing Humphrey Bogart in *Casablanca*, a testament to the power of imagery in the course of ideas.

The Importance of Technology

Even if we presume that the influence of ideas is mostly top down, the process is more complex than in Hayek's day because of subsequent changes to the market for "second hand dealers." As ideas spread through different mediums and technologies, for example, the influence of the second hand dealers changes dramatically. Movies have been a particularly powerful medium. For example, today's younger generations are especially likely to view World War II through the lens of a handful of great movies—*Band of Brothers*, *Flags of Our Fathers*, *Saving Private Ryan*, and *Schindler's List*. This helps explain why the one man who directed these movies, Steven Spielberg, is a force in Hollywood (where ideas are distilled into entertainment) as well as in Washington (where ideas are distilled into law).

Talk television and radio have been highly influential as well. For years Oprah Winfrey recommended books and important thinkers to her millions of viewers, and sales figures showed that America took her advice. Soon a number of presidential candidates, including Barack Obama, were lining up to appear on her show and win her endorsement. From another point of view, once candidate Obama became president critics such as Bill O'Reilly and Glenn Beck argued that his administration's policies promoted socialism in America. Glenn Beck told his listeners about Hayek's *Road to Serfdom*, and sales of Hayek soared. CNBC reporter Rick Santelli ignited the Tea Party movement with a live television rant about the government's bailout of Big Auto.

As "second hand dealers" in ideas, Hayek likely would count among today's intellectuals such figures as Oprah and O'Reilly, Glenn Beck and Rachel Maddow, Rush Limbaugh and Jon Stewart. And he would count far more of them today than at any time before. The climate of ideas has far more competitors in it compared to the past six or seven decades. Intellectuals are not as unified behind a single ideology as they were during the middle of the twentieth century. Most commentators and public intellectuals after World

War II believed that government should command the most critical aspects of society. In contrast, today's highly competitive intellectual landscape supports an array of viewpoints that transcends a simplistic left-right categorization.

In fact, in important ways, the marketplace of ideas is more competitive and less dominated by ideology than at any time in history. There are well over 6,000 think tanks around the world, for example, with about nine in ten having been founded since the end of World War II.[15] The evolution of news media has generated a diversity of viewpoints that could scarcely have been imagined in the age of Walter Cronkite, and that's just considering radio and television. If today's consumer of ideas has more options than could even have been imagined only a few decades ago, it seems almost a quaint notion that a few biased "intellectuals" will decide which ideas filter into the mass of public opinion. With a click of the mouse or television remote, ordinary people can control more of the information they receive.

Thus, today, the marketplace for ideas is far more competitive than it was in 1949, or even 1999. It's probably true that Oprah and Jon Stewart have affected people's beliefs about human affairs, but they haven't held the monopoly on public opinion suggested by Keynes's academic scribblers or Hayek's intellectuals. It's not all top down. If ideas about the proper role of government emerge at least partially from the bottom up, it bears taking a slight detour into the science of individual beliefs, how they form, and why some are not likely to change anytime soon.

The Importance of Biology and Culture

Ideas are accepted or rejected by individuals, but each individual comes to his or her set of beliefs in a specific context. These ideas are shaped by nature as well as nurture.

By *nature*, we mean genetic endowment, what each individual inherits at birth. Obvious examples include physical traits like body type, hair and eye color, hereditary disease, and so forth. Can genetic differences explain why millions of people have certain ideas about family, faith, law, and politics? Perhaps it can, at least in part. For example, it is reasonable to expect that, as compared to other societies, there may be notably different laws and policies in a society with a large percentage of its members suffering from anxiety or depression. Ideas about policy are simply in front of a different audience, who may see those ideas differently or even be affected differently by them.

By *nurture*, we mean the environment in which an individual is raised, including family, faith, community, culture, and country. What language a person speaks is a product of environment. For example, one of us speaks broken Spanish, and the other is fluent. Unless you knew which of us has lived in Latin America for many years, you might guess wrong based on our surnames. Like language, peoples' worldviews and ideologies are influenced by family, friends, teachers, religious leaders, politicians, and any number of other people, living or dead, famous or not famous. Remember the essay on Japanese politics that Mrs. Parsons made you write in the eighth grade (or that paper on French philosophy or Italian history)? Not only did it reflect her love of that country's culture; it may have instilled the same in you. Your minister's devotion to the poor may have done more than encourage you to volunteer your summer vacations as a teenager; it may have influenced how you approach social policy today.

The biological sciences that describe the influence of nature and nurture are complicated, at times controversial, and certainly beyond the scope of this book. A few contributors, however, tie in directly and help us better understand how nature and nurture may ultimately affect how we choose the rules by which we live together with other human beings.

Consider, for example, the work of evolutionary biologist Richard Dawkins. His 1976 classic *The Selfish Gene* ignited a decades-long conversation on traits and characteristics that tend to endure in plants, animals, and that most social of animals, humans. In a sense, the book is an extension of the work of Charles Darwin, especially the idea of natural selection, by which better-performing traits enhance survivability and thus are more likely to be passed on.

Twenty-six years before Dawkins's classic, the economist Armen Alchian penned a related article, "Uncertainty, Evolution and Economic Theory." While focused on economic behavior, the link to evolution is clear. Adaptive, imitative, and "trial-and-error" behavior are modes of economic competition. Firms do not maximize profits, as the standard neoclassical model dictates. Firms instead continuously adapt in a marketplace that punishes inefficient use of resources; otherwise they don't survive. Efficient behaviors, like better-performing physical traits, are more likely to survive. Other economists have tried to link biology and economics, with varying degrees of success. No less a pioneer economist than Alfred Marshall, one of the founders of neoclassical economics, observes a connection in his 1890 text. But one need not see biology and economics as equal to recognize that both can be evolutionary.

For economists and other social scientists, the big questions are not about blue eyes or baldness; the interesting themes strike closer to the core of survival traits like aggression and altruism, competition and cooperation. As Adam Smith and his forbears believe, the mix of these and other qualities are more likely to make a human society free, peaceful, and prosperous, or instead oppressed, violent, and poor. To his credit, Dawkins is careful to avoid playing psychologist. Rather, he argues that individual selfishness and individual altruism coexist as part of "gene selfishness" that is rooted in survival—that is, in the desire to perpetuate or, in Dawkins's terminology, to replicate. The selection that drives this process does not exist to benefit the group (whether market or species); it occurs to benefit the gene (Alchian's firm or individual people).

But how do individuals relate to the rest of their group, and in what ways do their ideas, attitudes, beliefs, and the like get transmitted over time? Is there a genetic (nature) component to such transmission? Here Dawkins is more careful, though his speculation is worth examining, as it has been a part of the social sciences for more than three decades. Here is a key passage:

> The gene, the DNA molecule, happens to be the replicating entity that pre-vails on our own planet. There may be others . . . But do we have to go to distant worlds to find other kinds of replicator and other, consequent, kinds of evolution? I think that a new kind of replicator has recently emerged on this very planet. It is staring us in the face. It is still in its infancy, still drifting clumsily about in its primeval soup, but already it is achieving evolutionary change at a rate that leaves the old gene panting far behind. The new soup is the soup of human culture.[16]

Dawkins introduces a new word to our vocabulary—*meme*—to describe culture as such a replicator. A meme is, in short, a unit of cultural transmission. Examples can range from the mundane (a tune, a phrase, a fashion), to the practical (ways of making cookware or building arches), to the sublime (faith). To what extent do humans hold memes? How are they transmitted? And what effect does such transmission have on individual attitudes and beliefs about the rules they should use to guide behavior? These questions remain of interest to social scientists of all sorts, but the answers are incomplete. What seems clear, however, is that something—an idea, an attitude, a skill, a habit—is transmitted. The cause and effect may be unclear, but the interrelatedness of it all—a type of soup of life—remains.

Ten years later, Richard Lewontin, Steven Rose, and Leon Kamin weighed in with their book and its telling title, *Not in Our Genes*. The authors offer a contrasting position to Dawkins' *Selfish Gene*, and the debate has been fierce. If taken to an extreme, their argument against nature produces a straw man, a point easily grasped by anyone with a serious genetic disorder, let alone the rest of us with bad vision or flat feet. On the other hand, Lewontin, Rose, and Kamin have an important point to make. Much of who we are as individuals is a product of social conditioning, and much though not all of this conditioning can be shaped and improved. A summary of their argument is made clear with a quotation: "We have the ability to construct our own futures, albeit not in circumstances of our own choosing."[17] A fervent desire to "construct our own futures" sounds inherently human, and indeed it is. Great minds from across the ideological spectrum maintained as much. Once again, Karl Marx gets to the pith of the matter: "Men make their own history, but they do not make it just as they please; they make it under circumstances directly encountered, given and transmitted from the past."[18]

The roles of nature and nurture, then, may not be mutually exclusive. This is an argument closely associated with the cognitive neuroscientist Steven Pinker. According to Pinker, it is helpful to think about how nature and nurture interact:

> In some cases, an extreme environmentalist explanation is correct: which language you speak is an obvious example, and differences among races and ethnic groups in test scores may be another. In other cases, such as certain inherited neurological disorders, an extreme hereditarian explanation is correct. In most cases the correct explanation will invoke a complex interaction between heredity and environment: culture is crucial, but culture could not exist without mental faculties that allow humans to create and learn culture to begin with.[19]

In other words, history and culture and personal experience matter, but they do not tell the entire story. In most cases, who we become is not entirely because of a "bad seed" (nature) or an abusive caregiver (nurture), powerful as such effects may be. Our genetic and environmental influences interact in a way that is at once complex and powerful. Parsing the two may be a fool's errand; ignoring either in its entirety may be worse.

As the anthropologists Robert Boyd and Peter Richerson argue, cultural evolution is a process determined "not by genes alone" (a catchy line that also is the title of their book). They describe culture as "information" that is "acquired or modified by social learning, and affects behavior."[20] Individuals *choose* among an infinite array of attitudes, beliefs, customs, and dogmas. Over time these become part of the culture. Individuals consider new ideas or information within a context that includes all information that is commonly held.

The Importance of Geography

On the other hand, a different form of nature argument says that biology may be trumped by geography, at least according to Jared Diamond. In his successful 1997 book *Guns, Germs and Steel*, Diamond argues that the earliest causes of success of certain societies precede political and religious institutions, deriving instead from climate, types of domesticated animals, and ease of human travel. Better soil and climate helped agriculture to emerge earlier in some places as compared to others, for example, which is why the Fertile Crescent got its name. Regions with navigable rivers and natural harbors were more conducive to migration and commerce. If agricultural development favored certain regions (neither too hot nor too cold, for example) and if trade followed specific routes (more often East–West than North–South), then specialization, trade, and economic development would be more likely in some places than in others. And if traders also brought exposure to new ideas, then a fertile intellectual climate might be as predestined as a good harvest.

The Importance of Psychology

The ideas that work their way into public opinion are not always good ones. Research that blends fundamental insights of psychology and economics has shed much light on how—if not why—people often hold seemingly irrational preferences. For example, the psychologists Daniel Kahneman and Amos Tversky have shown how individuals often revert to the status quo, to that with which they are familiar, even when an obviously better option is available to them. Similarly, individuals often place greater weight on avoiding losses than on achieving gains, when economic theory predicts that a rational person would weigh them equally under the same odds. For example, the average person prefers a certain payout of $500 over a 50 percent chance of winning $1000 combined with a 50 percent chance of winning nothing, even though the expected value of those two scenarios is the same.

Such research offers insights into human behavior in everyday economic affairs, in business and politics and more. For example, how a company structures its retirement plan often will determine the extent to which employees participate in it. If a company's policy (or a government rule) establishes that employees automatically will have a minimum percentage of their salary deposited into a personal retirement account, participation in the savings plan will be greater than if employees are given the option of contributing to this same type of account. Even if employees may choose to opt out of such savings plans, there generally is more saving if the default policy is for the employee to participate. As we saw in the discussion of public choice theory in Chapter 3, rules matter. The insights of evolutionary psychology simply remind us that rules should take into account people's predispositions.

Kahneman, a psychologist, shared the 2002 Nobel Prize with an economist, Vernon L. Smith (born 1927), for their contributions to understanding how individuals make decisions under different circumstances and with different frames. To the extent that those frames change—either as a direct result of social policy or an indirect consequence of other factors—people's views may change as well.

Individuals also have biases when it comes to politics, and these biases affect how they participate in politics. The economist Bryan Caplan's 2007 book *The Myth of the Rational Voter* identifies four areas where voters' beliefs clash with the actual effects of public policies. For example, Caplan points to surveys where most voters support import tariffs to support domestic job growth, yet the vast majority of economists agree that such policies would not produce the intended effect and in fact are quite harmful.

And likewise, Kahneman and Tversky's behavioral anomalies don't go away. Behavioral research has shown it can be disruptive and difficult for people to change their minds about the world. If you grew up believing that the sun revolves around the earth, for example, and if your family and friends believe the same, it can be startling to discover proof that the solar system is heliocentric—so much so that you may choose to ignore such proof. When individuals' understandable, perhaps even rational, biases inform their support for certain public policies over others, politicians might have little choice but to enact the inefficient policies that a free and democratic people demand. As H. L. Mencken once quipped, "Democracy is the theory that the common people know what they want, and deserve to get it good and hard."[21]

From Collective Belief to Institutional Change

Aggregation forms another layer of the problem. How do we go from genetic predisposition and personal psychology—the combination of nature and nurture that makes up each individual's unique history—to collective belief? The cognitive anthropologist Dan Sperber argues that, in many ways, the spread of ideas and beliefs resembles the spread of infectious diseases. This theory explains why statistical models that help the U.S. Center for Disease Control estimate the spread of deadly viruses have a new set of users: anthropologists and other social scientists who model the dissemination of ideas. If voters are biased toward certain interests or have mistaken beliefs about the consequences of government, they might support bad policies. Their biases could spread through the marketplace of ideas, and they can be as difficult to overcome as some biological epidemics.

The idea is not that radical or unfamiliar, even to nonscientific audiences. Malcolm Gladwell's best-selling books, *Outliers* and *The Tipping Point*, show how the right conditions (place of birth, ethnicity, years of practice, or working at something others ignore), combined with an accumulation of other factors (shared beliefs and attitudes, for example), can make some outcomes almost inevitable. Yet the same author's other best-selling book, *Blink*, demonstrates how quickly we process information with little apparent thought, almost as if we were hardwired to see some things and not others.

Other experts argue that the way we are wired has changed over time, as humans adapt to changes in our environment. Over the last few decades, much light has been shed on this question by evolutionary psychology, a field that borrows heavily from anthropology, genetics, psychology, and economics. Robert Wright, a journalist and former science editor, provides one of the earliest contributions to this field of thought in a classic work, *The Moral Animal: Why We Are, the Way We Are: The New Science of Evolutionary Psychology*. Matt Ridley, a science writer with a doctorate in zoology, follows with *The Origins of Virtue: Human Instincts and the Evolution of Cooperation*. Paul Rubin, an economist, offers *Darwinian Politics: The Evolutionary Origin of Freedom*.

A central theme in these popular explanations is that human beings have evolved to better take advantage of the benefits of cooperation. This does not mean that selfishness or self-interest has been purged from the human gene pool. Rather, societies converge on institutions that channel self-interest (individual survival) into activities that promote the general interest (group survival). Human interaction has evolved in ways that allow people to experience the benefits of cooperation, and social norms develop in support of mutual gains. The lesson is that societies evolve to avert the Hobbesian jungle and instead adopt rules that let people generate Adam Smith's invisible hand.

In a more recent book, *The Rational Optimist: How Prosperity Evolves* (2009), Ridley takes the metaphor of natural selection in social arrangements even further, using it to explain the ongoing success of some societies. Ridley argues that the wealth and well-being of a society is not determined by the average IQ of its brightest intellectuals—disheartening news for academic scribblers and social critics everywhere—nor is it determined by the average IQ of the masses. Rather, argues Ridley, a society's material well-being hinges on its ability to integrate the best ideas available.

Taking a figurative cue from Darwin, Ridley argues that societies evolve to better and better conditions when "ideas have sex"—the process whereby ideas interact and produce new ideas. As with natural selection in its original sense, the ideas that best meet our needs gain a reproductive upper hand. In the long run—and evolution is about the long run—better ideas tend to be recognized and rewarded and replicated. This optimistic tone has much in common with contributions from scientists like Richard Dawkins and economists like Armen Alchian.

In fact, optimism about our ability to improve the human condition has a long history in social and political thought, dating at least to Adam Smith, who lays out clearly why specialization and the division of labor promote social cooperation and, ultimately, human well-being. It is in *The Theory of Moral Sentiments* that Smith first points the way to social cooperation. Here Smith argues that it is our ability to engage in sympathy, putting ourselves in the shoes of others, that allows us to form rules of just conduct. A social environment that combines rules of just conduct with an imagination that can think of the needs of others will facilitate exchange, production, and cooperation, the secret ingredients to human prosperity. A good environment for the marketplace of ideas matters to the flourishing of a society.

Two centuries after Adam Smith, his namesake, Vernon Smith, was awarded the Nobel Prize for pioneering the field of experimental economics and, like Kahneman, contributing to our understanding of human decision-making. Vernon Smith's work combines his findings in laboratory and field experiments with a deep reading of political philosophy, especially the classical liberals. In his *Rationality in Economics: Constructivist and Ecological Forms* (2008) the modern Mr. Smith describes the cognitive origins of two types of rules in society, designed and emergent. The first, constructivist rationality, invokes Bacon and Descartes (whom we met in Chapter 2) to present the case for reason as the basis for rules in society. A single mind (or a small group of minds) develops solutions that apply to all. The effects can be beneficial, such as Internet protocols that help organize all communication between very different kinds of information systems and technologies. The effects can also be devastating, especially when a select few are given economic control of an entire society; just ask anyone who has ever lived in the former Soviet Union or today's North Korea. And the effects sometimes can be negligible, for example when a law is technically on the books but not enforced.

The second, ecological rationality, is the set of informal rules and norms in society that coordinate behavior spontaneously. People reach positive-sum outcomes without a central plan, thus obviating the need for hierarchical, central control. Instead, evolution can favor the best ideas. In his 2002 Nobel lecture, Smith offers a dozen observations on human behavior in general and markets in particular. Among these are two gems. First, he notes that "markets are rule-governed institutions." Second, he argues that "rules emerge as a spontaneous order—they are found—not deliberately designed by one calculating mind."[22]

The 2009 economics Nobel Prize winner, Elinor Ostrom (1933–2012), spent her career studying the spontaneous design of rules that emerge when people are allowed to coordinate behaviors over time. Ostrom studied resources to which everyone has common access, or "common pool resources." Too easily scholars fall into a false dichotomy of centrally planned versus private property regimes. When in the real world, many valuable resources, such as inland fisheries and underground water basins, don't respect borders and can't easily be centrally planned or treated as private property. Ostrom's research shows that the right type of rule can emerge through repeated trials among the same groups of people. The best outcomes tend to be when the rules reflect local knowledge about the resource and how other locals are using it. Oftentimes the outcome is best under a system of communal rights, with well-defined rules regulating access and use that are appropriate to the circumstances on the ground.[23]

The implications of Smith's and Ostrom's ideas for social and political change are immense. For the most part, rules do not have to be imposed hierarchically, even if in the beginning a brilliant mind conceives them and in the end a dictator decrees them. Rather, rules emerge through a variety of parallel processes through which ideas about just conduct and a better society slowly work their way into a society's shared beliefs systems and eventually become embodied in its shared institutions. There's no equilibrium in this kind of economics. And whether the social scientist concludes that people are rational or not, as Vernon Smith likes to observe, in the end, "markets will do their thing."

The Framework

If we think back to the triangle in Figure 5.2, the area at the top labeled Ideas gives us a lot to consider. Through a number of parallel forces at the individual and group levels, shared beliefs about the proper scope and function of government take shape, and their continual evolution exerts pressure

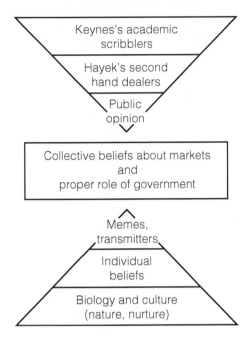

Figure 5.3　The top-down and bottom-up process of idea formation.

for political change. Figure 5.3 organizes these forces into a simple hourglass, showing both the top-down and bottom-up components involved in the formation of collective beliefs.

In the top section of the hourglass, ideas take shape from the pens of Keynes's academic scribblers. Certain ideas are then selected by Hayek's "second hand dealers" competing in a marketplace of ideas. These ideas are then selectively absorbed by masses of people into the general climate of public opinion and collective beliefs about commerce and government. It is these ideas that will shape the message delivered by madmen in authority.

Every hourglass can be turned over. In the bottom section of the hourglass we lay out the individualistic origins of beliefs as we've discussed them these last few pages. Starting from the bottom, we have "Biology and culture" representing the influences of genes, upbringing, life-changing experiences, and so forth. People's "Individual beliefs" come out of this experience, and "Transmitters" make ideas available for selection by others, as with Dawkins's meme. Unlike the single top-down cone from above, the highly individualist bottom section has a cone for each person in society. In the United States there are about 300 million bottom cones like this. Each has its own story, of course, because each represents an individual who has come to his or her beliefs over a lifetime.

Completing the relationship between these top-down and bottom-up processes, an increasingly large number of individuals in a society may, through their combined experiences and endowments, come to a particular belief that they may or may not even know they share. These beliefs in turn may be given voice by an academic scribbler and then looked on favorably by intellectuals. In this way, a seemingly self-generating, bottom-up process ultimately may merge into the type of top-down influence that Keynes and Hayek described.

At the confluence of these top-down and bottom-up forces, collective beliefs take shape about the proper role and function of government. These beliefs are continually evolving under the influence of ideas circulating in society. Now when we think back to the nexus of ideas, institutions, and incentives in Figure 5.2 we have a road map for thinking about what forces might cause a shift. Figure 5.4 combines our hourglass with the adapted Hayekian triangle to complete our framework for understanding political change. On the left is the hourglass of ideas taking shape through both top-down and bottom-up forces in society. This shift might take place over many years—in a roundabout process that involves many further relays—and may perhaps not even be visible to the casual observer. As this process shapes collective beliefs about the proper role and scope of government, new ideas move their way to the right side of the diagram. As ideas shift in the top of the triangle on the right, they exert pressure on institutions, which in turn shape incentives and outcomes. To create political change, this pressure on institutional arrangements must be

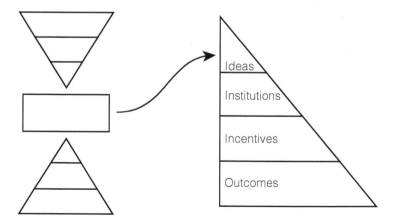

Figure 5.4 The framework of political change.

sufficient to overcome status quo interests. For those ideas that eventually *do* surmount vested interests, new institutional arrangements emerge, which in turn present policymakers and ordinary people with revised incentive structures, and outcomes will change from there, for better or worse.

Significantly, rule change is seen as an emergent process in this model. It is a product of rational individuals engaging in that most human of activities—exchange. The exchange of ideas and their effects on institutions and incentives in a society always take place in the context of a particular time and place, and it cannot be planned.

Nonetheless, the temptation to plan is strong. Indeed, a casual glance at Figure 5.4 might lead one to conclude that the process of political change is mechanistic, a somewhat complicated system which, if properly engineered, can yield the social outcomes that people desire. But a more careful look suggests a more profound conclusion: There is no starting point. The search for such a magical point—a lever with which to change the world—is a fallacy common to madmen and intellectuals everywhere. It is akin to the constructivist error Hayek warns us about. Because humans are rational creatures, and because they respond to incentives, we can and should expect them to adjust to changing conditions in their world, to include new rules.

Answering Question 3: Why Only Some Failed Policies Get Repealed
The wasteful and unjust policies that simply do not seem to get reformed—Tullock's transitional gains trap—may describe the vast majority of political outcomes. But they do not describe all of political reality. Sometimes, things can actually get better. Sometimes, reform is possible.

The opportunity for reform emerges in specific issues or policies, in particular times and in particular places. In our language, a "loose spot" emerges in the nexus of ideas, institutions, and incentives. It becomes possible for a new idea to overcome the vested interests. But this possibility must first be noticed by alert people in the society. In short, political change happens when entrepreneurs notice and exploit those loose spots in the structure of ideas, institutions, and incentives.

In the following chapter, we discuss case studies of exactly this type of political change, focusing on ideas that have gone on to change institutions and the incentives they create. Then, in the concluding chapter, we look specifically at the political and intellectual entrepreneurs who produce institutional change in our framework.

6

Four Stories of Political Change

I'd go anywhere for a check this big.
—*President Bill Clinton, April 2, 1995, at a Federal*
Communications Commission press conference

Is it any wonder that I ask myself every day: Is this action
necessary? Is this what my mother raised me to do?"
—*Alfred E. Kahn (Quoted in Thomas K.*
McCraw, Prophets of Regulation, p. 272)

In the previous chapter, we saw how madmen, intellectuals, and academic scribblers interact to create political change. The process involves ideas that influence institutions—the rules of the game—which in turn create the incentives that drive the outcomes we see. In this chapter, we consider four examples of political change and the ideas, institutions, and incentives behind them. The first three cases—spectrum license auctions, airline deregulation, and welfare reform—represent examples of significant policy changes that came from better ideas and that brought increased economic well-being. The last example—the housing bubble that began in the late 1990s and burst in 2006—illustrates what happens when the rules of the game create perverse incentives.

Spectrum License Auctions and Ronald Coase's Big Idea

In April 1995, newspapers across the country ran a front-page story with a photograph of President Bill Clinton, Vice-President Al Gore, and Chairman of the Federal Communications Commission (FCC) Reed Hundt. While this federal agency seldom led the news, and even less frequently warranted an appearance with the president, something big had just happened. As the federal entity charged with overseeing the nation's airwaves, the FCC had just auctioned ninety-nine licenses to use valuable radio frequency spectrum, hauling in a handsome $7.5 billion for the deficit-pounding Clinton administration, all with the promise of more to come. The front-page photograph said it all. In it, a beaming Chairman Hundt delivers to President Clinton an oversized check from the FCC, payable to "The U.S. Taxpayer" for seven and a half billion dollars. "I'd go anywhere for a check this big," the president joked.[1]

Those too young to remember the Clinton years might be forgiven for missing the self-effacing humor (or perhaps utter lack of embarrassment) in this clever line. President Clinton had been criticized by both the political right and left for inviting large campaign donors to enjoy overnight stays in the famed Lincoln bedroom of the White House. Here was a politician who really would go anywhere or do anything for a big check. In this case, however, the check was not destined to benefit a political party. The beneficiaries were the U.S. taxpayers.

Who would pay over $7 billion to the U.S. government? Aspiring providers of wireless services. And why would they do so? Because the spectrum licenses they receive in return are a necessary input for the mobile voice and data services they provide. Why would they pay so much? Because consumers value these wireless services even more. In fact, since its first auction in 1994, the FCC has raised over $50 billion in approximately ninety auctions for licenses to use the spectrum. U.S. mobile communications providers have used these licenses to form the backbone of an industry that generates over $160 billion in sales, and much more in consumer value, every year.[2]

It wasn't always this way. As economist Thomas Hazlett documents in a number of studies of the U.S. wireless industry,[3] the use of auctions to assign licenses starting in the mid-1990s represented a radical departure from the inefficient, highly politicized license assignment process that had originated in the 1920s and 1930s.

Didn't anyone have the idea to auction spectrum licenses sooner? Well, yes, someone did. In 1959, a third of a century before auctions became standard practice, our friend from Chapter 3, Ronald Coase, suggested exactly that. Coase published a paper titled "The Federal Communications Commission."[4] In it, he argues that the airwaves (radio frequency spectrum) share many characteristics with real property, that is, with land. We don't have governments controlling routine decisions with how land is used, and Coase shows that there's similarly not much reason why the government ought to be in command and control of the airwaves.

A History Tied to Politics

In the earliest days of radio communication and up until the mid-1920s, decades before Coase first wrote on the issue, the rules of the game for assigning spectrum use rights paralleled the distribution of land parcels in the West during the previous century, with "first in time, first in right" as the order of the day. While disputes over rights to spectrum bands inevitably arose, the Department of Commerce enforced users' rights and generally tried to minimize interference. The Radio Act of 1927 turned this arrangement on its head, however, requiring centralized control of the license assignment process. The Communications Act of 1934 replaced the legislation of seven years earlier and further codified this approach, requiring what would come to be known as "comparative hearings" (or "beauty contests") in which potential licensees were chosen based on their ability to best satisfy the "public interest," a standard that henceforth would be frustratingly difficult to define.

From legislation in the 1920s and 1930s to well past Coase's 1959 paper, the dominant players in the communications industry were first radio and then television broadcasting. Indeed, until the emergence of mobile telephony (cellular service) and the Internet during the latter part of the twentieth century, the big money was largely to be found in broadcasting. It is not surprising that here we also find the political influence and the political interest.

Government provided broadcasters with licenses to use the spectrum at no cost but also established obligations to help meet the "public interest," such as children's programming, limits on speech related to obscenity, public service announcements, and the like. There was a quid pro quo that gave to and demanded from the broadcasters, and it was unique. For example, First Amendment rights were limited for broadcasters in a way not seen with the print media. On the other hand, while broadcasters simply could not exist without access to the spectrum, newspapers did not receive any such valuable asset from the government.

The quid pro quo was not perfectly defined, however, and over time the Supreme Court had to clarify the rules of the game. In a 1943 decision, it ruled that government administration of the spectrum was appropriate, given the scarcity inherent in the spectrum resource.[5] A 1969 ruling again reasoned that regulation was justified because spectrum was scarce, and it further affirmed, as Congress had done in 1927 and 1934, that license holders had no property interest in this resource.[6]

In contrast, Coase's argument is that the U.S. government *could* treat radio spectrum as if it were property. It is not a legal argument; it is an economic and ultimately a practical argument. Continuing the analogy between airwaves and land, Coase argues that the price system could assign the resource to those who most value it. After all, just like land, the airwaves can be divided by frequency band and by geographic area, and some parcels are more productive and thus more valuable than others.

Coase carefully distinguishes between the question of *how* a particular band may be used (for example, broadcasting, voice communications, and the like) and *who* will be given the right to use it. Again, the analogy to land is apt. Government often determines which neighborhoods in a city will be set aside for industrial use and which for residential use, while allowing market processes to determine who will be doing the using on each lot in each area. Indeed, Coase states, "I would not argue that regulations such as zoning are necessarily undesirable or that there ought not be need for their counterpart in dealing with the radio frequency spectrum."[7]

This argument by Coase is not a call to the barricades; it is a proposal to make an important market significantly more efficient. Yet, at the time, the idea seemed strangely radical. Citing a congressional hearing the year prior, in 1958, Coase notes that the president of CBS was caught off guard when asked whether competitive bidding could be used by the government to assign spectrum use licenses, calling this a novel theory. We mentioned Coase's lifelong fascination with the invisible hand, ever since learning the idea at the London School of Economics in 1929. Here, thirty years later, Coase reminds his readers that this theory for allocating rights to use the spectrum is "novel with Adam Smith," and in fact it represents how resources commonly are allocated in a market economy.[8]

But to allow the market to determine even the question of assignment meant a significant change in the status quo. When he was called to testify before the agency shortly before his FCC paper was published, Coase's reception was indicative of how political institutions—especially Congress but also the FCC—would view his idea for decades to come. Commissioner Philip Cross began with the question, "Is this all a big joke?" It was not; Coase was serious.

Coase enjoyed a better reception among fellow academic scribblers and intellectuals. In 1962, for example, the economist Harvey Levin proposed that government specifically address the ambiguities in the quid pro quo.[9] He noted that obligations on broadcasters could be made more explicit or, alternatively, that licenses could be made available to the highest bidder, with auction revenues used to subsidize various public interest goals such as children's television programming. The problem with the first approach was that extremely explicit rules might thwart innovation or even be deemed illegal. The problem with the second approach was that it had no political support. Inertia trumped efficiency, and auctions lost.

In 1965, Coase published another paper that explains the problem in more detail. He begins with a citation to the "Report on the Regulatory Agencies," which had been produced in 1961 for the incoming President John F. Kennedy. Written by James M. Landis, a former dean of Harvard Law School and advisor to the Kennedys and to President Franklin Delano Roosevelt, the report notes that "more than any other agency," the FCC "has been subservient, far too subservient, to the committees on communications of the Congress and their members. A strong suspicion also exists that far too great an influence is exercised over the commission by the networks."[10]

The Landis Report provides a glimpse into the institutions and interests that would be most resistant to Coase's proposed policy change over the next several decades. Landis simply points out what Coase already knew and what George Stigler would later refer to as "regulatory capture." As applied to this market, Stigler's point is that artificially restricting the number of valuable broadcast licenses and simultaneously entrusting the FCC with the responsibility of distributing these licenses is a recipe for political mischief. The rent seeking was rampant, producing what Coase calls an "anti-poverty campaign for millionaires."[11]

It is not hard to imagine what Landis is getting at. Within Washington, D.C., throughout the last half of the twentieth century the National Association of Broadcasters enjoyed a reputation as one of the most powerful lobbies in town—and for good reason. Most members of the House of Representatives have congressional districts that fit nicely into the geographic license area of a few broadcasters, such as the local affiliate of ABC, CBS, NBC, and

Fox. The politicians who represent these districts know the reporters, editors, and managers of the news stations affiliated with these broadcasters, and they care about their opinions.

Like Landis, Coase recognizes the power of vested interests. His argument in 1965 simply builds on his point from six years earlier. He notes that "the American economic system manages to work without having a Commission for each resource which is entrusted with the task of allocating that resource to those who are to be allowed to use it."[12]

While government might decide the general type of use in a given spectrum band (broadcasting or something else), it need not determine who would be the user, a process that inevitably becomes political. And broadcasters already face market rather than political pressure at some level, producing programming that audiences value in order to sell commercials. This means that incentives are aligned because only by producing something of value can a broadcaster make money. Once again, an obvious point traces to Adam Smith, but given the other obvious points that were overlooked in the debate, Coase decides to be more clear: "In a commercial broadcasting system the object of the program is to attract an audience for the commercials. It is not from the benevolence of the butcher, the brewer and the baker that we expect our radio and television programs."[13]

The closing paragraph of Coase's paper provides a measure of the economist's balance. A society's choice of institutions matters, while platitudes about "the government" or "the market" are not helpful. This is no bomb-throwing anarchist arguing for the end of government oversight:

> The policy choice should not be put in terms of government action versus the market in the field of radio and television. I am arguing for sensible government action. I am arguing for a properly functioning market. These aims are not inconsistent. Of course, the task of building social institutions is not an easy one. But it is not made easier by syrupy talk about broadcasters acting in the public interest. What is wanted is more economics and less humbug.[14]

Despite this plea, the humbug was not far behind. In fact, it appears on the following page in the same journal in which Coase had just published. Written by Hyman H. Goldin,[15] the rebuttal builds on a simple but fundamental objection: The market couldn't handle it. In short, the many different frequencies, the hundreds of thousands of licensees, and the millions of consumers in this market "make the pricing mechanism unworkable for frequency allocation." As a professor and former FCC economist, Goldin represents the view of many in government charged with managing the spectrum resource.

While sympathetic to Coase's concern about powerful broadcasters, Goldin nonetheless holds that the proposal's main ideas are unworkable. Still, he concludes his essay on a note of confidence: "The Commission has absolutely no intention of considering them now or in the foreseeable future. They are purely the mind-spinning of an academic bureaucrat."[16]

Yet the debate among academic bureaucrats continued. In 1969, the RAND Corporation commissioned Coase, along with two of its economists, William Meckling and Jora Minasian, to produce a report on "Problems of Radio Frequency Allocation."[17] The arguments closely parallel those made by Coase in his 1959 and 1965 papers. To describe the challenge faced by the FCC, the authors offer an analogy in which the government is tasked with managing a warehouse full of steel. The authors point out that the challenge for the government is not to determine whether there is a demand for the resource but to determine how the resource should be assigned among competing uses. Exactly what criteria should be used? The authors argue that the FCC faces a similar problem in assigning licenses to use the spectrum. Slowly but surely, academics were adopting the argument that the "problem" of spectrum allocation was like that surrounding the use of any other resource.

Yet despite its first-rate economics team, the RAND Corporation was not merely a group of academic bureaucrats. Rather, RAND proved to be politically savvy in a way most economists, Coase included, were not. Proof is found in the history of the Coase/Meckling/Minasian report, which was produced in 1969 and released in . . . 1995. In a case of bureaucratic understatement, the introductory note states: "This manuscript on 'Problems of Radio Frequency Allocation' was originally intended to become a RAND research memorandum (RM). For various reasons, it never reached the publication stage."[18]

These "various reasons" are not trivial. The RAND Corporation's management vetoes the economists. Decades later, Coase would describe his experience by quoting an internal memo that expressed concern over public relations "in government quarters and in the Congress." The commenters recommend that the report not be published, and if it were to be published, that several alternative solutions be proposed, to avoid "the fire and counterfire of CBS, FCC, Justice, and most of all—Congress."[19] In short, while Coase's idea was gaining ground among academics in the 1960s, its reception among politically powerful—and politically connected—interests was going nowhere.

This does not mean that all was paradise for the broadcasters. Despite the government's apparently clear authority in regulating the broadcast industry, not all policymakers were happy with the status quo. In 1961, not long after Coase published his FCC paper, the then-FCC Chairman Newt Minow gave a speech that half a century later is well known among those who work in telecommunications and broadcasting policy. Unhappy with the sorry state of television programming in the U.S. at that time, Chairman Minow challenged his audience:

> I invite each of you to sit down in front of your television set when your station goes on the air and stay there, for a day, without a book, without a magazine, without a newspaper, without a profit and loss sheet or a rating book to distract you. Keep your eyes glued to that set until the station signs off. I can assure you that what you will observe is a vast wasteland.
>
> You will see a procession of game shows, formula comedies about totally unbelievable families, blood and thunder, mayhem, violence, sadism, murder, western bad men, western good men, private eyes, gangsters, more violence, and cartoons. And endlessly commercials—many screaming, cajoling, and offending. And most of all, boredom. True, you'll see a few things you will enjoy. But they will be very, very few.[20]

While the "vast wasteland" speech resonated with many, broadcasters were not amused. Like most industries with vested interests, broadcasters do not take kindly to harsh criticism by high-ranking government officials. At the same time, most industries are not well positioned to do much about it or are afraid to do so. But broadcasters, especially in the second half of the twentieth century, were in a unique position due to their influence over public opinion, a power that garners the attention of government officials.

Sometimes the message would be subtle, on the order of an inside joke. Exhibit A in the response to Chairman Minow applies only to those old enough to remember television shows from more than three decades back. "Gilligan's Island" was a popular sitcom based on a fictitious ill-fated party who found themselves stranded on an island following a shipwreck. The wrecked ship was named, not coincidentally, S.S. *Minnow*.

Less anecdotally, within Washington, D.C., the National Association of Broadcasters had plenty of power. The trade association lobbied effectively, aided by its many members who knew the halls of Congress and were well acquainted with the politicians who served districts in their broadcast area.

This does not, however, mean that broadcasters were all-powerful in Washington, D.C. Rather, the pressure went both ways. While the examples are many, two stories illustrate the conflict.

As a member of Congress and prominent figure in the Democratic Party, Lyndon Johnson used his contacts at the FCC to help his wife acquire television and radio stations. Later, Johnson would become president of the United States. And like most modern-day presidents, he would complain that the press did not treat his policies fairly. Shockingly, in at least one case he also complained to CBS that it overcharged his wife's stations for television programming. CBS resolved the matter by providing the president's wife with the desired programming for free.

Decades later, a prominent figure in the Republican Party and majority leader of the Senate, Bob Dole, would prove that political heavy-handedness is a bipartisan affair. As reported by the *Washington Post*, in the debate that preceded the Telecommunications Act of 1996, Dole met with top executives from the major broadcast networks, who had come to lobby about the pending legislation. In a none-too-subtle link between the value of spectrum licenses that broadcasters originally had received for free and the content of the news their stations were providing, Dole was quoted as asking, "Why should I give you a $40 billion giveaway when you're driving my (approval rating) numbers through the floor on Medicare?" A spokesman for the senator subsequently clarified that no link was intended between licenses and news content, but the *Washington Post* did not see it that way. Apparently, neither did the broadcast executives. As one attendee later observed: "Everyone took the comment (about news) very seriously."[21]

Change Comes to the Congress

As the 1960s gave way to the 1970s and then the 1980s, change was everywhere, from hemlines and hairstyles to social attitudes and civil rights. On the economic front, deregulation came to airlines, trucking, oil and gas pipelines, and more. Even the telecommunications market saw dramatic upheaval with the breakup of the monopoly telephony company, AT&T. But the rules for use of spectrum—for broadcasting, wireless communications, or anything else—pretty much stayed the same.

Coase's ideas had gained some traction with academics and intellectuals in the 1960s. The ideas also made some headway in Washington, but not with the FCC and especially not with Congress. In 1977, when one FCC commissioner suggested that serious consideration be given the proposal to auction spectrum licenses, two other commissioners dismissed the idea, arguing that its odds of adoption were "as those on the Easter Bunny in the Preakness."[22]

Yet the Easter Bunny had already left the gate. In 1972, the Department of Commerce had produced a study arguing for consideration of auctions for spectrum licenses. A year later, the White House Office of Telecommunications Policy had made a similar argument. By the end of the decade, the Carter administration advocated spectrum license auctions; the idea even merited a mention on one occasion in a State of the Union address. The Reagan administration took a similar position.

By the 1980s, the FCC was on board with the White House, favoring spectrum license auctions at least in some circumstances. Throughout the administrations of Ronald Reagan and then George H. W. Bush, almost every year the White House Office of Management and Budget, with the FCC, would propose that Congress grant the FCC the authority to auction spectrum licenses. It didn't happen.

But while policy was changing slowly, technology was not. By the 1980s, advances in technology meant new communications services could be made available to consumers; further, existing spectrum bands could be used more efficiently, and other bands that previously were of too high a frequency could now be put to use. A license to use the spectrum remained a valuable asset, but now it was possible to do even more with that same asset.

Among the "new" communications services that changed the political and technological dynamic was mobile telephony. The technology was not exactly new, of course, given that since the 1960s there had been bulky, car-mounted devices that let users communicate via radio transmission with a base station operator, who in turn would connect the caller to the public switched telephone network. The FCC started a proceeding on this matter in 1968. By the 1980s, it was time to assign licenses for this new service.

The question was how to assign these licenses. In 1982, the FCC proceeded with its first strategy. We'll call it Plan A. The agency would use comparative hearings, also known as "beauty contests" and essentially the same process used since the 1930s, with competing applicants trying to demonstrate to the FCC why they, rather than any other applicant, deserved to have the license in question. The country was divided into local service areas, 734 at the end of the day. Two licenses would be assigned in each market. One would be given to the local telephone company to enable it to expand from wireline to wireless service, and one license would be given to the applicant that won the beauty contest.

The FCC used this process to award licenses for the thirty largest markets in the country but was surprised to receive over 200 applications, many prepared in great detail. The agency was not prepared to carefully scrutinize so many competing claims. Something had to be done. It was time for Plan B.

For the remaining markets, the FCC decided to use lotteries to assign spectrum licenses. Just one year earlier, in 1981, Congress had granted authority for the FCC to use lotteries to assign licenses for mobile telephone service. Congress did not allow auctions, nor did it allow lotteries for other services, such as broadcasting. Nonetheless, this was a major policy change. A newly elected President Reagan and the first Republican Senate in a generation meant that a little experimentation could be tried.

As Michael Calhoun describes the experience in *Digital Cellular Radio*, this was a major investment opportunity.[23] At least, that's what potential investors were told in ads that featured the afternoon talk show host Mike Douglas and in newsletters that called it the "opportunity of the century." Not since the development of the railroads could so much money be made, proponents claimed.

Investors rushed in. While in theory the FCC required that applicants demonstrate an ability to actually build a wireless network, such details could be addressed after a license was won. The trick, as many perceived it, was getting in the lottery. Thus, many applied. As the FCC proceeded to assign licenses in the next thirty markets, more than 500 applications were filed. For the next thirty markets, 700 more applications came in.

The agency was overwhelmed. As Calhoun describes it, FCC staff lacked the resources to handle the administrative burden. Even the physical burden was too much. Applicants were directed to send their paperwork to the FCC's licensing center in Gettysburg, Pennsylvania, and the weight of so many filings caused the agency's shelving to collapse.

Despite the chaos, something good came of it. According to a study prepared by the FCC for Congress, by moving from beauty contests to lotteries the agency cut the time needed to assign spectrum licenses from 720 to 412 days.[24]

But lotteries were not auctions. Yes, they were efficient in one sense, in that spectrum licenses eventually ended up in the hands of those who valued them the most. But similar to what happened with beauty contests, a lot of resources were wasted in the process of trying to acquire these licenses. A few individuals literally won the lottery and became rich because all a lucky winner had to do was to sell the spectrum use rights to a real wireless services provider. Meanwhile, everyone who participated in the lotteries had to pay fees to law firms to file their applications. In the end, the FCC received almost 400,000 applications, which meant a lot of legal fees.

In Chapter 4 we mentioned Gordon Tullock's idea that rent-seeking costs are unproductive and therefore socially wasteful. A study by Thomas Hazlett and Robert Michaels estimates that between $500 million and $1 billion in social losses accrued due to this type of unproductive activity—thousands of people paying fees for a chance to strike it rich—which continued throughout the 1980s.[25] As Tullock says in his original 1967 paper, "The cost of a football pool is not measured by the cost of the winner's ticket but by the cost of all tickets."[26]

It would not be until the next decade that U.S. policy moved to Plan C. Finally, auctions were possible. With the Omnibus Budget Reconciliation Act of 1993, Congress granted the FCC the authority to use auctions to assign licenses for certain types of wireless services. It was a product of President Clinton's political skill and of his urgent need for something just like this.

If the idea for auctions of spectrum use rights had been part of the public debate since at least 1959, why didn't the relevant institutions change sooner? What interests stood in the way? Hadn't Coase convinced a large number of academics, as well as experts in public policy? In fact, he had. Hadn't the FCC itself come to support this policy? Yes, since at least the 1980s. And hadn't every U.S. president since Jimmy Carter supported this policy? Well, yes, they had.

The sticking point was, and had always been, Congress. Not necessarily the institution as a whole, but certainly the relevant committees with jurisdiction over the FCC and the industry: the Commerce Committee of the Senate and the Energy and Commerce Committee of the House of Representatives. Other committees had responsibility for the federal budget, appropriations, and other issues related to government taxes and spending, which meant they were interested in the revenues auctions could bring. But until the 1993 legislation, the committees of jurisdiction opposed the policy. It was a rational strategy: Additional funds in the U.S. Treasury brought few if any benefits to a member of a committee with jurisdiction over communications, whereas any change in regulation brought significant lobbying and potential political support. As Landis had observed three decades earlier, the commerce committees held tremendous power.

So why the change in 1993? One big motivator was money, or more specifically, a need to address the federal budget deficit. The seriousness of the deficit issue gave budget committee members an upper hand in dealing with commerce committee members; the former would tend to favor revenue-generating auctions over lotteries. This argument was made more powerful after a decade of experience, during which it became obvious that the value of spectrum licenses was going to a handful of lucky lottery winners, rather than the taxpayers as a whole.

Still, if they were going to give up political control (a valuable asset to a politician), the commerce committee members would need to get something in return. They did. Most notably, they retained control of license assignment in ways that mattered politically. Licenses to use spectrum for broadcasting, for example, would not be auctioned. Rather, auctions would apply to spectrum used for commercial wireless services like mobile telephony, where their value would bring big revenues to the U.S. Treasury. Yet even with commercial wireless services, commerce committee members remained relevant. Special allowances were granted to give a financial incentive (bidding credit) to auction participants who were women, minorities, or small business owners. In the end, everyone with a decisionmaking role in Congress got something, either more revenues or more political oversight. The country got an efficient way to help pay for government and a much more efficient way to assign spectrum use rights.

While the move from beauty contests to lotteries cut by more than 40 percent the time needed to assign spectrum licenses, according to the FCC Report to Congress, the move from lotteries to auctions cut this time again, from 412 to 233 days.[27] As a result, rights to use the spectrum were placed in the hands of mobile providers sooner, competition emerged sooner, and consumer benefits were larger. The estimates of the consumer benefits associated with this more efficient, more competitive market run in the tens of billions of dollars.

The Improbable Path of a Big Idea

Every story of social and political change is unique, even as common lessons can be gleaned. In the case of spectrum reform, change would not come until the relevant members of Congress got on board. Members of the commerce committees were especially resistant to auctions to assign spectrum use rights, given the political control that might be lost. Unsurprisingly, other members, especially those who controlled the funds that might be raised from these license auctions, supported the idea much sooner, as did presidents of both parties. Over time, acceptance of the good idea spread from academics to some political institutions, then others. For the key decisionmakers who were last to get on board, once the benefits of the new policy idea outweighed the cost, change was possible. But it took a long time for a good idea to overwhelm some important interests.

At first glance, Ronald Coase's eventual influence in the auctioning of licenses to use spectrum appears to be a classic case of the top-down transmission of a big idea, however slowly it came about. But even the origin of this good idea does not perfectly fit our simple model. In fact, to be precise, the idea did not exactly start with an academic scribbler with the stature of a Professor Coase. Just ask the professor himself.

In a twist that turns the top-down model on its head—and shows just how much good ideas can come *to* academic scribblers, rather than *from* them—Coase credits Leo Herzel, a law student at the University of Chicago, with the idea of auctioning rights to the spectrum. In 1951, a young Herzel published a paper in his university's law review, in which he introduces the basic question: Why not treat the spectrum like other resources and assign it to those who value it most highly?[28]

The student author was quickly put in his place. Dallas Smythe, a former FCC economist turned professor, criticized the proposal as misguided and unworkable.[29] Coase decided to look into the debate, though he was reasonably sure it was the expert economist and not a young law student who had the right answer. After a careful reading of the arguments, however, Coase changed his mind. The young law student had been scolded for not recognizing that spectrum was special, not to be subjected to the rigors of the market. As Coase later recalled, if there were no better arguments than this for not taking a market-based approach, Herzel probably was right. A famous paper followed in 1959.

In the end, an idea worked its way from academic scribblers to intellectuals to madmen in authority. The latter at first included stubborn FCC commissioners and later applied to politicians with an interest in the status quo. They were not Third World dictators; they were simply political actors who were rationally resistant to change. But once it was expedient to do so, the madmen in authority embraced the idea and the policies it represented. And consumers won.

Airline Deregulation and the Triumph of Good Policy

On a typical evening in 1978, well after normal office hours, Alfred Kahn's phone rang. As head of the Civil Aeronautics Board (CAB), the federal agency charged with regulating business practices in the airline industry,

Kahn was used to airline executives calling to plead for permission to fly a new route or change an existing fare. But this call was unique. On the other end of the line was a businessman who needed the CAB's approval to transport a flock of sheep from the United States to England. This unusual business venture was stuck in the CAB's usual level of red tape. In this case, however, time was of the essence; the sheep were of a very high quality, they were in heat, and they were about to be bred with equally prized rams across the Atlantic. If the flight was not approved right away, the English sires would lose their interest and a private company would lose its investment. Kahn got the flight approved. He also got to thinking critically about U.S. airline regulation.[30]

A former economics professor at Cornell who went on to head the New York Public Service Commission before being named to the CAB, Alfred Kahn did not arrive in Washington, D.C., with the goal of dismantling economic regulation of the airlines. He simply wanted things to work. Given the level of complexity that had built up in airline regulation, it was a lot to ask.

Economists often complain that they are ignored on matters in which they broadly agree (such as the benefits of free trade) and paid too much attention on matters in which they do not agree (such as the ideal tax policy). The case of airline deregulation was a happy exception. The ideas of economists and intellectuals in the 1970s were nearly unanimous in expressing the need for airline reform, and, while the existing political and market institutions resisted at first, reform came relatively quickly once the ideas reached a few well-connected intellectuals and motivated madmen. With the help of Alfred Kahn, an academic turned bureaucrat, and Teddy Kennedy, a politician, good ideas were transformed into better policy. Significant consumer benefits followed. How did they do it?

Clearly Inefficient Regulation, Clearly Attacked

The CAB was a poster child for what was wrong with economic regulation. It had been created by Congress in 1938. Twenty years later, in 1958, Congress had created the Federal Aviation Administration (FAA). While the FAA had (and continues to have) authority for regulating air safety by setting standards for pilots, aircraft, and airports, the CAB was given authority for economic regulation of the industry. Specifically, the board had three key powers: to permit or deny entry into markets, to set airfares, and to approve agreements that would be immune from U.S. antitrust laws. Imagine working for the government and explaining to your neighbors that you are responsible for keeping new airlines out of markets, setting fares, and not allowing carriers to charge less. This is not a job that would get you invited to a lot of parties.

But in the middle of the twentieth century, in the earliest stages of reform, the problems with airline regulation did not weigh heavily on the public's mind. There was essentially no interest apart from academics and intellectuals with an interest in public policy. Consumers were not mobilized and provided no constituency for reform. While business executives did not like the high cost of air travel, this was not the first issue they raised when lobbying policymakers. There was no push for reform from the regulated airlines, at least not from the major carriers. In short, the idea to reform the economic regulation of airlines did not get started by a grand coalition of consumers, business travellers, potential new carriers, or anyone else in the market. Instead, ideas about reform started with academic scribblers. And in contrast to Ronald Coase's big idea to auction spectrum licenses, in the case of airline regulation, quite a few academics were studying the issue.

For much of the 1960s and early 1970s, many economists published research that was critical of various U.S. regulatory agencies, noting how their policies did not appear to promote the most basic goals, such as competition and lower prices. The CAB came under especially heavy intellectual fire at this time, perhaps because it published many statistical reports (perfect for young graduate students to use in their dissertations) or perhaps because it regulated the relatively sexy airline industry (sexy, at least, when compared to electricity, gas pipelines, and similarly regulated industries).[31]

Building on the economic analysis of regulation that had emerged in the 1960s, in 1970 the *Bell Journal on Economics and Management* was launched. It would go on to publish a broad array of research on the regulation and deregulation of industries, especially electricity, telecommunications, and airlines. In 1971 the *Bell Journal* published George Stigler's article on regulatory capture. Then in 1975 it published Gordon Tullock's "Transitional Gains Trap." Another important role during this era was played by the left-of-center Brookings Institution, which sponsored policy papers on economic regulation. In so doing, the intellectuals at Brookings provided a forum in which the academic scribblers, usually safely housed in universities, could have their ideas translated and communicated to policymakers, who operated in the rather different environment of government. When Brookings ended its program in the mid-1970s, many of these research projects (and researchers) migrated to the right-of-center American Enterprise Institute (AEI). While the labels and the political affiliations may have changed, both groups criticized much of the economic regulation of the day. Among the academics and intellectuals, even those inside the Washington, D.C., beltway, this was a bipartisan conversation.

But when it comes to changing the institutions of government—say, the regulation of an entire industry—the attention of academics and intellectuals matters little by itself. The game changed only when key political players stepped onto the field.

Enter Kennedy and Kahn

All that research in the universities and think tanks got a political boost in 1974 when the Ford administration hosted a conference on inflation. The conference produced little agreement on monetary policy but considerable agreement on regulatory policy. Specifically, it was the conclusion of virtually all participants that economic regulation of airlines and trucking was not working and probably contributed to higher prices in these industries.

President Ford's Council of Economic Advisors (CEA), especially Paul MacAvoy and James Miller, started looking more closely at airline regulation. They didn't have to look far. If you are an academic economist, a call from the White House tends to make your day. Sure, it's not the president, but it is his economic advisor, who at any rate is more likely to understand what you're talking about. To say the least, you try to be helpful. And of course, the Brookings and AEI experts were always available to translate economic ideas into policy recommendations for staff in the White House or Congress. For policymakers with an interest in airline regulation, plenty of material was at hand. Thus began a conversation that went beyond academics and intellectuals and extended into the realm of the madmen in authority.

An even bigger political boost came at roughly the same time, from a subcommittee of the U.S. Senate Judiciary Committee that had jurisdiction over administrative practice and procedure. It was led by Senator Edward Kennedy (Democrat from Massachusetts), assisted by special counsel (and later Supreme Court justice) Stephen Breyer. Many lawyers consider administrative procedure to be the most boring part of law school, a three-year experience not known for its exciting subjects. At least constitutional and criminal law introduce you to Johnny Cochran and O. J. Simpson. In contrast, administrative procedure is about the rules that make for good government. It's sort of like the digestive system: We want it to work, and we're glad there are people who know how it works, but we all would rather not be bothered by the smelly details. Kennedy made the gastroenterology of government sexy.

The conservative Republican in the White House (Ford) and the liberal Democrat at the head of this subcommittee (Kennedy) were quite far apart politically, but in the airline industry they found common ground in criticizing the regulation of prices and limits on entering markets. The chair of the subcommittee on aviation in the Senate Commerce Committee, Senator Howard Cannon, who would later head the full committee, saw the obvious threat to his political turf and initiated his own hearings. But Kennedy's subcommittee was first out the gate, with hearings and reports that clearly showcased the silliness of the existing economic regulation of the airlines.

A powerful weapon in these public hearings was the use of real yet outrageous examples, and the committee exploited them to full effect. It showed that a traveller flying between Los Angeles and San Francisco, an intrastate market not regulated by the CAB, would pay half as much as a traveller flying between Washington and Boston, or flying between two cities that were roughly as far apart and, importantly, that were regulated by the CAB.

Reporters rationally avoid reading academic papers because they usually have little to say that interests their readers and because the useful gems are hard to parse from all the math and complicated language. Similarly, reports from government bureaucracies can be case studies in minutia. But the Kennedy committee made the lesson easy. A one-hour flight from Washington to Boston was not much different from a one-hour flight from Los Angeles to San Francisco, so it almost certainly shouldn't cost twice as much. Even a 100-word article in *USA Today* could make the point in ways an average consumer could understand. The press eagerly reported on the hearings, and the public started to understand.

It doesn't require a doctorate in economics to recognize that high prices are common in markets with little competition, and the committee showed just how little competition there was. In a report released in 1975, the committee observed with indignation that, over the previous twenty-five years (1950–1974), the CAB "had received 79 applications by companies who wanted to enter the domestic scheduled airline industry. Not one was granted!" Kennedy's committee would conclude that entry into the major markets was "effectively blocked" by the CAB.[32]

Reaching back to the legislation that established the CAB in 1938, the committee offered a helpful review of the congressional deliberations that preceded it. Kennedy's committee concluded that the congressional sponsors of the enabling legislation almost certainly had not intended to exclude entry in the airline industry. Clearly aware of the value of a good witness, it even drew on a little star power from a hearing in the 1930s, citing an exchange between a sponsor of the legislation, Senator McCarran, and the witness, Amelia Earhart. Dismissing the witness's concern that the CAB could deny a "pioneer" the right to serve two population centers, the senator replied:

"He could apply for a certificate of convenience and necessity . . ."

Miss Earhart: "Perhaps so. But you know that the mills of any legislative body grind exceedingly slow."[33]

Thus the aviation celebrity proved that she was not only an expert pilot but also an expert judge of the incentives inherent in government. Decades later, the Kennedy committee demonstrated that the CAB's consistent denials of applications to serve a market—in the form of "certificates of convenience and necessity"—likely were not consistent with the original intent of the law. In short, competition was slim as a result of the regulatory institution in place, and consumers were getting screwed.

In concluding its 1975 report, the Kennedy committee offered that commercial air travel could enjoy lower prices, that increased competition would likely help to lower prices, and that the CAB had not effectively promoted competitive conditions. In response to this heightened scrutiny, in 1975 the CAB conducted its own in-house analysis, with surprising results. The staff recommended elimination of price and entry regulation in this market. It would be a significant understatement to say that this was an unusual recommendation from an agency whose job it was to provide exactly this type of regulation. The CAB's staff economists and analysts were well aware of the academic research that had been going on for well over a decade. They understood the economics. The ideas had already won in this particular institution, the regulatory agency itself. All that remained to be overcome were some vested interests and a handful of madmen in authority.

In 1976, Jimmy Carter defeated Ford for the presidency, changing the party in the White House from Republican to Democratic. White House support for reforming airline regulation, however, remained strong. President Carter's new head of the CAB was to be Alfred Kahn, who was busy serving as chairman of the New York Public Service Commission. Previously, as an economics professor at Cornell, Kahn had authored the widely respected treatise *The Economics of Regulation*. Here was a highly regarded academic scribbler.

As an important public figure, Kahn had climbed down from the ivory tower and now was deeply enmeshed in political institutions. Still, he was not someone who had spent decades thinking about the airlines. In fact, early in his CAB tenure, Kahn was given a tour by airline executives and succeeded in exasperating his audience by proclaiming an inability to tell one plane from another. "To me," he sighed, "they're all marginal costs with wings."[34]

Indeed, Kahn's experience at the New York Public Service Commission had focused on regulation of the electricity and telecommunications industries, and he had hoped to be head of the Federal Communications Commission, not the Civil Aeronautics Board. Professor Ronald Coase, who had written about spectrum policy and who had so much intellectual firepower to offer the FCC, remained an academic all his life. Professor Kahn, who left academic life to regulate the telecommunications industry at the state level and who aspired to be its chief national regulator, was sent to regulate the airlines. Such is fate.

Early on, Kahn brought in new leaders to serve as division chiefs within his agency. One was Philip Bakes, a former staffer to Senator Kennedy who had helped orchestrate the highly effective hearings only a couple of years earlier. Another was Michael Levine, an attorney who in 1965 had written one of the first articles to examine intrastate airline competition, which had the unambiguous title, "Is Regulation Necessary?" Kahn's committed lieutenants were in place.

As described in Thomas K. McCraw's extensive biography, *Prophets of Regulation*,[35] the new chairman and his team had a unique opportunity. The momentum of the Kennedy hearings remained strong, and there was interest in some kind of reform. Yet the major airlines and their employee unions were deeply opposed to deregulation, and few in Congress were interested in reform via legislation. What was a deregulatory-minded regulator to do?

Kahn and his team had a number of options. They could take steps to allow competition in the area of prices or routes. They could allow entry by new competitors—not that any of this would be easy. Decades of legal precedent provided armies of attorneys with the fodder they needed to argue that countless administrative procedures must be followed. It seemed that slow going would be the order of the day.

Kahn pressed on. He complained to anyone who would listen about the regulatory details that were part of life for an overburdened regulator who, incidentally, was overburdened because of unnecessary rules and regulations. McCraw provides a compendium of Kahn quotations:

May a carrier introduce a special fare for skiers that refunds the cost of their ticket if there is no snow? May the employees of two financially [solvent] airlines wear similar-looking uniforms? . . . Is it any wonder that I ask myself every day: Is this action necessary? Is this what my mother raised me to do?[36]

There was plenty to do. Fortunately, the previous chairman of the CAB had left Kahn the perfect present on leaving the agency. Kahn came into office with an "experiment" in place that allowed discount fares for interstate travel. Southwest Airlines and Pacific Southwest Airlines already had intrastate bargains available in Texas and California, and now other airlines wanted in on the action. American Airlines, for example, proposed a "Super Saver" fare for off-peak travel between New York and California. For Kahn, the decision was easy. A formal investigation would not be necessary, and the experiment would proceed.

On the issue of entry, the new CAB would be just as deregulatory. When questions arose as to how the agency would address questions of possible new service between Midway Airport in Chicago and Oakland Airport in California, the answer was clear. The CAB would allow new entry. Further, it would not protect new entrants or any other carrier from competition by giving it exclusive rights to serve a particular market; in other words, no short-term (or not-so-short-term) monopoly privileges.

With exciting experiments taking place in the market and increased public awareness of the issue, Kahn saw that the idea of airline deregulation was tilting in his favor. A legislative fix was necessary, however; otherwise the economic benefits of deregulation likely would give way to rent seeking by vested interests. Unsurprisingly, Congress was resistant. Kahn was up against the major airlines, their employee unions, and politicians who found the current arrangement to work in their favor. These politicians of course included representatives with districts hosting the headquarters of American, Delta, Eastern, United, and the like. They also included a number of representatives from rural areas, who naturally worried that a deregulated market would mean fewer flights to small towns. (This likely outcome suggested a certain level of inconvenience for the business executives and pleasure travellers who lived in these areas, along with a huge level of inconvenience for the politicians who returned regularly to visit their constituents.)

At the same time, the opportunity for reform was ripe. Kahn had many allies, a mix that spanned the political spectrum, including representatives from the political right such as the American Conservative Union, representatives from the political left such as Common Cause, business interests such as the

National Association of Manufacturers and the National Federation of Independent Business and various consumer groups, including those affiliated with Ralph Nader. They made strange bedfellows, but they prevented easy dismissal of reform proponents as lackeys of the left, right, or any special interest.

The political pieces were in place, probably as well aligned as they ever would be, and it was time to sell the idea to Congress. The master communicator was up to the task.

Most academics are good at presenting complicated ideas to their peers. A few know how to communicate with broader audiences. Kahn excelled at both. He was smart, funny, congenial, and committed. As an academic, he could fill a college classroom and keep his students engaged. As a public intellectual at the head of a bureaucracy, he warranted interviews by major newspapers and magazines. Now he simply had to reach a different audience.

The master communicator pressed on. Kahn spoke with anyone interested in the issue—allies, opponents, the press, and many, many politicians. He made himself available to members of Congress and their staff, he took their calls, and he responded to their letters. He didn't mind repeating his carefully honed and reasoned arguments.[37]

After hearings by the Commerce Committee and the Judiciary Committee in the Senate, as well as their counterparts in the House of Representatives, with support from President Ford and then President Carter, and with the press reporting stories that informed the public on the inefficiencies of regulation, for more and more members of Congress it was becoming politically popular to support deregulation. Kahn built on this momentum with effective "experiments" that clearly demonstrated the benefits of price and entry deregulation, giving the term "Super Saver" real meaning in this market. Meanwhile, the Kennedy committee hearings from 1974 and 1975 were followed with the last great hurdle, hearings by the committees of jurisdiction for airline regulation, the Senate Commerce Committee and its counterpart in the House of Representatives. Congress then passed the Airline Deregulation Act of 1978, which arranged for the economic regulation of airlines to be phased out by 1982. The CAB itself was phased out two years later, officially closing January 1, 1985.

Welfare and Its Reform

To the average person, few policy issues are more clearly linked with the central lesson in economics—incentives matter—than welfare reform. Yet the specific shape of U.S. welfare policies and the incentives they foster are a result of the institutions that administer these policies and, even more so, of the ideas that the bureaucrats, politicians, and ultimately the public have about exactly what welfare policy should do.

An example is the 1996 welfare reform. At the end of the twentieth century, the average citizen held ideas about welfare that were fairly simple. These attitudes and beliefs built on ideas from previous efforts to address the plight of the poor in society, ideas that have gone on to become part of our political vocabulary today. The argument was that welfare was designed to be a hand up, not a handout. Yet the existing system had failed to achieve this. As Bill Clinton famously remarked in a campaign speech, it was time to "end welfare as we know it."

This idea—that the welfare system was broken for specific reasons and that it needed to be fixed in specific ways—would have a profound effect on social policy and, ultimately, on social outcomes. It would change institutions designed to help the poor, which in turn would change the incentives faced by the poor and those less fortunate. And these new incentives would change social outcomes.

But why were the existing social outcomes so bad? And if outcomes were so bad, why weren't the incentives changed sooner? What institutions allowed bad incentives to stay in place once it was clear they produced undesirable results?

The Nineteenth Century to the 1930s

In fact, welfare policy had taken many forms and had been debated and reformed well before the 1990s. In the nineteenth century, financial support for the poor most often came from private institutions—Catholic and Protestant social service agencies, the Salvation Army, trade associations, and mutual aid societies. But early in the twentieth century, policymakers began to take an interest as well. In 1909, President Theodore Roosevelt convened a conference on the needs of children, especially orphans and those with parents who were too poor to care for them. Over the next decade, "mothers' pensions" emerged in a number of cities and states, as the earliest government support for the poor came from nonfederal sources.[38]

By the 1930s, the country was in the middle of the Great Depression, an economic downturn such as it had never experienced before. The average person's faith in the market economy was deeply shaken. President Franklin Delano Roosevelt and Congress responded with the New Deal, the largest expansion of government in the history of the country.

Driven by economic desperation, ideas about the role of government in the economy changed dramatically in the 1930s, sowing seeds that quickly bore fruit in terms of government programs. Prior to this era, politicians were less inclined for the government to take actions that were not stipulated in the Constitution. For example, in 1887 President Grover Cleveland vetoed a bill to grant disaster aid to drought-stricken farmers because he did not see authority for such action in the Constitution.[39]

But in Depression-era America, desperate times called for new ideas and new solutions. Some of the most respected minds of the day—intellectuals and especially academic scribblers—were enlisted in the effort. As we saw in Chapter 3, John Maynard Keynes changed the terms of debate and provided intellectual support needed to expand the role of government in an effort to address serious economic distress. The Keynesian recommendation for government to spend to boost demand found a receptive audience among policymakers and among much of the public, not least the unemployed.

FDR was a particularly receptive audience for the Keynesian remedy and a particularly powerful policymaker. He successfully framed his new government programs and involvement in the economy, the New Deal, on the basis of rights. It was similar to earlier ideas about the role of government during the founding of the country but with a much broader definition of rights. Now there were new rights, which government was to protect. They are best illustrated by FDR's "Four Freedoms": freedom of speech and expression, freedom of religion, freedom from want, freedom from fear.

The first two rights were familiar, enshrined as they were in the First Amendment. The last two—freedom from want and fear—were different. For example, the right not to experience want, even when construed narrowly to mean freedom from deprivation, was not stipulated by the Constitution and clearly involved a more expansive role for the state. And the state expanded.

This sea change in ideas prompted an equally dramatic shift in institutions. The New Deal's most transformative example would be Social Security, one of the most expansive government social programs in the history of the country. Originally designed to provide a financial safety net for individuals in their later years, Social Security would become an institution in its own right. For decades, a politician who dared touch what was called the "third rail" in politics would get the same punishment as a person foolish or unlucky enough to touch the third rail on an electric train track—a quick and certain death.

While politically less important than aide to the unemployed or drought-stricken farmers, federal support for the poor nonetheless advanced during the New Deal. For example, included in the legislation establishing Social

Security was a program called Aid to Dependent Children, which later would become Aid to Families with Dependent Children.[40]

The 1960s

Fast forward three decades to another historic era for the United States, the era of civil rights and massive social reform in the 1960s. It was the biggest social reform since the New Deal, and President Lyndon Johnson called it the Great Society. Improving social welfare was part of the Great Society, which was to be accomplished through the War on Poverty.

The ideas that emerged in this decade and carried into the 1970s were so new and radical that the "sixties generation" still evokes memories—fondly by some, with disgust by others, but seldom with indifference by those who lived it. A generation of young singers and songwriters like Janice Joplin, John Lennon, and Neil Young took up protest against the Vietnam War, racial discrimination, and poverty. At the same time, philosophers and writers like Jack Kerouac and Tony Hendra made moving arguments for a society that could do better by its least fortunate.

One of the most prominent names responsible for social change during this era is the Reverend Martin Luther King Jr. He is the embodiment of leaders who helped change ideas, institutions, and even social outcomes. Less known, however, is that this civil rights leader who did so much to change ideas on race and equality also addressed poverty. King spoke of vast numbers of poor, often in forgotten places across the country. In Appalachia, for example, he pointed out that the poor were both black and white, and numerous. There were so many, in fact, that it was hard to dismiss their plight as simply due to bad luck or lack of effort. Some institutional failure had to be at least partly responsible. Something was wrong with the rules of the game. Some change in the current rules therefore was warranted.

Not only did ideas about racial discrimination start to change at this time, so too did ideas about whether and how all individuals could succeed in the U.S. economy. This dramatically changed the previous view of the average person, who had held that support should be tailored to the "deserving" poor. It was becoming harder to say someone was not deserving.

Despite the protests, sit-ins, love-ins, and the like, the average person in the street was not clamoring specifically for reform, or at least not as it related to policy towards the poor. The obvious discrimination was against blacks, especially in the South, which formed a blot on the country's self-image of a land of opportunity. This is what had to be eliminated. As a result, while civil rights enjoyed broad popular support, welfare reform was much less on the public's mind. Welfare reform mattered, but there was little time for the details.[41]

This meant the details of welfare reform were to be left to the experts. Years later, the scholar Charles Murray would observe exactly how this came about:

> The group is with no pejorative connotations best labeled the intelligentsia— a broad and diffuse group in late-twentieth-century America, but nonetheless identifiable in a rough fashion. It includes the upper echelons of (in no particular order of importance) academia, journalism, publishing, and the vast network of foundations, institutes and research centers that has been woven into partnerships with government during the last thirty years. An important and little-recognized part of the intelligentsia is also found in the civil service, in the key positions just below the presidential appointment level, where so much of the policy formation goes on . . . I do not mean to provide a tightly constructed definition, but a sense of the population: people who deal professionally in ideas.[42]

Murray's description is a simple telling of a complex process, highlighting especially the role of professionals who deal in ideas—Keynes's academic scribblers and Hayek's intellectuals.

Perhaps unique to a policy debate was the fact that the intellectuals themselves—or at least some of them—recognized how important they were in this process. As Senator Daniel Patrick Moynihan observed, welfare reform in the 1960s and 1970s "was from the first an affair of scholars and bureaucrats."[43] And Senator Moynihan was both. His thoughts on the importance and challenge of welfare would not have much influence until the next wave of welfare reform three decades later. But he first came on the intellectual and policy scene in 1965, with what became known as the Moynihan Report.[44]

The Moynihan Report provided shocking statistics to policymakers and the public. Families with no father present were on the rise, and these numbers were particularly striking in the black community. Moynihan's arguments are poignant and readily summarized by headings within the report: "Nearly One-Quarter of Negro Births Are Now Illegitimate"; "Almost One-Fourth of Negro Families Are Headed by Females"; "The Breakdown of the Negro Family Has Led to a Startling Increase in Welfare Dependency." These arguments were not well received, especially among Moynihan's peers in progressive and socially liberal circles. Ironically, Moynihan's arguments would gain even greater weight in the reform efforts three decades later, when the percentage of households headed by white females was higher than the 1960s-era rate for black females, and the 1990s-era rate for black females was higher still.

If welfare reform was an affair of scholars and bureaucrats, an even better example of someone who met both criteria was Mollie Orshansky. She developed the first poverty index in the United States, a measure that is still used today. The poverty index estimated the cost of an adequate diet, with food assumed to take up one-third of the income of the poor. Thus, the poverty rate was set to be three times the cost of an adequate diet, and any income below this level was an income for someone in poverty.[45] With this one statistic, real numbers could be used to represent real people, a powerful way of illustrating the poor among us.

Other intellectuals caught the public's attention in other ways. Michael Harrington's *The Other America* (1962) would sell over a million copies and have a lasting impact on ideas about poverty.[46] A similar portrait was painted by Kenneth Clarke's *Dark Ghetto* (1965), which was widely shared by those working to alleviate poverty.[47] The ideas were simple and powerful. The poor were like us but less fortunate. Welfare policy previously had distinguished between the aforementioned "deserving" poor—those who were willing to work but had experienced a bit of bad luck—from those who, with more effort on their part, could avoid poverty. The former were the focus of welfare policy, not the latter.

Harrington and Clarke argued forcefully that the environment in which the poor lived was not just unfortunate; it limited their economic opportunities and ultimately isolated them from the rest of society. The media picked up on this message as well, thus making it part of the national consciousness. It didn't matter if one hadn't read Harrington or Clarke. There were pictures of Martin Luther King touring Appalachia. And there were the numbers, developed by Orshansky and reported by the press, saying these were the faces not of social outliers, but of a large part of American society.

The experts got to work. Interestingly, considerable agreement was to be found for the simple idea that government should guarantee a minimum level of income. This was to be achieved through the tax code, in the form of a negative income tax. (With a negative income tax, people whose incomes fall below a certain threshold receive a check from the government on a sliding scale of their earnings, while people with incomes above that threshold pay taxes to the government, a tax payment.)

The two most prominent supporters were academic scribblers at opposite ends of the political spectrum—Milton Friedman and James Tobin. As we shall see with other reforms, a broad political coalition often is an extremely effective way to get change. But bipartisan intellectual support was not enough in this case. The idea of a negative income tax never caught on with the public. Nonetheless, President Richard Nixon, hardly a social liberal as was President Lyndon Johnson before him, would attempt welfare reform based on a framework that would include a guaranteed minimum income.

But as author David Ellwood summarized it in 1988: "The plan was never adopted. It was ultimately defeated by conservatives who wanted work to be a more central part of the aid and liberals who worried that the plan was still too punitive . . . Thus, contrary to popular belief, the great social planners did not get the policy they really wanted for their War on Poverty."[48]

The 1990s

Again fast-forward another three decades, this time to the mid-1990s. The 1996 Welfare Reform Act—one of the most far-reaching reforms of the welfare system—clearly was built on a foundation of ideas, many of which dated to the Moynihan Report. That study had prompted much soul searching, reflection, and analysis, all of which was reflected in works published in the 1980s and 1990s.

Depressing statistics appeared in books such as Nicholas Eberstadt's *Prosperous Paupers*, David Ellwood's *Poor Support*, and Charles Murray's *Losing Ground*. Most notably, government spending had increased dramatically since World War II, while social outcomes—in terms of the percentage of the population on welfare, for example—had grown worse. Eberstadt observes that, six decades after the New Deal, per capita income had increased by roughly a factor of four, chronic unemployment was eliminated, legalized segregation was abolished, and yet half of all African Americans were receiving some form of public assistance, which was double the rate expected by the New Deal policymakers.[49]

While working with similar facts, these authors differ in approach; Eberstadt tends to support more government intervention to improve welfare policy, while Murray is skeptical. Others make similar observations but speak more of the breakdown of the traditional roles. For example, George Gilder argues that the welfare state has removed men from their natural role as providers and undercut their relationships with their wives and, ultimately, their families.[50]

Whether one approached the issue from the political left or right, the increasingly common view among the intelligentsia was that the welfare system created incentives for both socially and individually destructive behavior. Specifically, under welfare policies in effect at the time, an unemployed male who fathered children had an incentive not to care for them, and the mother had an incentive not to have the father in the household.

This idea that welfare policies create perverse incentives increasingly became part of the attitudes and beliefs held by the public. And it became part of the public conversation.

Some attempts to fix these incentives had been attempted only a decade earlier. President Ronald Reagan had signed the Family Support Act of 1986, which restructured Aid to Families with Dependent Children. Under the new rules, one parent in a two-parent household would be required to work. For single-parent households, there would be education and employment opportunities. To help support the children of absent parents (usually fathers), child support payments would be automatically withheld from these parents' paychecks. But it was not enough, and the public sensed as much.

Suddenly, Daniel Patrick Moynihan's original thesis was fashionable in a way it had not been when it first emerged in the 1960s. But now he was Senator Moynihan and, notably, chairman of the Senate Committee on Health and Human Services, which meant he had great influence over welfare policy. His favored approaches, however, did not mesh perfectly with the then-occupant of the White House.

As already noted, the now-memorable call to "end welfare as we know it" had been made famous by then-Governor Bill Clinton, who opened his presidential campaign with an address that chose these words. The first two years of the administration of President Bill Clinton, however, focused on another big idea, health care. Senator Daniel Patrick Moynihan protested, arguing that there was not a real health care crisis in the United States, but there *was* a welfare crisis. His fellow Democrats in the White House and Congress, however, did not agree. A sweeping health care reform would be the issue de jure for the new Clinton administration, though no legislation would be enacted.

The 1994 elections brought a Republican majority to Congress, along with new priorities. Health care reform was out. Welfare reform, slowly, would be in. The early work of Moynihan was cited often by pundits and policymakers, as was the more recent work of other scholars, especially Charles Murray. Reform was coming.

The Republican-controlled Congress eventually sent President Clinton a welfare law, which was vetoed. Another was sent, only to be vetoed again. Finally, Clinton and the Congress found a mutually agreeable political solution.

Aid to Families with Dependent Children was eliminated. Federal support was to be distributed with a greater focus on block grants administered by the states. And time limits were established for recipient families. The new rules would create some very different incentives.

Critics of the new law, especially those on the left, were furious. Senator Moynihan passionately argued that many children would be hurt. The Urban Institute went further, arguing that millions of children would be condemned to poverty.

It didn't happen that way. Ten years after the welfare reform of 1996, the number of children living in poverty in the United States was greatly diminished, while the number of welfare recipients who had found work increased. Programs to alleviate poverty remained, in most cases administered at the state level. But welfare as we had known it really had come to an end. As compared to the experience with spectrum reform, the story of welfare reform does not really start with one or two academic scribblers. Popular beliefs changed in the 1930s, again in the 1960s, and once again in the 1990s. Influential intellectuals—from Martin Luther King and Daniel Patrick Moynihan to Charles Murray—helped lead this move. In fact, their role was pivotal, as the government institutions charged with providing welfare would not respond to obvious failures until political pressure forced them to do so. And public opinion, guided by these intellectuals, sooner or later was ready for it and in fact demanded exactly this sort of change.

The American Dream and the Housing Bubble

At 3:00 p.m. on Monday, October 13, 2008, Treasury Secretary Hank Paulson met with the CEOs of the nine largest financial institutions on Wall Street. The purpose was to inform them of the terms of the Troubled Asset Relief Program (TARP), approved by Congress only ten days earlier. The U.S. Treasury had received authorization to purchase up to $700 billion in distressed assets from these institutions to prevent a financial crisis.

The historic meeting and events leading up to it have been researched and documented in painstaking detail. Important histories include Bethany McLean and Joe Nocera's *All The Devils Are Here: The Hidden History of the Financial Crisis*; Andrew Ross Sorkin's best seller, *Too Big to Fail: The Inside Story of How Wall Street and Washington Fought to Save the Financial System—and Themselves*; and John Taylor's *Getting Off Track: How Government Actions and Interventions Caused, Prolonged, and Worsened the Financial Crisis*.[51] Countless other economists and financial experts provide even more material.[52]

For political observers on both the left and right, and for average citizens of any political persuasion, the Paulson meeting was seen by many as the beginning of the bank bailouts. Yet the discussion had an important twist. The CEOs were told that they *would* accept the money. The idea was to bring everyone together, the nearly bankrupt and the merely weak, and project an air of strength in the financial system. As treasury secretary to President George W. Bush, Paulson made the point forcefully. He was supported by Timothy Geitner, who attended the meeting in his role as president of the Federal Reserve Bank of New York and who later would become treasury secretary to President Barack Obama.[53]

The bipartisan nature of this "bailout"—Paulson hated the term—was not limited to the executive branch of the U.S. government. Congress had established the TARP program as part of the Emergency Economic Stabilization Act of 2008, legislation with a goal clearly indicated by its name. Both Washington and Wall Street wanted to prevent the failure of key financial institutions, which could lead to economic crisis. Behind the failure or near failure of banks and brokerages were assets held on Main Street—homes and the mortgages that financed them.

How could mortgages cause such a mess? Isn't home ownership part of the American dream? And haven't mortgages been used successfully for decades to facilitate home ownership?

The idea that home ownership is part of the American dream has been embedded in the culture since at least the 1930s. This idea or belief or attitude may have multiple sources, from the early experiences of settlers and pioneers, to the independent spirit that remains in American thought and politics, to a simple desire for financial security. It grew in popularity following World War II, the rise of the middle class, and the growth of suburbs. In contrast to the influence of ideas on improved spectrum policy, welfare reform, or airline deregulation, it is unlikely that a single great mind or group of intellectuals planted this seed in the American consciousness.

In response to this bottom-up demand for the American dream, and at times in an attempt to build on it for political or economic gain, politicians spent the better part of the last century trying to facilitate home ownership. Various institutions emerged, prompted by both political and market forces. Indeed, it is hard to separate these two influences, as they are intimately linked.

The cast of characters among these institutions, and those affected by them, is long. They are star players in the biggest financial crisis since the Great Depression, and they include Congress, the White House, the Federal Housing Administration, Fannie Mae and Freddie Mac, the Federal Reserve, other federal agencies, independent financial ratings agencies, banks, and mortgage brokers—and, just as importantly, the homebuyers themselves. Everyone responded rationally to the incentives before them. In short, the rules that guided homeownership changed over time, which in turn changed the incentives of these actors. And bad things happened.

Key Players and the Incentives They Created, or Responded to

The exact causes of this crisis remain an issue of debate. Even the ten members of the Financial Crisis Inquiry Commission, established to investigate the causes of this event, could not agree. Four of the ten dissented on the final report.[54] Still, the average American knows that the financial crisis of 2008 had something to do with mortgages gone bad. Some people bought homes when they could barely afford the monthly mortgage payments or with conditions that established low "teaser" rates for two years and then reset the monthly payments at unaffordable levels. While risky, these were rational decisions for anyone who believed that real estate prices were rising and the house could soon be sold at a profit. Other people bought at the top of the market, then watched in horror as the price of their home fell below the amount they owed, the dreaded status known as being "underwater" that also provided an incentive for borrowers to walk away from their homes. Not only did homeowners lose; investors holding these mortgages lost billions as well.

These undesirable outcomes came from many sources. If success has many fathers and failure is an orphan, the orphan nonetheless has a paternity and, in this case, a complicated one. Its lineage traces at least to the 1930s, the last major economic crisis in the country.

The Great Depression had seen a housing crisis of its own, with banks unwilling to lend or extend loans for homes. In response, the Federal Housing Administration was created in 1934, primarily to insure loans for mortgages and thus give lenders an incentive to offer home loans. To prevent moral hazard—that is, to give the borrower an incentive to fulfill the terms of the mortgage when failure to do so would be covered by the insurance—the FHA sets a minimum down payment and other requirements. For approximately the first six decades of its history, the agency maintained conservative rules, for example, requiring at least a 10 percent down payment. Only home loans issued by commercial banks were insured, while loans from other institutions such as investment banks and mortgage brokers were not protected.

Another product of the 1930s is the Federal National Mortgage Association, better known as Fannie Mae. Congress established Fannie Mae in 1938 to purchase mortgages from banks. In 1968, Fannie was split in two. One half became the Government National Mortgage Association, or Ginne Mae, which focused on loans backed by the FHA and the Veterans Administration and which enjoyed the full backing of the U.S. government. The other half remained Fannie Mae, which became a publicly held corporation—a term with little meaning outside of Washington, but that allows the government to keep the entity's profits and losses off its books. In 1970, Fannie Mae was authorized to invest in mortgages that were not backed by the U.S. government. That is, banks could now issue "conventional" mortgages that were not insured by the FHA or VA, then sell these loans to Fannie. That same year, Congress decided to foster competition in the secondary mortgage market by creating a competitor to Fannie Mae, the Federal Home Loan Mortgage Corporation, or Freddie Mac. These institutions also are referred to as Government Sponsored Entities (GSEs).

Fannie and Freddie provide liquidity for lenders in the mortgage market by purchasing their mortgages. By selling their mortgage loans to the GSEs, banks and other mortgage issuers acquire the funds needed to provide more loans to other homebuyers. At the same time, Fannie and Freddie need liquidity, too. To achieve it, the mortgages they purchase are bundled and sold as mortgage-backed securities (MBSs). The interest payments by homeowners with mortgages provide a stream of income to the holders of these securities.

Interestingly, while "securitized" mortgages ultimately would provide the vehicle for so much of the financial crisis, these special entities, created by Congress, were the leaders in this important innovation that greatly facilitated mortgage lending and put more people in their own homes. Ginnie Mae first securitized loans in 1970, and Fannie Mae followed only one year later.

That same decade, Congress passed the Community Reinvestment Act (CRA) as part of a larger piece of legislation, the Housing and Community Development Act of 1977. Depending on one's political leanings, the evolution of the CRA over the subsequent three decades is either largely responsible for or entirely irrelevant to the 2008 crisis. It is certainly true that the higher-risk loans that were promoted in response to the CRA and other influences did not make up a majority of the loans issued. It also is true that rules adopted as part of the CRA helped shape the regulatory environment in which both banks and borrowers had to operate.

In its original charter, the CRA required "each appropriate Federal financial supervisory agency to use its authority when examining financial institutions, to encourage such institutions to help meet the credit needs of the local communities in which they are chartered consistent with the safe and sound operation of such institutions."[55] Over time, this "encouragement" would become rather forceful. Legislation passed in 1991 and 1992, signed by President George H. W. Bush, added new rules, such as the requirement that financial regulators score the institutions they examine on the criteria of meeting the needs of the communities they served, including low-income and disadvantaged borrowers. Legislation passed in 1994, advocated and then signed by President Bill Clinton, added another wrinkle. In evaluating mergers or expansions by interstate banks, regulators would now have to consider the CRA ratings of these institutions. Advocates for the poor and other community organizations now had a powerful tool with which to pressure banks to increase lending to marginal borrowers. Many banks had a strong appetite for expanded operations and little interest in a political fight, which meant that increased loans of higher risk were simply a cost of doing business.

Both President Clinton and his successor, President George W. Bush, went well beyond the CRA to promote home ownership. In 1994, Clinton launched the National Home Ownership Strategy. In a speech, Clinton observed that four decades of increasing home ownership had been reversed in the 1980s, presumably due to the policies of his opponents, and he argued that these policies hurt 1.5 million families who otherwise would be in their own homes.[56] Clinton's plan aimed to increase home ownership by eight million families in six years. It would find "creative" ways for public and private institutions to lower costs for would-be homeowners, especially those with limited means who lacked sufficient cash to make a down payment.

Less than a decade later, in 2002, President Bush launched his Blueprint for the American Dream. The goal was remarkably familiar, as were the policy prescriptions. This time, the focus was on adding an additional 5.5 million homebuyers, especially minorities. Among the ideas put forth in the Bush plan were expanding options and creating new opportunities for homebuyers to overcome the hurdles faced by high down payments and closing costs.[57] It was another call for creativity. For good measure, in some speeches Bush added that homeownership was good for a *secure* America, nicely tying financial policy with national security policy.

While the creative policies were many, two in particular stand out. The first, which went hand in glove with the CRA, was an effort to increase the number of loans to people considered to be higher-risk borrowers, perhaps due to their credit history. Known as subprime loans, they would become the face of the crisis. The second was the effort to lower the required down payment, that bane of homebuyers everywhere. At the start of the new century, half of all new mortgages in the United States began with a down payment of 10 percent or less. The FHA would eventually insure loans with only a 3.5 percent down payment. At the peak of the market, before the crisis, private options existed for purchase with no down payment, and FHA-backed loans became a small portion of all mortgages. These riskier loans, which were carried on the books of many financial institutions for reasons explained in the following paragraphs, would contribute to a trend of rising national homeownership rates and eventually would contribute to a crisis.

The interest in home ownership under the Clinton and then the Bush administrations was a rational effort by madmen in authority to give the people what they wanted, or what they thought they wanted. It also fit perfectly with the mission of Fannie and Freddie, which were becoming increasingly important in both financial and political markets. In the years leading up to the crisis, Fannie would grow to become the third-largest corporation in the country, with significant advertising in Washington and beyond, as well as one of the largest charitable foundations. Its political prowess was even more impressive. In 1992, the same year Clinton won the White House, a new leader took charge at Fannie Mae. Jim Johnson was a seasoned political operative. As McLean and Nocera describe it, Johnson's experience was hard to match: manager of Walter Mondale's 1984 presidential bid; co-founder of Public Strategies, a public relations and lobbying firm; chairman of the Brookings Institution, a respected left-of-center think tank; head of the Kennedy Center for Performing Arts, the leading arts organization in the nation's capital; and once referred to as "chairman of the universe" by the *Washington Post*.[58] In other words, he was expert in all things political and thus perfect for the job.

To a great extent, Fannie and Freddie's interests aligned with those of politicians, both in the White House and in Congress. Everyone understood that the GSEs made more loans possible by buying and bundling mortgages. Most everyone also understood that this benefit came at a cost. For example, Fannie and Freddie received an implicit subsidy, as they borrowed money at lower rates because the market viewed their securities as guaranteed by the federal government, even if this guarantee was implicit and not in writing. In 2004, the Congressional Budget Office estimated that the previous year's subsidy to these entities was $23 billion, and it further noted that borrowers received less than two-thirds of this subsidy in the form of lower rates, while Fannie and Freddie retained one-third in the form of higher earnings.[59] A study published by the Federal Reserve in 2003 had concluded much the same, arguing that a significant portion of the GSE's subsidy was not passed on to borrowers.[60] Fannie and Freddie would reply by arguing they were "private tax-paying corporations that operate at no cost to taxpayers" and, of course, that they promoted home ownership. This tie to the attitudes and beliefs of the masses—the American dream—gave the GSEs significant political power in resisting any proposed change to the rules of the game.

Most politicians saw little to gain from a critical review of the GSEs. Those who ventured into this territory were labeled "antihousing" and met with the full force of Fannie and Freddie. The GSEs were not everyday petitioners before Congress, and they were always heard. Not only were their CEOs politically powerful, they also employed an army of lobbyists. As an example of their effectiveness, any hearing or critical meeting that involved members of Congress often included what came to be known as the Fannie Pack: a folder with a list of all the constituents holding GSE-backed loans in a member's congressional district.

As a number of experts have observed, Fannie and Freddie did not use political muscle to get permission to enter the subprime market. In fact, they were slow to buy subprime mortgages, and they likely did so simply to maintain their massive book of business and the profits that came with it. Yet the GSEs did succeed in protecting their implicit subsidy and in fighting off efforts to raise their capital requirements. A number of highly placed people favored higher reserves for the GSEs, from Clinton's treasury secretary, Larry Summers, to the head of the Committee on Financial Services in the House of Representatives, Richard Baker. They would fail. Still, these efforts were prescient. The Financial Crisis Inquiry Commission would report, far too late, that Fannie and Freddie had an average leverage of 75 to 1, which meant that for every $75 in mortgage debt only $1 in capital was held to back it up in case of an emergency. This ratio was substantially higher than the 40 to 1 ratio held by the big financial institutions on Wall Street, which also would prove to be a disastrous degree of leverage.

But the government's influence on the housing market over the last three or so decades is not limited solely to the Executive Branch, the Congress, and its creation, the GSEs. The Federal Reserve plays a key role here as well, both as a regulator of financial institutions and as the central bank in charge of monetary policy.

In an important sense, monetary policy improved during the decades of the 1980s and 1990s, with fewer swings in interest rates and a more systematic response to inflation. Yet, as a number of economists have observed, this changed at the beginning of the new century. For the first half-decade, roughly from 2001 to 2006, the Federal Reserve pursued a highly expansionary monetary policy. The federal funds rate was lowered from 6.5 percent to 1.25 percent. This key rate then was kept so low that for over two years it did not even match the rate of inflation. That is, for banks, the cost of borrowing was less than the cost of inflation, which made taking on debt a very rational decision. Banks acquired the funds and loaned them out. According to Professor John Taylor, a leading expert on monetary policy and originator of the Taylor Rule (which recommends interest rate adjustments by central banks in response to macroeconomic changes), these low interest rates had a strongly positive effect on housing starts.[61]

Alan Greenspan, the Federal Reserve chairman from 1987 to 2006, was the star player here. It is hard to overstate the credibility he enjoyed during most of this period. The Federal Reserve's response to the stock market dive in 1987 earned Greenspan praise on Wall Street and in Washington. Following the demise of the technology bubble in 2001, the Federal Reserve could be seen as just another rational actor trying to make the world a better place by providing a monetary stimulus, even if a drop from 6.5 percent to 1.25 percent is rather large. But the effect was not benign. It seldom is.

Significantly lowering the federal funds rate was not simply a stimulus, it was artificially lowering the rate borrowers would have to pay for access to funds. In a free market, the interest rate reflects the time preferences of individuals. When many people postpone consumption now to have more resources in the future, this increase in savings pushes interest rates lower and encourages capital investments—in factories, farms, even homes. This is the same story we saw in Chapter 5 with Hayek's capital theory. An artificially low interest rate provides a false signal to invest in more roundabout production because there is no real savings behind it and no real demand for the good that this capital will produce. The amount of capital investment far exceeds the true demand. After 2008, empty neighborhoods in Las Vegas, southern Florida, and other distressed markets would provide a clear example.

But the story does not end here. Apart from many government institutions, a number of private institutions also helped facilitate the financial crisis. Among these players, the ratings agencies had a starring role. They are easy to follow because there are only three of them: Fitch Ratings, Moody's, and Standard and Poor's. These private firms supposedly competed among themselves to provide financial institutions with the information they needed to evaluate the mortgage-backed securities. In practice, however, they more often competed for the fees that were earned from evaluating these securities. The financial institutions that paid these fees wanted securities that paid high returns and provided little risk, that nirvana state sought by investors everywhere.

Why were ratings so important? In short, mortgage-backed securities with the highest rating, AAA, required banks to hold less capital as compared to lower-rated securities. The pressure was on for Fitch, Moody's, and Standard and Poor's to provide increasingly high ratings, even for subprime loans. These three firms did not have to worry about alternative evaluations—either positive or negative—by other ratings agencies, because the Securities and Exchange Commission had decreed in 1975 that the ratings of these agencies, and only these agencies, would conform to various federal regulatory guidelines. The big three faced no other competitors for their services and thus had a strong incentive to provide unrealistically high ratings, which they did.

For their part, major players on Wall Street, from commercial banks to investment banks, had every incentive to keep the party going, too. While these entities clearly were motivated by greed, this very human condition was not new to Wall Street, Main Street, or any other venue. Rather, far too many financial institutions simply relied on the ratings agencies, without further due diligence about what they were buying. Profits came from having highly leveraged balance sheets because highly rated securities meant more could be acquired with less capital.

Indeed, capital requirements are too often overlooked in this story, even though they play a key role in determining profitability for financial institutions. The rules are international in reach, part of the Basel Committee on Banking Supervision, which first gathered in 1974 but did not adopt its first set of rules, known as Basel I, until 1992. In theory, these capital requirements for banks were designed to reflect risk, much as capital requirements for banks always had done. But things were changing rapidly in the world of finance. While previous rules had required the same amount of capital for any asset a bank held—for example, 8 percent, or $8 of capital for every $100 a bank held in loans or other assets—financial innovations in the 1990s and beyond meant that there was huge variation in the types of assets that might be held.

When it came to mortgage-backed securities, the Basel I rules changed the game entirely. The capital requirements for a mortgage-backed security not insured by Fannie or Freddie were set at one-half the capital needed for a commercial loan. A mortgage-backed security that was insured by Fannie or Freddie needed only one-fifth the capital required for a commercial loan. A simple rule change provided huge incentives, and banks responded accordingly, taking on more and more securities tied to mortgages. Taking the game even further, banks looked for additional investment vehicles that could operate with still lower capital requirements. Thus was born the idea to issue insurance that protected the security holder against default, which allowed the bank to operate with lower capital, at least once the Federal Reserve approved. The insurance product was called a credit default swap.

While Washington was busy looking for ways to increase home ownership, and Wall Street was hungry for high-paying securities that did not require a correspondingly high capital base, a number of nonbank mortgage originators stood ready to help. They needed no greater incentive than the higher fees associated with subprime loans. Indeed, these loans provided more opportunities for the broker to profit from upfront fees and for the holder of the mortgage-backed security to profit from the higher rate of interest that went with it.

Leading these brokers were companies that eventually would become household names, names on a football stadium or names across players' jerseys. They included Ameriquest, Countrywide, and Washington Mutual. These companies started small but grew quickly as they provided the most "creative" financing, some of which genuinely helped people get in homes, some of which set up borrowers for failure, but all of which increased their market share.

In the early days, prior to securitization, these nonbank mortgage issuers had to borrow from Wall Street, use these funds to make loans for homes, then attempt to sell the mortgages to raise more funds for more loans. It was a tough business. Fannie and Freddie bought only loans that were insured by the FHA or the VA. All this changed in 1989 when Congress granted Fannie and Freddie authorization to buy conventional mortgages, that is, those without FHA or VA backing. The nonbank issuers went from just under 20 percent of the market to over 50 percent of the market in four years. But it was still the mid-1990s, and calamity was far off.

Much like the ratings agencies, the mortgage originators had every incentive to compete, but along all the wrong margins. As McLean and Nocera describe it, front-line employees seldom faced disciplinary action for egregious behavior, and stories of "revised" income statements were not uncommon. And while the cost of fraudulent behavior appeared low to these brokers, the benefits were just the opposite. Those who produced were handsomely rewarded. The anecdotes abound, with college-age mortgage brokers earning six-figure salaries, huge bonuses going to those who closed the most mortgages, and the parties, always the outlandish parties. As P. J. O'Rourke once remarked, giving money and power to politicians is like giving whiskey and car keys to teenage boys. The policies and practices leading up to the 2008 crisis did both. Perhaps the only group that could rival politicians in responding to the incentives of money and power would be mortgage brokers not far from their teenage years.

Failure and the Framework of Ideas, Institutions and Incentives

The financial crisis of 2008 was remarkable for the large number of institutions that created bad incentives and the predictably bad outcomes that followed. But unlike the examples of reform in spectrum policy, airlines and welfare, at the end of the day, there was no academic scribbler, no one with a big idea about how to increase homeownership the way Ronald Coase spoke about spectrum reform. There was no critical mass of intellectuals arguing that important institutions were failing the least fortunate in society and that specific policies should be directed to get people in homes, the way Daniel Patrick Moynihan or Charles Murray argued that specific policies needed to be advanced to deal with welfare. There was, instead, significant interest in homeownership among millions of average Americans.

And Washington responded. With a web of artificial incentives forged in political deals that made sense to the parties exchanging but wrought havoc as markets eventually saw these policies to their logical conclusions. Their message found great purchase in the collective beliefs and ideas of a modernizing America. Because there was a general belief that homeownership was a good thing, politicians found the public with open arms to these creative solutions. Everybody was winning—except Alfred Marshall, whose supply and demand curves were difficult to see through the haze of excitement at the time, and except Friedrich Hayek, whose competition as a discovery procedure was befuddled by the many creative ways that market prices were distorted from carrying information about true cost and value. In short, once politicians started getting credit for homeownership rates, the housing market was doomed.

7

What Is to Be Done?

Assembling the Wisdom

The philosophers have only interpreted the world, in various
ways. The point, however, is to change it.
—Karl Marx, *Theses on Feuerbach* (1845)[1]

Ideas and the Human Condition

In the 1960s, farmers in India and Pakistan produced far too little grain to feed their people, and experts predicted mass starvation. It didn't happen. Instead, a humble plant pathologist named Norman Borlaug (1914–2009) came up with a bold innovation: high-yield, disease-resistant wheat. Away in far-off Mexico, a country that imported a significant portion of the grain it consumed, Borlaug toiled and perfected his innovation—a hybrid wheat with a shorter stalk that could bear the weight of more grain. It would eventually produce soaring yields in India and Pakistan, turn Mexico into a grain exporter, and launch a "green revolution" that over four decades would double the world's wheat production.[2] Awarded the Nobel Peace Prize in 1970, Borlaug made contributions that saved perhaps a billion people from starvation.

Norman Borlaug's story seems too good to be true, a great idea that directly improves the human condition, without the messy details. What interests would stand in the way of feeding hungry people? Yet Borlaug faced many obstacles. Environmentalists wanted his hybrid plant to be banned.

Bureaucrats in India's agriculture office responded with skepticism. Customs officials in India were loath to let unknown seeds into their country. Even U.S. politics complicated the picture, as riots in Los Angeles threatened the timely shipment of seeds.

Borlaug pushed back, lobbying politicians and peasants alike. At first, just a few Indian farmers and a prominent bureaucrat planted his seeds. But, after finding those initial loose spots, the higher yields of these pilot projects caught the attention of other farmers. Soon, there was a mass cry for the new seeds, and the rules of the game changed.

While we started this book with Danny Biasone saving basketball, we end it with Norman Borlaug saving a billion lives. These stories are not that different. Both faced vested interests, which were reinforced by popular beliefs that things should be a certain way—that is, until a better idea came along.

In this closing chapter, we assemble the lessons learned and use our framework to review the elements that combine to create political change. We illustrate how people see and seize opportunities to effectuate this type of change, whether at the level of ideas, institutions, or incentives. Sometimes it takes the courage of a Mart Laar walking on water. Sometimes it takes the alertness of Alfred Kahn and Teddy Kennedy. And usually in the mix there is an academic scribbler, a Ronald Coase or a Paul Samuelson, patiently sowing the intellectual seeds of a revolution to come.

As we have described it in this book, political change generally involves key players and inputs. Ideas are conceived by the brilliant (and not-so-brilliant) minds of Keynes's academic scribblers, from Aristotle and Aquinas, Machiavelli and Marx, and Hayek to Keynes himself. These innovative ideas then circulate in society, where they face off with vested interests and long-held beliefs in an attempt to change the institutional rules of the game that shape people's incentives. These incentives, in turn, have a direct impact on outcomes in society. It is through these channels that ideas have consequences.

The process can be revolutionary, creating new institutions through a crisis, such as a war or a revolution. Lenin and the Bolsheviks come to mind; so do the American Founders. At other times, this process can be evolutionary, not born out of a crisis but emerging as part of a nonviolent battle of ideas.

Indeed, in more open societies, ideas compete with each other, and in such an environment political change has a better chance of creating beneficial rather than destructive results. In contrast, if intellectuals face little competition, they can more easily align behind a single and perhaps misguided worldview, exactly the problem that prompted Hayek to pen his 1949 essay,

"The Intellectuals and Socialism." But, as Chapter 5 showed, with dozens of communications platforms, thousands of think tanks, and hundreds of thousands or even millions of websites that have emerged over the past few decades, the modern marketplace of ideas has become more competitive and therefore less aligned behind a single ideology. Perhaps more than ever, ideas have tremendous power to change the world, but it is harder for any one idea to dominate modern public discourse.

In addition, democratic societies are reasonably good at giving people what they want. And over long intervals in U.S. history we see vastly different attitudes toward government and what people want from it. As mentioned in Chapter 6, President Grover Cleveland refused to sign a $10,000 relief package for drought-stricken farmers because he said the action was not justified in the U.S. Constitution.[3] But over a century later, public opinion had evolved, and by the time hurricanes Andrew (1992) and Katrina (2005) had worked their destruction, federal disaster aid had become another third rail in politics, threatening political death to any president who would take the position President Cleveland took more than a century ago. Shifting attitudes, beliefs, and ideas explain much of why governments today look very different from governments of past centuries, even the past few decades.

This entire process of political change—where ideas influence institutions, which shape incentives, which in turn ultimately drive outcomes—appears to be inherently top down in both its revolutionary and evolutionary forms. As Keynes conjectures, madmen in authority, whether they realize it or not, usually get their big ideas from academic scribblers. But, as we've shown, the process also is bottom up. People tend to have ideas that conform to their endowments and their environments—both their nature and their nurture. Not every idea originates in the ivory tower of academic scribblers. Sometimes enough people have an idea about a shared experience that an academic scribbler notices this experience, sees the idea, and gives it voice.

Whether an idea bubbles up from the masses on the street to a scribbler in an ivory tower or instead is conceived by an academic, political change requires scribblers and intellectuals to connect with enough of the masses to gain a following. In short, as J. S. Mill reminds us in Chapter 5, ideas are powerful only when they combine with specific circumstances. Marx certainly found followers, and his success had much to do with the circumstances that surrounded him. The ideas of Marx found fertile ground in the struggling, newly industrialized society of nineteenth-century England. Would they have been as favorably received in the context of agrarian South

Asia or colonial America of that time? Evidently not, or at least, not until much later. And that's because societal and historical context matters. Political change does not occur in a vacuum. It happens in the hubbub of human affairs; it grapples with the forces of inertia that define a particular status quo.

By definition, the status quo is all around us, and inertia is tremendously powerful. When it does happen, when the right elements come together at the right time and place and overwhelm the status quo, it is because special people make it happen. We call them political entrepreneurs.

Political Entrepreneurship in Theory and Practice

There's nothing more powerful than an idea whose time has come.
—Victor Hugo, *The History of a Crime* (1877)[4]

At the start of the twentieth century, African Americans were denied the right to vote in many places in the United States, were welcome in few institutions of higher learning, and were rarely found in the professions or in corporate management. Prominent leaders such as Booker T. Washington and W. E. B. Du Bois struggled against this reality with arguments that would, over the course of many decades, work their way into mainstream opinion. The arguments of these intellectuals built on the everyday achievements of lesser-known African Americans. These included the many who studied at "negro colleges" or went to more mainstream universities, others who became professionals despite the obstacles, and those who made contributions in the arts and sciences and in the military. By the 1960s, after decades during which black and white Americans slowly witnessed these events unfolding before their eyes, the words of Martin Luther King finally found fertile ground.

As we have seen throughout this book, the public face of political change may be that of a madman, an intellectual, or an academic scribbler. But whatever form these leaders may take, they are political entrepreneurs—people whose ideas and actions are focused on producing change. Such change may come quickly or through many further relays, but it always focuses on an improvement in the ideas, institutions, and incentives that guide human behavior within a society.

Martin Luther King was a political entrepreneur. While his idea was not original—King built on a long tradition of thinkers who had argued for individual rights for all—it was an idea whose time had come. Thus, we would not call King an academic scribbler, a label that better fits someone like Karl Marx. Rather, we would call King an intellectual in the sense described by Hayek, someone whose vision, sense of timing, and extraordinary communication skills sold an important message to the masses.

The lines are often blurred as to whether a political entrepreneur is a madman, intellectual, or academic scribbler. For example, we have seen that Charles Murray and a few other intellectuals provided the books and essays and arguments that so clearly laid out the problems with the U.S. welfare system prior to its reform in 1996. And as a savvy politician—one of the madmen in authority—Bill Clinton saw the opportunity to make welfare reform a winning issue as popular beliefs had moved in this direction. Interestingly, Daniel Patrick Moynihan played important roles as both an academic scribbler in the 1960s and one of the more important madmen in the 1990s.

Similarly, Alfred Kahn left a university position to lead regulatory agencies, where one of his most important roles was to explain to politicians why certain regulations, especially those related to the airlines, needed to be reformed. His approach was innovative and effective. It was entrepreneurial. And so was Teddy Kennedy's. He saw an opportunity to make a mark for himself as a young senator, and he wound up closing a federal agency.

What, exactly, do these political entrepreneurs have in common? How do they promote change, especially when current institutions are generating wasteful and unjust outcomes? The political entrepreneur looks for opportunities in the nexus of ideas, institutions, and incentives to create change. The political entrepreneur looks for an idea whose time has come.

Entrepreneurship in Politics and Entrepreneurship in Markets

To many people, the role of an entrepreneur is a mystery. And too often, those who think they understand the term believe an entrepreneur is someone who runs a business. But this perspective confuses entrepreneurship with management, the skill of directing how defined sets of resources are used to produce specific goods or services. Entrepreneurship is also frequently confused with bearing risk, a specialized activity (called insurance) that only captures a slice of what entrepreneurs do.

An economist who spent a lifetime studying entrepreneurship, Israel Kirzner (born 1930) describes the entrepreneurial process as a phenomenon that goes beyond the neoclassical notion of rational, maximizing behavior that we saw in Chapter 3. He recognizes that human behavior entails choosing one's ends among an endless variety of options, applying the most effective means to achieve these objectives, and constantly reevaluating both ends and means under changing circumstances, evolving personal preferences, and the dynamics of life in general.

Kirzner argues that an entrepreneur is someone who is *alert* to new ways to create value for others and thereby earn profit for him- or herself. Market prices convey information about profit opportunities. The alert entrepreneur compares prices in different markets to reveal where resources are under-utilized or undervalued and by how much. The entrepreneur responds by buying resources at a relatively low price and combining them in a way that creates more value. This process could be as simple as transporting lobsters from Maine to Minnesota or as complex as turning sand into silicon chips.

To the casual observer, an entrepreneur's alertness to and success with opportunities for value creation might be ascribed to luck, but this attribution is misleading. While luck plays a role, as the entrepreneur must be in the right place at the right time, this alone will not guarantee success. Indeed, oftentimes, other people are in this magical time and place as well. Yet it is the entrepreneur who recognizes the opportunity, who visualizes what could be, and who acts on this very local knowledge. Similarly, the political entrepreneur has a vision and willingness to act, whether it is Marx seeing an opportunity to speak to social conditions in nineteenth-century England or King noticing that the time was right for his ideas in the United States of the 1960s. In this sense, luck and local knowledge are necessary but not sufficient conditions. The additional elements, the vision and decisiveness, are precisely what the entrepreneur provides, both in the market and in politics.

The opportunity to earn a profit is a powerful incentive to seek more and better ways to create value. In this sense, Kirzner says that competition *is* entrepreneurship. The two are inseparable, and they make markets work. While entrepreneurs engage in competition to make profits as they better meet consumers' needs, they improve resource allocation along the way. They help better match supply and demand, and thus equilibrate markets. In the same way, political entrepreneurs supply the combination of ideas and institutional reforms that are right for the circumstances at a particular moment.

A complementary view of entrepreneurship is offered by the economist Joseph Schumpeter (1883–1950). In one sense, Schumpeter's entrepreneur is not that different from Kirzner's, because both are alert to opportunities. On the other hand, Schumpeter argues that competition is *not* about reaching equilibrium as taught in most economic textbooks and reinforced by Kirzner's entrepreneur. Rather, Schumpeter emphasizes:

> . . . competition from the new commodity, the new technology, the new source of supply, the new type of organization . . . competition which commands a decisive cost or quality advantage and which strikes not at the margins of the profits and the outputs of the existing firms but at their foundations and their very lives.[5]

In the Schumpeterian vision, the entrepreneur is someone who disequilibrates, who disrupts, who destroys. These are not concepts we normally associate with value creation, but on net that's ultimately what happens. In the seeds of destruction something new and more valuable emerges. Schumpeter calls this process "creative destruction."

Creative destruction implies that old models are cast aside in favor of new models that provide benefits unimaginable a generation earlier. The telegraph is destroyed by the telephone; the carriage is destroyed by the car; the album record is destroyed by digital music. In politics, rigid regulation of airline prices and routes is replaced by deregulation, and welfare services go from minimal to expansive and back to minimal in less than a century. What comes next is anybody's guess. Or to be more precise, it is the guess of entrepreneurs, whose imagination and alertness to opportunity destroy today's business models and replace them with others that create even more value for consumers—and maybe for voters, too. In short, entrepreneurship is what gives life to a market economy. It plays just as important a role in political change.

Like entrepreneurs in markets, political entrepreneurs also must decide where to invest time, talent, and treasure to effectuate the kind of political change they believe will create the most value. Both economic and political entrepreneurs can create value through peaceful, cooperative behavior. A key difference is that political entrepreneurship can be used to enrich oneself at the expense of others in an entirely legal yet socially destructive manner. This harmful behavior within the political process we earlier described as "unproductive entrepreneurship" or, more simply, rent seeking. Because the rules of politics often make rent seeking tempting, there is great opportunity for the political entrepreneur to either create or destroy value. In contrast, under the rules of market competition economic entrepreneurs generally fulfill Adam Smith's invisible hand concept, creating net value for society. They only can impose *net* costs on others through coercion or deception, such as theft, breach of contract, or fraud.

As we saw in Chapter 4, rent seeking is a type of political entrepreneurship that contributes to democracies generating failed policies. Subsidies for corn ethanol offer a clear example. Because corn is a relatively costly way to produce ethanol, energy companies wouldn't naturally have the incentive to produce it. The market test would mean corn goes in people's cupboards, not in their gas tanks. But when political entrepreneurs secured a 45-cent-per-gallon "blenders' credit" for corn ethanol produced in the United States and combined it with strict quotas on sugar ethanol imported from Brazil, it became "profitable" for energy companies to start refining corn into fuel. Meanwhile, without government interventions, energy companies couldn't exist if their costs exceeded the value created for consumers. In short, the political system is vulnerable to destructive entrepreneurship, and rent seeking imposes net costs on society when it is allowed to emerge.

Another key difference is that political entrepreneurship focuses on what are rather abstract concepts—the ideas, institutions, and incentives in a society that must be changed to create value for others. Whereas an entrepreneur in the market may offer the world the next iPhone, a value-creating political entrepreneur offers new ideas, or new institutions that implement those ideas. In recent years the two forms increasingly have merged, as bottom-up political entrepreneurs coordinate through social networking and mobile handsets.

Examples of Entrepreneurship in Politics

He who wants to improve conditions must propagate a
new mentality, not merely a new institution.
—Ludwig von Mises, *The New York Times* (1943)[6]

We can see political entrepreneurs all around us. Consider, for example, the MacArthur Foundation's "Genius Grants," which award $500,000 to individuals over five years, with no strings attached. Winners are asked only to continue working on creative projects that interest them. Previous grant recipients have included anthropologists and architects, educators and economists, physicists and physicians, playwrights and poets. The Foundation's website describes the program as follows:

> The MacArthur Fellows Program awards unrestricted fellowships to talented individuals who have shown extraordinary originality and dedication in their creative pursuits and a marked capacity for self-direction. There are three criteria for selection of Fellows: exceptional creativity, promise for important

future advances based on a track record of significant accomplishment, and potential for the fellowship to facilitate subsequent creative work.[7]

Grant winners essentially are told to carry on with their big ideas. Some of these individuals will offer ideas about how to change specific institutions in society. Others will build our understanding of how institutions have evolved at different times and places, and still others will affect attitudes and beliefs through indirect avenues such as art and literature. But directly or indirectly, if the MacArthur Foundation invests well, the ideas of these grant recipients will have a favorable impact on the human condition.

Genius grants are a unique approach to political entrepreneurship, but far from the only one. In 1971, a Guatemalan entrepreneur and intellectual, Manuel Ayau, together with several of his like-minded countrymen, decided to start a university. After witnessing decades of public support for populism, Marxism, and other ideologies that were hostile to markets and economic liberty, Ayau and his friends decided that the change their country needed would have to come from bright young minds who would be the country's future leaders. In response, they established Universidad Francisco Marroquín with a well-defined mission: To teach and disseminate the ethical, legal, and economic principles of a society of free and responsible persons.

Ayau's vision was to provide students an excellent education in business or economics (disciplines such as architecture, education, law, medicine and dentistry, and psychology were added later). They also would learn the economic principles that support market economies, principles that were (and still are) rarely taught in that part of the world. Equipped with better ideas and the moral and intellectual capacity to advance them, perhaps later these young minds would go on to change their country. While Universidad Francisco Marroquín stays out of Guatemala's messy politics, its graduates are well positioned to participate in that country's civic discourse, as entrepreneurs and business leaders, as academics and intellectuals, and as political entrepreneurs.

The ventures of the MacArthur Foundation and Manuel Ayau are focused on ideas and intellectuals. The people they help are, or hopefully will become, "academic scribblers" or "intellectuals" or other influencers in society. That is, they will create or promote ideas that affect their societies, often in the long run, and perhaps over many further relays.

On other occasions, entrepreneurs focus on specific existing institutions. Reform of public school (K–12) education in the United States is a good example. In the late 1990s, a couple of billionaires, Teddy Forstmann and John Walton, saw a large and growing demand by poorer families for alternatives to public schools, especially in inner cities, where low-quality public education is common. Ideas for how to improve this institution have been around for years but usually have been met with significant political opposition. The institutional framework that supports public schools includes teachers, administrators, and others with a strong distaste for many of the proposed changes.

Rather than support additional research into ideas for reform, and rather than focus directly on changing institutions that were opposed to being reformed, Forstmann and Walton took a different route. Together with other rich and generous friends, like Michael Ovitz of the Disney Company, the philanthropists started the Children's Scholarship Fund. In 1998, they announced they would fund $200 million in scholarships to give children from poor families the means to attend the secondary school of their choice. In addition to the obvious benefit to so many families, significantly more people have come to appreciate the value of choice in secondary education. Attitudes, beliefs, and ideas are changing.

On still other occasions, rather than focusing on the reform of existing institutions, some seek to create entirely new ones. Rather than reform existing societies and their governments, they suggest new communities that would serve as an alternative for investors and immigrants alike. Among these reformers are the economist Paul Romer, who leads a project to establish Charter Cities—special economic zones that are based on the laws of a friendly country, that are large enough to accommodate millions of people, and that have rules that would attract them. The experience of Hong Kong is a powerful example. Another reformer is Patri Friedman, whose Seasteading Institute has garnered millions of dollars in funding to build new cities in international waters. A similar model called Free Cities, proposed by Michael Strong and others, would establish autonomous areas based on their own emergent laws and institutions.

These different ventures—the MacArthur Foundation's Genius Grants, Universidad Francisco Marroquín, the Children's Scholarship Fund, Free Cities—share a common goal of trying to improve the human condition by altering human institutions. They also illustrate several principles of political entrepreneurship. Why donate money to creative types? Why start a private university in a developing country? Why fund scholarships to give poor kids in rich countries an alternative to government schools? Why start a new country? In short, for each of these examples as well as for any other, one could ask the proponents: Why *this* effort and not any of thousands of other opportunities?

Principles for Political Entrepreneurship

No eternal reward will forgive us now for wasting the dawn.
—Jim Morrison, "The Wasp (Texas
Radio and the Big Beat)" (1971)[8]

Whether one tries to change the world by investing one hundred dollars or one hundred million, whether one dedicates an hour of labor or a lifetime, these allocations—like every other aspect of human action—involve tradeoffs. Simply put, choosing how to effect political change is an economic act because it is a decision about how to devote resources among competing alternatives.

Whether implicitly or explicitly, anyone who gives hundreds of millions of dollars to the Children's Scholarship Fund has a theory that such an investment will yield a better return than the alternatives. It is this *theory* that drives home the practical implications of our framework. Because, if they are wrong, then these generous philanthropists will not have simply wasted their money, they will have foregone the chance to succeed elsewhere. No one wants to waste a hundred dollars or a hundred million. Even more importantly, like Jim Morrison, no political entrepreneur wants to waste what little time he or she may have in life.

So, what is to be done? The question is relevant whether you're a recent college graduate, a market entrepreneur, a member of Congress, a schoolteacher, a billionaire philanthropist, or anyone who wants to improve the human condition—whether down the street or around the globe. In all these cases and more, if the goal is to be an agent of change to the fullest potential that one's resources afford, then the question of *how* warrants deep reflection. The answer can suggest how to spend one's career, or how to give away—that is, *invest*— one's fortune to charity. Our framework speaks to the question at hand because it helps you—yes, you—to find the loose spots in the nexus of ideas, institutions, and incentives. With those open doors in sight, you can work your magic.

Drawing on the framework developed in this book and the principles of economics developed over centuries, here are a handful of proposals for how to effect political change.

A Focus on Comparative Advantage

Where to invest one's time or treasure depends on one's comparative advantage. With the power of his pen, Karl Marx understood this. So did Martin Luther King. While King's talent as a writer has been questioned, few dispute that he was a world-class orator whose speeches changed an entire country.

Then there are Ronald Coase and Alfred Kahn. Coase got his fingers dirty looking carefully at different legal institutions in society, but he did all his work within academia. Kahn started out as an academic, then got his fingers dirty working at the highest levels of U.S. politics. All the examples we've been discussing involve entrepreneurs finding weak spots in the nexus of ideas, institutions, and incentives at a particular time and place.

Knowing one's comparative advantage matters for academic scribblers as well as for individuals working in corporations, foundations, educational institutions, and more. Some people are particularly good at thinking and writing about abstract concepts, and they are patient enough to let their ideas germinate over time, like Marx or Coase. Others, like Steven Spielberg, produce gripping films that teach history from a given perspective. Public intellectuals engage in the important debates of the day by writing thoughtful (and not so thoughtful) pieces on current affairs or debating at conferences, on talk shows, and YouTube channels. These intellectuals may read the works of academic scribblers to keep abreast of the best thinking and to consider ideas that they in turn will recommend to their broader audiences. Still others, call them political activists, do battle in the trenches, changing the rules of the game in the here and now toward more immediate impacts.

Comparative advantage in effectuating change applies whether someone is working in a foundation, a lobbying group, a think tank, a university, or anyplace else wanting to promote political change. Universities, for example, may have a comparative advantage in idea generation. Among think tanks, some may be good at this as well, while others select and translate the ideas of academic scribblers into language the rest of us can understand. As Hayek describes it, this is the role of intellectuals.

To get the most out of their donations, the most successful foundations and philanthropists invest in organizations that have a comparative advantage in the task at hand. Those that wish to promote specific principles—classical liberal or Marxist or something else entirely—might invest in academic scribblers and intellectuals. Such an investment could include a donation to a university or supporting filmmakers or novelists who tend to promote specific values. It may be less effective to invest in policy groups that specialize in responding to legislation and get-out-the-vote drives. Similarly, it may be less effective to invest in lobbyists who specialize in responding to the issues of the day.

Importantly, everyone has a comparative advantage, and everyone has a means to generate more of the good in life. A parent, a teacher, or a minister may introduce ideas that stay with future generations and that influence how they think for the rest of their lives. This is a long-run strategy. A politician may cultivate a reputation or build a coalition to get better laws in place next year. This is a more short-run strategy. But both are strategies. Successful entrepreneurs know their comparative advantages so as to better choose the right strategy.

Deep Knowledge of the Market

Young people in high school and college receive lots of advice—solicited and otherwise—about the opportunities available to them. It's a bad time to be a doctor, they're told, or a good time to be an engineer. These are statements about the market. Specifically, they are statements about how well some careers pay as compared to others, which at least in part gives information about what jobs may provide more value in society as compared to others.

The same applies to an investment in political change. Some investments pay more than others, by which we mean some investments are more effective in producing change than others. Where to invest depends on the state of the market. Teddy Forstmann and John Walton knew that; so did Manuel Ayau.

Ultimately, economics is economics, as Robert Tollison gently reminds us in Chapter 3. And markets are markets, both in potatoes and in philosophy, as Lionel Robbins puts it rather simply. Even in something as esoteric as *political* philosophy, the principles of economics still apply, and market realities must be respected. John Locke discovered this during his failed attempt to write a constitution for the Carolina colonies in 1669. His rules were rejected by most locals and didn't last a year. Yet a little over a century later, those same ideas found favorable conditions as the American framers wrote the U.S. Constitution.

The challenge, then, is to recognize opportunities for change in the market. This is not to say that the entrepreneur should not accept a challenge, entering a market where no one has entered before, selling an idea that no one dared offer before. Every entrepreneurial role risks failure. But in every instance, there is the expectation that a return may be had, that substantial value may be created, based on the comparative advantage that is brought to the table.

For an entrepreneur in the market, profit represents the difference between value created (reflected in the price paid) and the costs incurred to create this value. It is the same for an entrepreneur in the political market. The value created must be compared against what otherwise could have been done with the resources used—what economists call "opportunity cost." All of this information—the value of one activity versus another, the costs of the resources used—comes from the market, that is, from the interaction of exchange among human beings.

Getting the Greatest Marginal Return

While the savvy entrepreneur focuses on comparative advantage and gets to know the market at hand, even this is not enough. Oftentimes, there will be any number of attractive investment opportunities to choose from. What to do?

Suppose it is the 1990s, and we have a billionaire who wants to change the world. Suppose further that this philanthropist believes that secondary education is in need of significant reform. Given that Teddy Forstmann and John Walton already have contributed $200 million to support scholarships for young students to attend the secondary school of their choice, what should *this* entrepreneur do?

A little economic thinking goes a long way here, in particular the relevance of diminishing marginal returns. In this case, the first $100 million toward secondary school scholarship probably makes huge strides. Will another $100 million improve educational opportunities as much when piled on top of a $200 million base? Will it do more? Will it do less?

This is not a minor point. The question is whether the return to being the third $100 million in this market is greater than the return in another area where the same investment could be applied to a "fresh" cause. It may be difficult to calculate, but the calculation nonetheless is made, implicitly or explicitly, whether by studying history or mathematical models or by the seat of one's pants. This is what entrepreneurs do.

In our framework, this activity is called looking for loose spots in a market, looking for areas to gain leverage toward maximum return. Entrepreneurs think like this all the time. In markets and politics, entrepreneurs seek out opportunities to implement a different idea and create the most value. When this is done well, the effects on the human condition can be significant, and we can see both Kirznerian and Schumpeterian entrepreneurship at work. Only by destroying old ways of growing wheat did Norman Borlaug save perhaps a billion people from starvation. The young Senator Ted Kennedy also was Schumpeterian, helping to put an end to a regulatory agency while breathing new life into his political career. And James Buchanan was Schumpeterian, pitting the public choice model of government against the romantic public interest view. Yet all these innovators were first Kirznerians, recognizing loose spots in the status quo arrangements of their day.

Getting Lucky (Sort Of)

The three elements of successful entrepreneurship we have just outlined—knowledge of comparative advantage, knowledge of the market, and a focus on getting the greatest marginal return—are critical to effectuate change. To see why, imagine what happens if they are lacking. If one serves a market with huge demand and also somehow manages to focus on projects with the greatest returns, this matters little if one is poorly suited for the job. Someone else will come along and do it better. Similarly, focusing on the activities one does best but applying these efforts where they add little value also will fail a market test. The most successful entrepreneurs know what they do well, they know the market and the opportunities within it, and they choose those activities that create the most value. This is true in economic as well as political markets.

And yet, we all know examples of entrepreneurs who seem to consider all these factors and still fail. Despite all efforts to estimate market conditions, the fact remains that entrepreneurial ventures are precisely what their name implies—ventures, and speculative ones at that. Some succeed; others fail. Indeed, failure is common in entrepreneurship—so common it's often viewed as a rite of passage and even a vital feature of ultimate success. It is an opportunity for learning, of course, at the same time that it is a signal that something was missing in the approach taken.

It thus would appear that there is a certain amount of luck associated with success. Is "luck" simply being in the right place at the right time, focused on the right projects, with the skills and resources that happen to be needed and the vision to apply them? If so, "luck" sounds an awful lot like entrepreneurship, in economics or politics. Ultimately, what we call luck in political entrepreneurship may be nothing more than successfully combining the elements described here, at the right time and place. As Malcolm Gladwell points out in *Outliers*, Bill Gates had tremendous talent and applied it exceedingly well, but none of this would have produced Microsoft if Gates had been born thirty years earlier.

The Point Is to Change It

We must make the building of a free society once more
an intellectual adventure, a deed of courage.
—Friedrich Hayek, *Studies in Philosophy,*
Politics and Economics (1967)[9]

If you take just one notion away from this book, we hope it would be this: Ideas become powerful not simply because they are conceived by academic scribblers and then filtered into society by intellectuals but because political entrepreneurs discover ways to implement those ideas into society's shared institutions and ultimately change the incentives that drive human behavior.

The challenge, then, is for political entrepreneurs to look for and act on loose spots in the nexus of ideas, institutions, and incentives. Just as entrepreneurs in the market improve the human condition by seeing and acting on opportunities to meet the needs of consumers, so political entrepreneurs improve the human condition by seeing and acting on opportunities to promote ideas, institutions, and incentives that improve the rules of politics toward better outcomes in society: a society with justice; a society that produces wealth that enhances the lives of its members; a society that allows its members to live as they choose to live.

We all have the potential to be political entrepreneurs: perhaps as the academic who conceives a better idea; perhaps as secondhand dealers who relay ideas to the world through brilliant prose, powerful speech, or some other media; perhaps as a political reformer—yes, working among the madmen—creating or reforming institutions that improve millions of lives.

It is at least plausible that Keynes and Hayek are just wrong about the eventual dominance of ideas over interests and that the vast majority of ideas in human affairs never amount to anything—plausible, but not likely. As John Stuart Mill says, "When the right circumstances and the right ideas meet, the effect is seldom slow in manifesting itself."[10]

The best ideas for political change, and the way those ideas are selected, will always depend on the circumstances of time and place. What ideas matter most today? What media best convey them? We leave these questions to be debated by our readers, as students and practitioners of political entrepreneurship.

Whatever path we take as political entrepreneurs, each of us is more likely to succeed if we recognize not only the revolutionary but also the evolutionary nature of political change. In short, improving the human condition should start with recognizing that people respond to incentives, that incentives are part of institutions that neither rise nor fall overnight, and that the slow emergence of both good and bad ideas can change these institutions and thus have an enduring impact on the human condition. Tyranny or freedom. Poverty or wealth. War or peace. Ideas, indeed, can have consequences.

Notes

Chapter 1

1. The future NBA players in the game were Othell Wilson, Sam Perkins, James Worthy, Michael Jordan, and Ralph Sampson, the latter three of whom were to become NBA all-stars.

2. Ken Denlinger, "North Carolina Stalls off Virginia for ACC Title: A Classic Example of Overcoaching and Underplaying," *Washington Post*, March 8, 1982, C1.

3. Richard Goldstein, "In 1954, Shot Clock Revived a Stalled N.B.A.," *New York Times*, December 25, 2004; retrieved on December 4, 2011, from www.nytimes.com/2004/12/25/sports/basketball/25clock.html.

4. James A. Sheldon, "Basketball Rules Experiments May Net Results," *NCAA News*, June 16, 1982, 1.

5. Jeremy Gerard, "In $1 Billion Deal, CBS Locks up N.C.A.A. Basketball Tournament," *New York Times*, November 22, 1989; retrieved on December 4, 2011, from www.nytimes .com/1989/11/22/sports/in-1-billion-deal-cbs-locks-up-ncaa-basketball-tournament.html; and "March Money Madness: CBS Sports to Spend $6 Billion over 11 Years for Basketball Tourney," *Money Magazine*, November 18, 1999.

6. John Maynard Keynes, *The General Theory of Employment, Interest and Money* (Orlando, FL: Harcourt Brace, 1936), 384.

7. For estimates of the number of people dislocated by the use of eminent domain, see Ilya Somin, "Economic Development Takings as Government Failure," in *The Pursuit of Justice: Law and Economics of Legal Institutions*, ed. Edward J. López (New York: Palgrave Macmillan, 2010), 123–144.

8. John Stuart Mill. "The Claims of Labour," *Edinburg Review* (1845), in *Essays on Economics and Society Part I*, vol. 4 of *The Collected Works of John Stuart Mill*, ed. John M. Robson (Toronto: University of Toronto Press; and London: Routledge and Kegan Paul, 1967), 370.

9. "A 40-Year Wish List: You Won't Believe What's in That Stimulus Bill," *Wall Street Journal*, January 28, 2009, A14.

10. Mill, "The Claims of Labour," 370.

Chapter 2

1. Plato, "CRITO." In *The Dialogues of Plato: Translated into English with Analyses and Introduction by V. Jowett, M. A. in Five Volumes*, third edition (Oxford, UK: Oxford University Press, 1892); retrieved on November 9, 2011, from http://oll.libertyfund.org/title/766/93697.

2. Wikipedia contributors, "List of U.S. executive branch czars," *Wikipedia, The Free Encyclopedia*; retrieved on July 10, 2010, from http://en.wikipedia.org/wiki/List_of_U.S._executive _branch_czars.

3. Habeas corpus prohibits unlawful or arbitrary imprisonment of an individual by the government, a right enjoyed—if occasionally taken for granted—by citizens of stable and peaceful democracies yet longed for by citizens of abusive governments. Regarding limits on the government's

power of eminent domain, the earliest forms of the public use and compensation requirements appear in chapters 28 and 29 of the Magna Carta.

4. Harvey C. Mansfield, *The Prince: Second Edition by Niccoló Machiavelli* (Chicago: University of Chicago Press, 1998), ii.

Chapter 3

1. Paul A. Samuelson, "The Art of Economic Policy," *New York Times*, October 30, 1970, 41.

2. James M. Buchanan, "What Should Economists Do?" (Presidential Address, Southern Economic Association, November, 1963) *Southern Economic Journal* 30:3 (1964), 213–222.

3. Robert D. Tollison, "Economists as the Subject of Economic Inquiry" (Presidential Address, Southern Economic Association, November 26, 1985) *Southern Economic Journal* 52:4 (1986), 909–922.

4. Mark Blaug, *Great Economists before Keynes* (Atlantic Highlands, NJ: Humanities Press International, 1986), 262.

5. Associated Press, "Biofuel Brews up Higher German Beer Prices," May 30, 2007.

6. Mark Blaug, *Economic Theory in Retrospect* (Cambridge, UK: Cambridge University Press, 1985), 302.

7. N. Gregory Mankiw, "The Pigou Club Manifesto," *Greg Mankiw's Blog,* October 26, 2006; available at http://gregmankiw.blogspot.com/2006/10/pigou-club-manifesto.html.

8. Henry William Spiegel, *The Growth of Economic Thought: Revised and Expanded Edition* (Durham, NC: Duke University Press, 1983), 615.

9. Mark Skousen, "The Perseverance of Paul Samuelson's *Economics*," *The Journal of Economic Perspectives*, 11:2 (Spring 1997), 137–152.

10. Samuelson, "The Art of Economic Policy," 41; Mark Skousen, "The Perseverance of Samuelson's Economics."

11. Leonard S. Silk, "Samuelson Contribution: Nobel Prize Winner Has Demonstrated the Uniformity of All Economic Theory," *New York Times*, October 28, 1970, 67.

12. Ibid.

13. Samuelson, "The Pure Theory of Public Expenditure," *Review of Economics and Statistics* 36: 4 (1954), 387–389.

14. *The Concise Encyclopedia of Economics*, s.v. "Friedrich August Hayek," ed. David R. Henderson (Liberty Fund, Inc., 2008), Library of Economics and Liberty; available at www.econlib .org/library/Enc/bios/Hayek.html.

15. Citation counts are from Google Scholar. Comparisons to Friedman and Samuelson are from Avinash Dixit and Mancur Olson, "Does Voluntary Participation Undermine the Coase Theorem?" *Journal of Public Economics* 76: 3 (2000), 309–335.

16. Ronald Coase, "Intellectual Portrait Series: A Conversation with Ronald Coase." Interviewed by Richard Epstein at 42:00. Online Library of Liberty, 2002. Liberty Fund, Inc.; available at http://oll.libertyfund.org.

17. Dava Sobel, *Longitude: The Story of a Lone Genius Who Solved the Greatest Scientific Problem of His Time* (New York: Walker, 1995).

18. David E. Van Zandt, "The Lessons of the Lighthouse," *Journal of Legal Studies* 22: 1 (1993), 77–82; and Elodie Bertrand, "The Coasean Analysis of Lighthouse Financing: Myths and Realities," *Cambridge Journal of Economics* 30: 3 (2006), 389–402.

19. Coase, "The Problem of Social Cost," *Journal of Law & Economics*, vol. 3, October 1960, 18.

20. James M. Buchanan. "Better Than Plowing," in *The Logical Foundations of Constitutional Liberty*, vol. 1 of *The Collected Works of James M. Buchanan* (Indianapolis, IN: Liberty Fund, 1999), 11–27.

21. Ibid.

22. Ibid.

23. Buchanan. "An Economic Theory of Clubs," *Economica* 32 (1965), 1–14.

Chapter 4

1. U.S. General Accountability Office. *Sugar Program: Supporting Sugar Prices Has Increased Users' Costs while Benefiting Producers,* GAO/RCED-00-126 (Washington, DC: General Accountability Office: 2000), 5.

2. The transplant waiting list is updated in real time at the website of the United Network for Organ Sharing, www.unos.org. The historical data are from the interactive tables made available by The Organ Procurement and Transplantation Network, "Removal Reasons by Year, January 1995–October 31, 2007," available at www.optn.org/latestData/rptData.asp, based on OPTN data as of January 25, 2008. Report on file.

3. U.S. Department of Health and Human Services, Health Resources and Services Administration. *2006 OPTN/SRTR Annual Report: Transplant Data 1996–2005* (Washington, DC: Department of Health and Human Services, 2006); available at www.ustransplant.org/annual_reports/current/ar_archives.htm.

4. Gary S. Becker and Julio Jorge Elias, "Introducing Incentives in the Market for Live and Cadaveric Vital Organ Donations," *The Journal of Economic Perspectives*, 21: 3 (Summer 2007), 3–24.

5. Leonard S. Silk, "Samuelson Contribution: Nobel Prize Winner Has Demonstrated the Uniformity of All Economic Theory." *New York Times*, October 28, 1970, 67.

6. "This Year's Economics Prize Awarded for a Synthesis of the Theories of Political and Economic Decision-Making (Public Choice)," The Royal Swedish Academy of Sciences press release, October 16, 1986, on Nobel Prize website at http://nobelprize.org/nobel_prizes/economics/laureates/1986/press.html.

7. Jane Seaberry, "Nobel Winner Sees Economics as Common Sense; Buchanan Says His Public Choice Helps Explain Politics," *Washington Post*, October 19, 1986, C-1.

8. Ibid.

9. Hobart Rowen, "Discreetly Lifted Eyebrows over Buchanan's Nobel Prize," *Washington Post*, October 26, 1986, D-1.

10. Robert Lekachman, "A Controversial Nobel Choice? Tuning in to These Conservative Times," *New York Times*, October 26, 1986, 32.

11. Jane Seaberry, "In Defense of Public Choice; Chairman of Nobel Panel Discusses Economic Winner," *Washington Post*, November 23, 1986, K-1.

12. Rowen, "Discreetly Lifted Eyebrows," D-1.

13. James M. Buchanan and Gordon Tullock, *The Calculus of Consent: Logical Foundations of Constitutional Democracy* (Ann Arbor: University of Michigan Press, 1962), 22–23.

14. Gordon Tullock, "Problems of Majority Voting," *Journal of Political Economy* 67 (December 1959), 571–579.

15. Howard R. Bowen, "The Interpretation of Voting in the Allocation of Economic Resources." *Quarterly Journal of Economics* 58: 1 (1943), 27–48.

16. Kenneth A. Shepsle and Barry R. Weingast, "Structure-Induced Equilibrium and Legislative Choice," *Public Choice* 37: 3 (1981), 503–519.

17. Michael C. Munger, "They Clapped: Can Price-Gouging Laws Prohibit Scarcity?" *Library of Economics and Liberty*, January 8, 2007; available at www.econlib.org/library/Columns/y2007/Mungergouging.html.

18. Guido Pincione and Fernando R. Tesón, *Rational Choice and Democratic Deliberation* (Cambridge, UK: Cambridge University Press, 2006).

19. Tullock, "The Welfare Costs of Monopolies, Tariffs, and Theft," *Western Economic Journal* 5 (June 1967), in *The Selected Works of Gordon Tullock*, Volume 1, Charles K. Rowley, ed. (Indianapolis: Liberty Fund, 2004), 169–179.

20. Ibid., 174.

21. George J. Stigler, "Review," review of *Foundations of Economic Analysis*, by Paul A. Samuelson, *Journal of the American Statistical Association* 43: 244 (1948), 603–605.

22. Stigler, "The Theory of Economic Regulation," *Bell Journal of Economics and Management Science* 2: 1 (1971), 3–21.

23. Ibid., 4.

24. Sam Peltzman, "Toward a More General Economic Theory of Regulation," *Journal of Law & Economics*, 19 (1976), 211.

25. U.S. Government Accountability Office, "Understanding the Tax Reform Debate: Background, Criteria, and Questions," GAO-05-1009SP, September 1, 2005.

26. Tullock, "The Transitional Gains Trap," *Bell Journal of Economics* 6: 2 (1975), 671.

27. Michael M. Grynbaum, "Two Taxi Medallions Sell for One Million Each," City Room, *New York Times*, October 20, 2011; available at http://cityroom.blogs.nytimes.com/2011/10/20/2-taxi-medallions-sell-for-1-million-each/.

28. Winston M. Clifford, "Economic Deregulation: Days of Reckoning for Microeconomists," *Journal of Economic Literature* 31: 3 (1993), 1263–1289.

Chapter 5

1. John Stuart Mill, "The Claims of Labour," *Edinburg Review* (1845), in *Essays on Economics and Society Part I*, vol. 4 of *The Collected Works of John Stuart Mill*, John M. Robson, ed. (Toronto: University of Toronto Press; London: Routledge and Kegan Paul, 1967), 370.

2. Paul Belein, "Walking on Water: How to Do It," *Brussels Business Journal*, August 27, 2005; available at www.brusselsjournal.com/node/202.

3. John Maynard Keynes, *The General Theory of Employment, Interest and Money* (New York: Harcourt Brace, 1936), ch. 24.

4. F. A. Hayek, "The Intellectuals and Socialism," *University of Chicago Law Review* 16: 3 (1949), 373.

5. See in particular Hayek, *The Pure Theory of Capital* (London: Macmillan and Co., 1941) and *Prices and Production* (London: G. Routledge & Sons, 1931).

6. James Gwartney, Robert A. Lawson, and Joshua C. Hall, *Economic Freedom of the World: 2011 Annual Report* (Vancouver, BC: Fraser Institute, 2011).

7. World Bank, *Where Is the Wealth Of Nations? Measuring Capital for the 21st Century* (Washington, DC: World Bank, 2006), 87.

8. Paul G. Mahoney, "The Common Law and Economic Growth: Hayek Might Be Right," *Journal of Legal Studies* 30: 2 (2001), 503–525.

9. John Emerich Edward Dalberg, Lord Acton, "The History of Freedom in Antiquity" (address delivered to the members of the Bridgnorth Institution at the Agriculture Hall, February 26, 1877), in *The History of Freedom and Other Essays*, John Neville Figgis and Reginald Vere Laurence, eds. (London: Macmillan, 1907), 6.

10. Douglass C. North, "Economic Performance through Time" (Nobel Prize Lecture delivered in Stockholm, Sweden, December 9, 1993), *American Economic Review* 84: 3 (1994): 359–368.

11. North, *Understanding the Process of Economic Change* (Princeton, NJ: Princeton University Press, 2005), 69.

12. Deirdre N. McCloskey, "The Institution of Douglass North," MPRA Paper No. 21768, Munich Personal RePEc Archive (2009). More generally, see McCloskey, *Bourgeois Dignity: Why Economics Can't Explain the Modern World* (Chicago: University of Chicago Press, 2010) and *The Bourgeois Virtues: Ethics for an Age of Commerce* (Chicago: University of Chicago Press, 2006).

13. Adam Smith, *Lectures on Jurisprudence*, vol. 5 of *The Glasgow Edition of the Works and Correspondence of Adam Smith*, R. L. Meek, D. D. Raphael, and P. G. Stein, eds. (Indianapolis: Liberty Fund, 1982), 493.

14. F. A. Hayek, "History and Politics," introduction to *Capitalism and the Historians*, F. A. Hayek, ed. (Chicago: University of Chicago Press, 1954), 8.

15. James G. McGann, "The Think Tank Index," *Foreign Policy* (2010); available at www.foreignpolicy.com/story/cms.php?story_id=4598&page=0.

16. Richard Dawkins, *The Selfish Gene* (Oxford, UK: Oxford University Press, 1976), 192.

17. Steven Rose, *Lifelines: Biology beyond Determinism* (New York: Oxford University Press, 1997), 7, 309.

18. Karl Marx, *The Eighteenth Brumaire of Louis Bonaparte* (Moscow: Foreign Languages Publishing House, 1948), p. 16. (First edition published in German, 1852)

19. Steven Pinker, *The Blank Slate: The Modern Denial of Human Nature* (New York: Penguin, 2002), vii.

20. Peter J. Richerson and Robert Boyd, *Not by Genes Alone: How Culture Transformed Human Evolution* (Chicago: The University of Chicago Press, 2005), 5.

21. H. L. Mencken, *A Little Book in C Major*. (New York: John Lane Company, 1916), 19.

22. Vernon L. Smith, "Constructivist and Ecological Rationality in Economics (Nobel Address)," *American Economic Review*, 93(3, June 2003), 465–508.

23. Elinor Ostrom, *Governing the Commons: The Evolution of Institutions* (Cambridge, UK: Cambridge University Press, 1990).

Chapter 6

1. "Clinton Praises FCC Auction Process as 'Reinventing Govt. Model,'" *Common Carrier Week*, April 3, 1995; available at www.djnr.com.

2. "Wireless Quick Facts," CTIA–The Wireless Assocation; retrieved on November 7, 2011, from www.ctia.org/advocacy/research/index.cfm/aid/10323.

3. Thomas W. Hazlett, "The Rationality of U.S. Regulation of the Broadcast Spectrum," *Journal of Law and Economics* 33: 1 (1990), 133–175; "Physical Scarcity, Rent Seeking, and the First Amendment," *Columbia Law Review* 97: 4 (1997), 905–944; and "The Wireless Craze, the Unlimited Bandwidth Myth, the Spectrum Auction Faux Pas, and the Punchline to Ronald Coase's 'Big Joke': An Essay on Airwave Allocation Policy," *Harvard Journal of Law and Technology* 14 (2001), 2.

4. Ronald Coase, "The Federal Communications Commission," *Journal of Law & Economics* 2 (1959), 1–40.

5. *NBC v. United States*, 319 U.S. 190 (1943).

6. *Red Lion Broadcasting Co. v. F.C.C.*, 395 U.S. 375, 375-77 (1969).

7. Quoted in Harvey H. Goldin, "Discussion of 'Evaluation of Public Policy Relating to Radio and Television Broadcasting: Social and Economic Issues,' (Coase)," *Land Economics* 41: 2 (1965), 167–168, at 168.

8. Coase, "The Federal Communications Commission," 17–18.

9. Harvey J. Levin, "The Radio Spectrum Resource," *Journal of Law & Economics* 11: 2 (1968), 433.

10. Coase, "Evaluation of Public Policy Relating to Radio and Television Broadcasting: Social and Economic Issues," *Land Economics* 41: 2 (1965), 161–167.

11. Ibid., 165.

12. Ibid., 162.

13. Ibid., 166.

14. Ibid., 167.

15. Harvey H. Goldin, "Discussion of 'Evaluation of Public Policy Relating to Radio and Television Broadcasting: Social and Economic Issues,' (Coase)," *Land Economics* 41: 2 (1965), 167–168.

16. Ibid., 168.

17. Ronald Coase, William H. Meckling, and Jora Minasian, *Problems of Radio Frequency Allocation* (Santa Monica, CA: The RAND Corporation, DRU-1219-RC, 1995).

18. Ibid., iii.

19. Coase, "Comment on Thomas W. Hazlett: Assigning Property Rights to Radio Spectrum Users: Why Did FCC License Auctions Take 67 Years?" *Journal of Law & Economics* 41: S2 (1998), 577.

20. Newton N. Minow, *Equal Time: The Private Broadcaster and the Public Interest* (New York: Atheneum, 1964), 52.

21. Hazlett, "Assigning Property Right to Radio Spectrum Users: Why Did FCC License Auctions Take 67 Years?" *Journal of Law & Economics* 41: S2 (1998), 567, citing Paul Farhi, "Broadcast Executives Say Dole Vented Anger at Them," *Washington Post*, January 12, 1996, F8.

22. *Broadcast Renewal Applicant*, 66 F.C.C.2d 419, 434 n.2 (1977) (Commissioners Hooks and Fogarty, separate statement).

23. Michael Calhoun, *Digital Cellular Radio* (Norwood, MA: Artech House, 1988).

24. "FCC Report to Congress on Spectrum Auctions," Federal Communications Commission, WT Docket No. 97-150 (released: October 9, 1997), Appendix E: FCC Licensing Speed: Comparative Hearings, Lotteries, and Auctions.

25. Thomas W. Hazlett and Robert J. Michaels, "The Cost of Rent-Seeking: Evidence from Cellular Telephone License Lotteries," *Southern Economic Journal* 59 (1993), 425–435.

26. Gordon Tullock, "The Welfare Costs of Monopolies, Tariffs, and Theft," *Western Economic Journal* 5 (June 1967), in *The Selected Works of Gordon Tullock*, Volume 1, Charles K. Rowley, ed. (Indianapolis: Liberty Fund, 2004), 179.

27. "FCC Report to Congress on Spectrum Auctions," Appendix E.

28. Leo Herzel, "'Public Interest' and the Market in Color Television Regulation," *University of Chicago Law Review* 18 (1951), 802–816.

29. Dallas W. Smythe, "Facing Facts about the Broadcast Business," *University of Chicago Law Review* 20: 1 (1952): 96–106.

30. The anecdotes and details of Alfred Kahn's experiences are based on e-mail correspondence with the authors on February 18 and February 24, 2010. Records are on file with authors.

31. See Richard Caves, *Air Transport and Its Regulators—An Industry Study* (Cambridge, MA: Harvard University Press, 1962); Arthur DeVany, "The Effect of Price and Entry Regulation on Airline Output, Capacity, and Efficiency," *Bell Journal of Economics and Management* 6: 1 (1975), 327–345; George W. Douglas and James C. Miller III, *Economic Regulation of Domestic Air Transport: Theory and Policy* (Washington, DC: Brookings Institution, 1974); William A. Jordan, *Airline Regulation in America: Effects and Imperfections* (Baltimore: Johns Hopkins Press, 1970); Theodore C. Keeler, "Airline Regulation and Market Performance," *Bell Journal of Economics and Management* 3: 2 (1972), 399–414; and Michael E. Levine, "Is Regulation Necessary? California Air Transportation and National Regulatory Policy," *Yale Law Journal* 74: 8 (1965), 1416–1447.

32. Senate Committee on the Judiciary, Subcommittee on Administrative Practice and Procedure, *Oversight of Civil Aeronautics Board Practices and Procedures*, 94th Cong., 1st sess., 1975.

33. Ibid.

34. Quoted in Thomas K. McCraw, *Prophets of Regulation* (Cambridge, MA: Belknap Press, 1984), 224.

35. Ibid.

36. Ibid., 272.

37. Ibid., 291.

38. Daniel Patrick Moynihan, *Miles to Go: A Personal History of Social Policy* (Cambridge, MA: Harvard University Press, 1996), 26.

39. Robert Higgs, *Crisis and Leviathan* (Oxford, UK: Oxford University Press, 1989).

40. Moynihan, *Miles to Go*, 26.

41. Moynihan, "The Professors and the Poor," in *On Understanding Poverty*, ed. Daniel Patrick Moynihan (New York: Basic Books, 1968), 20.

42. Charles Murray, *Losing Ground: America Social Policy, 1950–1980* (New York: Basic Books, 1984), 42.

43. Moynihan, "America's Poor: What Is to Be Done?" (address delivered at Harvard University, Cambridge, MA, September 4, 1986).

44. Moynihan, *The Negro Family: The Case for National Action* (Washington, DC: U.S. Department of Labor, 1965).

45. Mollie Orshansky, "Counting the Poor: Another Look at the Poverty Profile," *Social Security Bulletin* 28: 1 (1965): 3–29.

46. Michael Harrington, *The Other America: Poverty in the United States* (New York: Macmillan, 1962).

47. Kenneth B. Clarke, *The Dark Ghetto: Dilemmas of Social Power* (New York: Harper & Row, 1965).

48. David T. Ellwood, *Poor Support: Poverty in the American Family* (New York: Basic Books, 1988), 37.

49. Moynihan, *The Negro Family*, 31.

50. George Gilder, *Visible Man: A True Story of Post-Racist America* (New York: Basic Books, 1978); *Wealth and Poverty* (New York: Bookthrift Company, 1984); and *Men and Marriage* (Gretna, LA: Pelican Publishing, 1986).

51. Andrew Ross Sorkin, *Too Big to Fail: The Inside Story of How Wall Street and Washington Fought to Save the Financial System—and Themselves* (New York: Penguin Books, 2009); Bethany McLean and Joe Nocera, *All The Devils Are Here: The Hidden History of the Financial Crisis* (New York: Penguin Books, 2010); and John Taylor, *Getting Off Track: How Government Actions and Interventions Caused, Prolonged, and Worsened the Financial Crisis* (Stanford, CA: Hoover Institution Press, 2009).

52. See, for example, Steven Horowitz and Peter Boettke, *The House That Uncle Sam Built: The Untold Story of the Great Recession of 2008* (New York: Foundation for Economic Education, 2011); Paul Krugman, *The Return of Depression Economics and the Crisis of 2008* (New York: W. W. Norton, 2008); and John Taylor, "Origins and Policy Implications of the Crisis," in *New Directions in Financial Services Regulation*, ed. Roger B. Porter et al. (Cambridge, MA: MIT Press, 2010).

53. See, for example, Sorkin, chapter 19.

54. U.S. Financial Crisis Inquiry Commission. *The Financial Crisis Inquiry Report: Final Report of the National Commission on the Causes of the Financial and Economic Crisis in the United States* (Washington, DC, 2011); retrieved on November 11, 2011, from http://fcic-static.law.stanford.edu/cdn_media/fcic-reports/fcic_final_report_full.pdf.

55. *Housing and Community Development Act of 1977*, Title VII, Sec. 802, 90 Stat. 1147 & 90 Stat. 1148.

56. William Jefferson Clinton, "Remarks on the National Home Ownership Strategy," (address delivered at the White House, Washington, DC, June 5, 1995), *The American Presidency Project*; available at www.presidency.ucsb.edu/ws/?pid=51448.

57. See *Blueprint for the American Dream*; available at www.nw.org/network/policy/pdf/blueprintbrochure.pdf.

58. McLean and Nocera, *All the Devils Are Here*, chapter 9.

59. *Updated Estimates of the Subsidies to the Housing GSEs*, Congressional Budget Office, Report to the Committee on Banking, Housing and Urban Affairs, U.S. Senate (April 8, 2004); available at www.cbo.gov/doc.cfm?index=5368&type=0.

60. Wayne Passmore, *The GSE Implicit Subsidy and the Value of Government Ambiguity*, Finance and Economic Discussion Series No. 2003-64, Board of Governors of the Federal Reserve System, 2003.

61. See John B. Taylor, "Housing and Monetary Policy," Proceedings, Federal Reserve Bank of Kansas City, (2007), 463–476. See also, Boettke and Prychitko, *supra*.

Chapter 7

1. Karl Marx, "Theses on Feuerbach" (1845), appendix to *Ludwig Feuerbach and the End of Classical German Philosophy*, by Friedrich Engels, 1888 ed. (Moscow: Progress Publishers, 1946), Thesis XI.

2. Gregg Easterbrook, "Forgotten Benefactor of Humanity," *Atlantic Monthly*, January 1997; retrieved on December 4, 2011, from www.theatlantic.com/magazine/archive/1997/01/forgotten-benefactor-of-humanity/6101.

3. Robert Higgs, *Crisis and Leviathan: Critical Episodes in the Growth of American Government* (New York: Oxford University Press, 1987), 83–84.

4. Victor Marie Hugo, "Conclusion," in *The History of a Crime* (Paris: Calmann Lévy, 1877), Huntington Smith, translator (University of Michigan Press, 2010), ch. 10.

5. Joseph A. Schumpeter, *Capitalism, Socialism, and Democracy* (New York: Harper & Bros., 1942), 82.

6. Ludwig von Mises, "Super-National Organization Held No Way to Peace," *New York Times*, January 3, 1943, E8. We are grateful to Ben Dyer for locating this reference for us.

7. Information on the MacArthur Fellows Program is available at www.macfound.org/site/c.lkLXJ8MQKrH/b.959463/k.9D7D/Fellows_Program.htm.

8. Jim Morrison, "The Wasp (Texas Radio and the Big Beat)" on *L. A. Woman*, with The Doors, Elektra Records, 1971. EKS-75011. LP.

9. Friedrich August von Hayek, *Studies in Philosophy, Politics, and Economics* (Chicago: University of Chicago Press, 1967).

10. John Stuart Mill. "The Claims of Labour," *Edinburg Review* (1845), in *Essays on Economics and Society Part I*, vol. 4 of *The Collected Works of John Stuart Mill,* ed. John M. Robson (Toronto: University of Toronto Press; and London: Routledge and Kegan Paul, 1967), 370.

Index

Acton, Lord: on institutions, 116
African Americans, 6, 160–61, 162, 178–79
Aid to Dependent Children/Aid to Families
    with Dependent Children, 159, 163, 164
airline deregulation, 6, 8, 9, 11, 81, 106,
    112, 135, 148–56, 165, 174, 181; Airline
    Deregulation Act of 1978, 156; role of
    Alfred Kahn in, 135, 148–49, 153–56,
    179; role of Edward Kennedy in, 149,
    151–53, 154, 176, 179, 188; vested interests
    in airline industry, 153, 154, 155
Alchian, Armen, 130; "Uncertainty, Evolution
    and Economic Theory," 124, 125
allocation of resources, 44, 71, 85, 89, 140,
    180, 185; efficiency in, 59, 60, 61, 64,
    81–82; vs. exchange, 49, 51–52, 67, 68,
    69, 72, 76, 77
American Airlines, 155
American Civil War, 34
American Conservative Union, 155
American Dream, 164, 165, 168, 170
American Economic Association, 48
American Economic Review, 98
American Enterprise Institute (AEI), 150–51
American Founders, 18, 24, 29, 32, 34, 176
American Political Science Association, 48
American Progressives, 45–48
American Revolution, 13, 39. *See also*
    American Founders
Ameriquest, 173
Angelou, Maya, 102
antigouging laws, 91–93
antitrust laws, 46, 149
Aquinas, St. Thomas, 25, 45, 176; and
    Aristotle, 25, 30; on the Church, 26–27;
    on monarchy, 26–27; on natural rights,
    30; on virtue, 26
Arab Spring, 111

aristocracy, 20–21, 22, 23, 26, 29, 32, 33, 35, 38
Aristotle, 16, 22, 57, 176; and Aquinas, 25, 26,
    30; on aristocracy, 20–21; on democracy,
    17, 20, 21; on division of power, 35; on
    golden mean, 19–21, 26; on the good, 16,
    19; vs. Hobbes, 32, 33; on human beings
    as political, 32; on master and slave, 30; on
    moral weakness, 19; *Nicomachean Ethics,*
    16; vs. Plato, 19, 21; on virtue, 20, 35
Arrow, Kenneth: Fundamental Welfare
    Theorem, 60–61, 66, 89; on general
    equilibrium, 60–61, 66; Impossibility
    Theorem, 89; on methods of voting, 89;
    relationship with Downs, 90
Athens: School of, 16–17, 21, 38, 118
Atlantic Coast Conference (ACC) basketball
    championship (1982), 1–3, 191n1
AT&T breakup, 143
Augustine of Hippo, St.: on the Church, 25;
    The City of God, 25; on the state, 25
Austrian School of economics, 53, 62, 67–70,
    113
Ayau, Manuel, 183, 187

Bacon, Francis, 130; empiricism of, 31–32; on
    Machiavelli, 28
Baker, Richard, 170
Bakes, Philip, 154
balance of power: checks and balances, 24,
    29, 37; Cicero on, 23, 29; Hobbes on, 33;
    Locke on, 38. *See also* separation of powers
Band of Brothers, 122
banks: bailout, 165; capital requirements for,
    172–73; deregulation of, 106; mortgage
    lending by, 166–68
barley prices, 57–58
Basel Committee on Banking Supervision,
    172–73

199